Two Decades
NAKED

Two Decades
NAKED

LEIGH HOPKINSON

hachette
AUSTRALIA

Pseudonyms have been used in this book and other details altered where necessary to protect the identity and privacy of people mentioned. While every effort has been made to recall past events accurately, the memories contained within this book are my own and may differ from those of others.

hachette
AUSTRALIA

Published in Australia and New Zealand in 2016
by Hachette Australia
(an imprint of Hachette Australia Pty Limited)
Level 17, 207 Kent Street, Sydney NSW 2000
www.hachette.com.au

10 9 8 7 6 5 4 3 2 1

National Library of Australia
Cataloguing-in-Publication data:

Hopkinson, Leigh, author.
Two decades naked/Leigh Hopkinson.

978 0 7336 3483 3 (paperback)

Stripteasers – New Zealand – Biography.
Stripteasers – Australia – Biography.

305.97927092

Cover design by Luke Causby, Blue Cork Designs
Cover image courtesy of Getty Images
Author photo courtesy of Tony Ryan
Text design by Luke Causby
Typeset in Garamond by Kirby Jones

Printed in Australia by Griffin Press, Adelaide, an Accredited ISO AS/NZS 4001:2004 Environmental Management Systems printer The paper this book is printed on is certified against the Forest Stewardship Council® Standards. Griffin Press holds FSC chain of custody certification SGS-COC-005088. FSC promotes environmentally responsible, socially beneficial and economically viable management of the world's forests.

FSC
www.fsc.org
MIX
Paper from
responsible sources
FSC® C009448

For my families – the clothed one and the naked one

One

HOLLY AND SABRINA

1.

IT WAS A MONDAY AFTERNOON IN OCTOBER 1993. I should have been studying for my first-year political science exam. Instead I was parked across the road from Pleasures massage parlour, killing time till my 4 p.m. appointment. Although I had fifteen minutes to spare, I wasn't about to take a walk around the block. I was wearing black heels from my school ball, a scarlet miniskirt and singlet from an op shop, and matching lingerie bought with the money my grandma had sent for my eighteenth birthday. I'd never applied for a job as a stripper before, so it was hard to know if I was underdressed or overdressed.

I checked my reflection in the rear-view mirror. Eyes rimmed jet black, lips painted fire hydrant red; it was my best slut impersonation, tried and tested on private school boys. I looked smoking hot, confident and in control. But my sweaty palms betrayed me. So did the butterflies in my belly. Winding down the window of my brown Vauxhall Viva, I lit a cigarette and peered up at the parlour.

Pleasures was on the third floor of the historic ANZ Bank Chambers building, which sat like a wedge of forgotten cake on a corner of downtown Christchurch. Its pistachio-green paint was flaking and in places the fire escape had popped its studs. A hand-painted sign hung from the sagging verandah: 'Pleasures' in hot-pink script, with a silhouette of a wild-looking woman, the kind that embellishes truck mud-flaps. A row of bare bulbs pulsed above the side entrance; a flight of crooked stairs led heavenward. As I sat there smoking and taking this all in, a voice in my head that sounded suspiciously like my mother's demanded to know just what I thought I was doing.

What I was doing was looking for a new part-time job because I'd stopped getting shifts at the Cotswold Hotel. Two afternoons a week at KFC wasn't enough to pay for food and booze, or fill the days a full-time arts degree left empty. Both bored and broke, I had been trawling the local paper, *The Press*, for a few weeks. There weren't many jobs for a school leaver, but I kept seeing the same ad: *Lingerie dancers required. No experience necessary, full training provided. Flexible hours, fantastic money.*

What did it involve? Could I do it? It certainly sounded promising. (I didn't yet know that if something sounded too good to be true then it probably was.) Girls like me weren't supposed to parade around in their undies, but as the days ticked by, the ad grew on me. It became an itch I longed to scratch, like an ingrown pubic hair.

4

That morning I mustered up the courage to make the call. My housemate Helen's fat tabby cat Gibson was shunting my hip with his head, egging me on. I felt light headed in the way you do when you're about to do something slightly dangerous. I did it anyway.

'Pleasures,' a woman said flatly.

'I'm calling about the ad in Saturday's paper,' I said.

'Which one?'

'The one for lingerie dancers.'

She sighed. 'You know we want strippers, don't you?'

'No,' I said.

'Is that all right?'

I thought quickly. 'I suppose so.'

'We need to see what you look like. When can you come in?'

'Anytime.'

'Well, give me a time!' she said irritably.

Taken aback, I stammered, 'Um, four o'clock today?'

'Four it is. Ask for Craig.' The phone went dead. I replaced the receiver, grinning like a champ.

In between making the call and parking on High Street, I discovered – courtesy of the Yellow Pages – that Pleasures wasn't a strip club but a massage parlour. Taboo of all taboos! The opportunity for a sneak peek into this gated realm was too good to pass up. When I finished my degree, I planned on becoming a journalist. Perhaps one day I would write about this escapade! It would be like an undercover assignment – only my cover would be coming off. And I'd be getting paid.

A soft-bellied, balding man appeared in Pleasures' doorway dressed in a sweatshirt, jeans and sneakers. He was an unmemorable bloke. He was also my first glimpse of a 'sex industry patron'. I'll admit to being disappointed. I don't know what I'd expected, but he looked … *boring*. Blinking furiously into the late afternoon sun, the man shuffled out onto the street. Then a dark-skinned girl in jeans and a t-shirt emerged and bounced down the stairs and up the footpath in the opposite direction. These were ordinary people, behaving as if they'd been running errands not transacting in illicit sex! Now I was even more curious.

I butted my cigarette and checked my reflection again, gave my shoulder-length strawberry-blonde curls a tussle. Then I got out of the car, strode purposefully across the road and through the doorway, took two steps and froze. It was simply too dark to see. The air was damp, rank with mould. As my eyes adjusted, I saw the stairs were turn-of-last-century narrow, worn down in the middle. Up I went, up and up. The higher I zigzagged, the more breathless I became and the more warped the stairs. I stopped to check it wasn't me, off kilter in my shoes. Even the walls slanted inwards. They were lined with hand-painted posters: 'XXX Entertainment!', 'Half-price Massage Mondays!', 'Oil Wrestling!' Oil wrestling?

I turned a corner and came face-to-face with a glossy black door and a small sign – *Ring buzzer and wait.*

I tried the door, it was as immobile as a bank vault. Through a tiny plexiglass window in the adjacent wall I spied a bench with a kettle and a neat pile of folded, white towels. Then I rang the buzzer. Its echo was met by a clatter of high heels that grew louder until the prettiest woman I'd ever seen was staring at me coldly through the glass. She had a halo of platinum hair, a heart-shaped face and the high cheekbones of a porcelain doll.

'Yes?' she mouthed.

'I'm here to see Craig,' I said loudly.

The door jolted open. I stepped into a triangular-shaped reception room, once grand, now dilapidated. Clouds of cigarette smoke hung in the stifling air. Although the sun was streaming in, the windows were closed and the heaters pumping.

Three black vinyl couches formed a U-shape around a low glass coffee table. Perched on the nearest couch was a scrawny brunette with wet hair. She wore a faded black singlet dress, had a cigarette dangling from Mick Jagger lips and looked at least thirty-five. Opposite her, two young Polynesian girls were curled into the armpits of a man who seemed awfully pleased with himself and who wore nothing but a towel. The two girls looked half his age. Appalled, I stood there staring. My friends would have run a mile from this guy, but these girls didn't seem at all grossed out.

The blonde clattered over to the middle couch and plopped herself down. She was immaculately dressed in a cream trouser suit, suggesting she wore the pants in this place. 'Have a seat. Craig'll be here soon.'

I sat next to the brunette and wished I hadn't. I could see straight up the man's towel to his wrinkled penis, lying on one pale, hairless thigh. My eyes widened. Noticing, he smirked. It was like a car accident: I found it hard to look away.

'What's your name?' asked the blonde.

'Leigh,' I said. Hers was Jacinta. Jacinta introduced 'the girls' but not the man, her shell-pink mouth soft but her blue eyes glacial. In my nervous excitement, I remembered only her name and the brunette's, which was Candy.

A gunshot rang out. I jumped, then realised it came from the TV. Everyone turned towards it. Craning my neck, I could see an old western was on featuring a young Clint Eastwood. On top of the TV, a goldfish swirled lethargically in its bowl.

'I don't watch telly,' said Candy. 'It's bad for you. Nothing but sex and violence and more sex and violence and shit like this.'

'Hah!' Jacinta snorted. 'You just sit there and smoke one cigarette after another – like that's not bad for you.'

Candy, appreciating the irony, snorted and lit a second cigarette from the first. Ash tumbled down the front of her dress. She scraped it away and twisted the butt into a fast-filling ashtray.

I could feel Jacinta's eyes on me. I fixed mine on the dust particles slow-dancing in the toxic air. Despite its neglect, the wedge-shaped room was stunning, with high windows, a corniced ceiling and a tiled chequerboard floor. My dad was an architect and I knew he would've appreciated the attention to detail. I also knew he would never see the inside of this room. There was a semi-circular balcony at its apex, with French doors and a 270-degree view. I longed to check it out, but doubted I could stand up without flashing my knickers at the towelled man. If I didn't want to do that then what was I doing here?

Jacinta was still eyeballing me. My neck had begun to ache and sweat was pooling behind my knees. Towel Man whispered in one of the girls' ears, she giggled. There were more gunshots.

Just as I was thinking up an excuse to leave, I heard raucous laughter and footsteps pounding up the stairs. Jacinta rose to open the door. A thickset man in blue denim barrelled in, barking into his mobile phone. The cuffs of his jacket were rolled up and his free hand hung like a slab of meat, each digit sparkling with a gold-and-diamond ring. He had a black mullet, a bulbous nose and sharp blue eyes that darted about but showed no sign of what they saw. This was Craig.

'If you didn't smoke so much fucking dope, you dumb prick, you'd remember,' he chuckled into the phone. He eased onto the arm of the couch and elbowed Candy in the ribs. She sighed and shuffled towards me. Craig's expression narrowed. '*Listen*. Sort it out.' He snapped shut the phone, nodded at Towel Man with a conspiratorial grin, then shot him down. 'Put on some clothes, mate. This isn't a fucking bedroom.'

As Towel Man heaved himself up, one of the girls stood too. He slid his arm around her and they disappeared through a side door.

'Girls, girls, girls!' Craig grinned again and spread his hands, preacher-like. He cocked his head at me. 'Who are you?'

'This is Leigh,' said Jacinta. 'She wants to dance.'

'Good, you showed up. I'll need you Thursday to Saturday.' Craig turned back to Jacinta. 'How are we going today?'

She shrugged. 'Okay. A bit slow.'

Craig twisted one of his rings, nodding thoughtfully. Then he glared at Candy. 'Go and dry your hair, you old slag.'

'Yeah, yeah, I'm going,' said Candy, making no effort to move.

'Excuse me,' I said, confused, 'where will I be dancing?'

'You don't know?' Craig frowned at Jacinta. His phone rang. Answering it, he beckoned to me and I followed him through the side door, into a hallway reeking of chlorine and wet carpet, past an alcove with an empty spa, down another corridor with six numbered doors, into a back room. Craig flicked on the lights.

The rear windows had been blacked out and packing crates were stacked in the corners. There was a bar made out of corrugated iron, guarded by a life-sized cardboard cowboy with pop eyes and a devil grin. The narrow stage – a five-metre-long platform – hugged the front wall and had a single pole at its centre. A handful of tearoom-style tables and chairs were scattered about, along with a few upended wine barrels. It looked like what it was: a converted storeroom, trying but failing to go country.

My face fell. I'd never been inside a revue bar, but thought 'lingerie dancing' would be glamorous. Lisa Malcolm had made it sound better than Broadway. We'd both been in the same production of *A Chorus Line* at Rangi Ruru private girls' school. She'd been a senior when she began lingerie dancing in her lunch-hour at topless club Route 66 and word of her antics had spread faster than athlete's foot in the shower room. Fed up with being good but not very good at being bad, I'd been awestruck by Lisa. Unfortunately her extracurricular activity had been short lived. Issued with an ultimatum – the pillar of society or the pole – she had opted to finish high school. Now I was about to follow in Lisa's footsteps and unleash my inner extrovert … only I wasn't sure I wanted to do it here.

While I hesitated, Craig yabbered into the phone, something about police and liquor licensing. I had the good sense not to interrupt. Besides, he was a fascinating distraction. Beneath his jacket, Craig's t-shirt, emblazoned with 'Pleasures massage parlour', had its neckband ripped out. He also had a third-trimester-sized paunch. No adult in my world had a potbelly, hacked up their clothes or sold sex. Craig was also the first person I'd met who owned a mobile phone.

Craig hung up and thumbed at the stage. 'This is it. Wear what you're wearing – it looks good. Bring some raunchy music and think of a fake name for yourself. Something exotic, like Candy, Paris or Frankie.'

Frankie sounded suburban, not exotic. I chewed my lip. 'Don't you want me to audition or something?'

Craig burst out laughing. 'You haven't got two left feet, have you?'

'No.'

His mobile rang again. 'Thursday eight o'clock, yeah?'

'Okay.'

Craig turned away. I found my way back to reception and murmured goodbye.

'See ya,' said Candy. Wordlessly, Jacinta buzzed me out.

Not until I'd pulled out into the rush-hour traffic did I realise I was drenched in cold sweat – and I'd forgotten to ask how much I would be getting paid.

* * *

When I got home Helen was still at work, so I didn't need to explain why I looked like a whore at 5 p.m. on a Monday. We lived close to the University of Canterbury in a two-bedroom unit owned by my parents. Helen had moved in three months earlier, after my best friend Sonia moved out. Sonia and I had argued because I chop carrots in rounds, not sticks. Before I knew it, she had left for a share house in the city.

I was sad and perplexed. Sonia had been my bestie since I was twelve. We both had the same unruly blonde hair, were exactly five feet six and came from Greymouth, a small town on the west coast of the south island. 'The Coast' is known for its wild seas and lush rainforests. It's the birthplace of the New Zealand labour movement, a place that breeds resilience, where it takes an outsider twenty years to become a local.

Local by birthright I grew up on a hobby farm twenty kilometres from Greymouth, surrounded by native forest. It was a quiet, mostly idyllic upbringing. We had a few sheep, several goats, a cat, a dog and guinea pig. Two boys lived next door for my younger brother to play with, but they often excluded me because I was a girl. I thought that was grossly unfair. After school I kept to myself, read Enid Blyton books, wrote stories with heroines in far-flung cities like New York, climbed trees or hung out with my pet goats. On Saturdays, Mum drove me into town for junior athletics, where I tried to beat the other kids, especially the boys. Soon our family holidays were geared around my regional athletics championships or Dad's yachting regattas.

Mum was a primary school teacher, committed to us kids, and Dad was always going somewhere exciting – business trips, yachting or skiing. He taught my brother and I how to ski and I adored spending time with Dad, when he had the time. Being grounded from these adventures was the ultimate punishment. And by age twelve, I was getting grounded a lot. Mostly for being a highly competitive, overachieving classroom nuisance, often inspired by the more experienced Sonia.

I distinctly remember Mum saying, 'If you stay in this town you'll end up barefoot and pregnant at fifteen.' The idea of procreating at all filled the child-me with horror. I yearned to be out in the world, not bound to small people in country towns. So when Mum asked if I wanted to go to boarding school in Christchurch I said yes. I couldn't wait to get out, and Sonia was going too.

Boarding school, however, wasn't the adventure I'd been looking for. Quite the opposite: it was strict, institutionalised living. Sonia found creative ways around the rules, but I couldn't seem to. They weighed heavily – as did the hierarchy, the privilege and the sacrifice my parents were making. To my surprise I missed the bush, my pets and my solitude. I even missed the boys next door.

For me, boarding school felt like a prison sentence: each year served was one closer to getting out. I set myself a rigorous extra-curricular routine of study and sport, tried not to be miserable, did my best to be good. Sonia was kicked out of the boarding house for smoking a joint. I finally got kicked out in my senior year, when they caught me sneaking back in after seeing a movie with my boyfriend Ben.

I'd met Ben skiing. He was quintessentially tall, dark and good looking, a quick-witted private school boy destined to become a lawyer like his father. Ben's mother had an open-door policy and I spent many contented hours at their house, reading poetry and trying to appreciate his parents' jazz records. Deep down, though, I felt too uncultured for Ben, so I broke up with him – and broke his heart – before he could do it to me. And I instantly regretted it. Since then we had been on-again, off-again, mostly off. Ben was busy with his new law-student friends and share-house living.

I had hoped to share a house with my friends Kim and Kate once university started, but my parents had refused, concerned I would be 'distracted'. They bought the flat and, fortunately, Sonia agreed to move in. *Un*fortunately, we disagreed about almost everything. Our lives were taking us in different directions – hers to art school, mine … well, I wasn't sure anymore.

In the wake of the 1990 Gulf War, I'd busted out of school wanting to be a war correspondent, convinced that if enough atrocities were reported, the world would surely prioritise peace. But journalism wasn't part of undergrad studies at the University of Canterbury. Neither, it seemed, was independent thinking. During my first politics tutorial I openly disagreed with the tutor and was told I didn't understand the material. But I understood it fine. Surely a point of disagreement was worth discussing? I complained to Ben's mother, one of the few adults I trusted and felt got me. 'Sadly, no one is interested in what you think until postgraduate level,' she explained. 'It's a case of doing your time.'

Fuck it, I thought. I'd been doing time in boarding school for years; I didn't intend to do any more. I vowed to cruise at uni and turn my naked ambition elsewhere.

* * *

On Thursday at 8 p.m., face painted and scarlet outfit on, I was ready for my nudie debut. Over my shoulder was a backpack containing some mix tapes and a muesli bar. Like my first day of school I was preened, prepped and bursting with nervous excitement.

Jacinta met my big smile with a cold stare. 'You can go straight out back. I'll send Candy through.'

The back room was empty but the overhead lights were on, tinting the corrugated iron piss-yellow. The room was even dingier than I remembered. It smelled dirty and yeasty, like my granddad's pot plants the Christmas he served up his undrinkable homebrew. Nevertheless, I tried to keep positive.

I dropped my bag, teetered up the raw wooden steps of the stage and surveyed the empty room. Who would occupy the tables and chairs – a procession of towelled men? God, I hoped not. I had no idea what to expect – a full house or a single unit.

Nor did I know what to do with the pole. Gripping the cold steel, I tried spinning around but spun out, landing with my legs splayed and my head reeling. I picked myself up and was holding the pole at arm's length – number one no-no in pole mastery, I would discover – when Candy walked in wearing the same old black dress.

'Hey, you look great up there,' she said.

'Thanks, but I have no idea what I'm doing.'

'I can show you a few moves. Mind you, I'm not very good.' Candy clomped up the steps and pulled aside a tatty piece of black fabric tacked across the sidewall. 'This is where we wait to go onstage.'

A hole had been sledgehammered out of the plasterboard, opening up the space between the walls. Three Occupational-Health-and-Safety-defying steps led down to a girl-sized mouse-house. A portable tape deck sat on the floor; an ashtray and a couple of glasses had been tucked into the wall studs. It was as much a dressing-room as a portaloo was an ensuite. Screwing up my nose, I stepped back from the dusty hole, and from Candy, who was standing too close. She reeked of rotting lilacs.

'How long have you been stripping for?' I asked.

Candy let go of the curtain. 'I'm not really a stripper; I'm a working girl. But they don't have enough strippers right now, so I'm helping out.' She shrugged. 'I don't mind, and it probably helps me get booked.'

Staring into her unblinking brown eyes, I wondered how many men had held those long, lean limbs – had poured themselves into her, hour after hour, night after night. I wanted to know, but didn't know how to ask. 'Do you like it?' I said finally.

Candy stared at me warily. 'It's better than some other jobs I've done. I work for myself, you know, and I get to be at home with my kids.' Her expression lifted. 'Two of 'em are all grown up, but my precious wee angel, she's nearly three.' Candy smiled a toothy yellow grin. 'Do you have any kids?'

I shook my head.

'Then you can work as much as you like! You'll get a lot of bookings here.'

Did she think I was a hooker? Shocked, I stammered, 'I'm only going to strip.'

'Oh. Well good for you! You could do anything you want; you're real pretty.'

'You too,' I lied, trying to be nice.

Candy frowned then, realising I wasn't being nasty, clattered over to the pole. She showed me how to grind and how to spin around without losing control. It was a bit like gymnastics, which I'd embraced too late at fourteen. Attempting to land a basic spin, I heard Craig's juggernaut footfall.

'Girls! How are we?'

'Good,' we chorused, filing down from the stage.

'I'm gonna put you on in a minute,' he told me. My heart rate doubled. Craig jerked his head at the bar. 'Cue up your music and give it to whoever's behind there, two songs each time. First song, take off your dress. Second song, take it all off – but don't flash us your cunt, it's illegal. Fuck knows why.' He pointed to the makeshift curtain, diamonds glittering. 'Wait back there till you hear your music. Got it?'

'Got it,' I said, more confidently than I felt.

A solid girl with frizzy hair and thick glasses trudged in, went behind the bar and flicked on the sole stage light, a red spot trained on the pole. She was wearing tramping boots, jeans and a polar fleece. There was just enough time to wonder if this was a disguise to ensure she never got asked for sex in here, ever, before 'Legs' by ZZ Top blared out.

'Go on, go,' said Craig.

I grabbed my pack, scrambled backstage and began to cue my tapes. During the week, I'd bought Madonna's single 'Fever' and the soundtrack from *American Gigolo*, which included 'Call Me' by Blondie. I'd also decided to call myself Holly, not realising it was a mash-up of my last and first names. We were approaching the festive season and the prickly plant with its bright red berries was lovely to look at, but not to be touched. Just like me in my scarlet ensemble, I hoped. Said ensemble was about to be plucked from the proverbial bush, but how to do it? While I'd busted out a few moves in the living room – carpet-burning my knees and scaring the cat – I hadn't thought to make up a routine. Now it was too late.

Hurrying out with the tapes, I was astonished to find two tables already occupied – and relieved to see all occupants fully clothed. The two men wore jeans, t-shirts and needy expressions. They were chugging down beers with a thirst I sensed alcohol wouldn't satisfy. Each guy had a female companion at his table, overdressed by comparison. One was a dead ringer for Paula Yates. She wore a short crimson dress and let her customer hold her hand. They sat frozen in awkward silence. The other woman looked like a happy Morticia Addams. Her raven locks were matted in what I would come to recognise as wig hair. She wore a black chiffon gown and chatted with her guy, a pack of cigarettes and a clutch purse in her lap. The scene looked like a sad, middle-aged dating debacle – with me as the inept distraction.

Presiding over it all was Craig, swaggering like a modern-day Al Swearengen from *Deadwood*. He flashed me a grin. 'Knock 'em dead!'

I grinned back, handed my tapes to Miss Polar Fleece and prepared to face the music.

Moments later I stood backstage, wiping my hands on my skirt and thinking panicky thoughts. What if I couldn't get my bra undone? What if I tripped over? What if I fell off the stage?

Too soon the guitar riff of 'Call Me' blasted out. Would someone call me? I waited. Nothing.

Taking a deep breath, I clambered up the steps, tossed aside the curtain and plunged onto the stage with a gymnast's fervour, headed straight for the pole – a glinting anchor in a sea of red. I smiled brightly and didn't dare look at the judges. Apparatus in hand, I demonstrated my dry-humping ability, then two-stepped around the pole. I was so busy mentally undressing myself I almost forgot to do it for real.

Leaning back against the pole, I eased one arm out of my singlet then the other, tugged both singlet and skirt down over my hips and wiggled like an epileptic caterpillar. Gravity did the rest. Carefully, I stepped out of the clothing pooled at my feet. So far, so good.

Although a size twelve and polar white, I didn't feel self-conscious in my red bra and G. I'd worn very little onstage before and lingerie this gorgeous deserved to be seen. Having successfully removed not one but two items of clothing, my confidence ballooned. While Debbie Harry repeated the chorus, I took a stab at pirouetting the length of the runway, lost my bearings and reeled out of the spotlight, dangerously close to the edge of the stage. I pulled up just in time. When the dizziness abated, I toddled back to the pole, threw a half-hearted kick and told myself to calm down.

'Fever' began and the slow, sultry song was an instant corrective. I started grinding in time with the music instead of rocketing around. And I got lost in the words. Just like at my primary school concert when I'd lip-synced 'Like a Virgin' into a deodorant bottle without knowing what a virgin was, I imagined I was New Zealand's answer to Madonna. That gave me the courage to unhook my bra. As it fell to the stage, there was a smattering of applause. This surprised me: I hadn't really done anything.

Daring to glance at my audience, I saw Candy wolf-whistling, the ladies clapping and the men eyeing me like a dog does a bone. Then I high-kicked some more – not a smart move without a bra on.

Wow, I'm topless in public! I thought. Why isn't this bothering me? Instead, my exposure felt delicious: the air cool, the spotlight warm on my skin. And my body knew instinctively what to do. It felt exhilarating and frightening and, although I didn't understand why, primal in its significance. *This* was bigger than *me*. At that moment stripping ceased to be an act of defiance. I felt alive.

As 'Fever' came to an end, I peeled off my G. The applause grew. I strode to the pole and ground at it until the song faded out. Then I gathered up the scattered pieces of clothing, floundered with the curtain and descended backstage. ZZ Top started up again.

Lathered in sweat, my mouth tinged with the metallic taste of adrenaline, I was gripped by a post-provocateur moment of shyness. I couldn't put my clothes back on fast enough. Just as I pulled up my skirt, Craig poked his head around the curtain.

'Come out when you're ready.'

The ladies and their customers had gone; Miss Polar Fleece was clearing the tables. A glass of lemonade bubbled on the bar.

'Not bad,' said Craig, handing me the glass. 'Try and slow down, all right. And *look* at the people you're stripping for. Eye contact is important.'

I met his sharp blue eyes, sipped the cold drink and nodded, disappointed he hadn't found me brilliant.

'From now on, you don't need to get here till ten. Shifts are ten till one, Thursday to Saturday. If you can't make it, call, all right? Pay is forty dollars a night, plus you get to keep all your tips. Monday is payday. You can pick your pay up from reception any time after two.'

I nodded again. Forty dollars wasn't 'fantastic money', but it was better than KFC and I could feasibly work both jobs. If I didn't like Pleasures, I could always leave.

'Basically, the guys are here to have a root. Parlours aren't supposed to serve alcohol,' Craig winked at me, 'but we can provide a little striptease, get the guys worked up so they stick around. Weekends are busier, so you'll need another outfit and some more music. I liked your songs, they were grouse. Any questions?'

'What do I do now?'

'Hang around till the next lot are ready.' Craig grinned and sauntered off.

The bargirl disappeared too, leaving me alone with the cardboard cowboy. I wondered if I should pretend to look busy. At first, I practised the pole. Then I ate my muesli bar. Eventually I sat around smoking, trying not to think about what my friends and family, especially my family, might say if they knew where I was. It was cold in the back room and I couldn't help but feel excluded. Reception with its overcooked air beckoned like a hearth with a roaring fire, but if I was propositioned for sex, how could I say no without sounding like a snob? I stayed where I was.

I stripped three times that night. With each six-minute 'set' the likelihood of me tripping over my knickers lessened, but I didn't learn a lot from studying Candy's two strips. Mostly, she leant against the back of the stage with her head to one side, thrusting like a disjointed stick insect and looking like she wished everyone would just go away.

My last set was at midnight. Afterwards, I dawdled backstage like a mouse in the wall, waiting for more cheese. It didn't come.

By ten past one I decided to leave. Even as I teetered down the wonky stairs, I half-expected someone to yell out, 'Where do you think you're going?' No one did.

Driving home I felt drained, as much from the downtime as the show time. Still, I had performed panty-free in public! It wasn't just what I'd done, but that *I* had decided to do it. I hadn't asked anyone's permission. After years of being told what to do, of being stifled by rules and regulations, it seemed I had found a way out.

* * *

At 9 a.m. the next morning I ached all over, from ankles to temples. Forcing myself out of bed for a lecture, I arrived late and absorbed little. Afterwards, I drove to Riccarton Mall to shop. The black bra and matching G both had a single diamante – dazzling by nineties New Zealand chain-store standards. They cost one night's pay but I figured it was worth it. I planned on wearing the lingerie with a short flip skirt.

Then I called into Sportsgirl to see Helen, who was the manager there. Helen had mahogany hair, wore platform wedges and chain-smoked rollies. And she was the only size sixteen I knew who looked sensational in stretch denim.

Her boyfriend Rich was an easygoing guy who spent his nights watching TV at our place and his days learning to play guitar, to impress Helen, I suspected. Then there was Gibson, whose mere presence turned the house into a sort-of home. I wasn't sure my parents approved of Helen, but I liked her a lot.

Seeing me, Helen beamed. 'Ooh, what did you buy?' She reached for the bag. 'Classy! He'll love it.'

I opened my mouth to explain then closed it again. I didn't think Helen would mind me stripping, but I couldn't be sure after Saturday night when I'd had impromptu ex-sex with Ben. We'd been so noisy we'd unknowingly woken her. Convinced an intruder was dismembering me, Helen fled the flat and locked herself in her car. When I'd gone for a post-coital cigarette I'd found her there, crying and waiting for the police. One shock this week was probably enough. Besides, Ben was the perfect alibi if Helen was to check on my whereabouts.

That evening I hacked twenty centimetres off my flip skirt, put my outfits in my backpack and wore jeans and a jumper to work. As I walked up High Street in the dark, carrying my covert life like a snail shell, I felt purposeful. The passers-by had no idea I was part of a small, select club. No one did. Stripping was my juicy secret – for now.

* * *

My second and third shifts at Pleasures were more challenging than I'd anticipated. Candy wasn't in Friday or Saturday, so I danced five sets both nights. I tried my hardest, making eye contact as Craig insisted, but the men were unresponsive. I wanted acknowledgement – generous applause, if not a tip. So I began leaving the stage and dancing around the tables, gyrating hopefully at the air. It wasn't quite begging, but it wasn't far off. My efforts went unrewarded.

In between sets, I attempted small talk while the couples finished their drinks. 'Nice to meet you,' I'd say politely. 'How are you?' In response, the men would ogle my breasts while the working girls looked peeved. Realising I was both cutting in and suggesting I was up for grabs, I went back to my mouse hole.

Luckily there was some reprieve. Each night a different girl from 'the club around the road' did a set. Friday's girl, Violet, was six feet tall with a magenta pixie cut. Violet wore all black: a fringed suede jacket, a miniskirt and a lace teddy. She greeted the working girls without moving her lips, which were deep purple and hung open non-compliantly, slashed across her porcelain skin like a blackening wound. Violet stripped to heavy metal, shuffling self-consciously, her eyes downcast. She was scarily fascinating to watch.

Saturday night's stripper was Lauren, who was slight with a hawkish nose and brown curls. She too wore all black, but didn't acknowledge anyone, handing over her cassettes with a scowl. Lauren wasn't a pretty girl, but she was an astonishingly beautiful stripper. She came alive at the pole, moving fluidly to Led Zeppelin's 'Whole Lotta Love', dancing for herself as much as for her audience. Every arch and writhe emphasised her lean limbs, full breasts and flat stomach. I watched transfixed. For the first time I became aware of the paradoxical nature of stripping: Lauren appeared soft yet hard, open yet closed, abandoned yet contained. I'd never seen anyone move like that and hoped one day to dance just as sensually.

Truth was, I had no idea what I looked like. There weren't any mirrors and the only feedback I received was from Craig. And that wasn't encouraging.

Around midnight, four young guys stumbled into the back room, rowdy and drunk. I was instantly on guard, but Craig materialised out of nowhere and sat in on my set. Grasping this opportunity to show my new boss how much I'd improved, I shimmied around the tables in my underwear, throwing in a few gymnastic moves.

After the guys had staggered out into the corridor, Craig squinted at me. 'What do you call that flip thing you just did?'

'A forward walkover,' I said proudly, thinking him impressed.

'Don't do it again,' he said. 'You know why?'

'No.'

'Because you can't do it properly. Until you can, don't do it. It made you look fat and unprofessional.'

True, I had put on weight since joining KFC and I hadn't done a walkover in years – and never in heels. Still, I pouted at Craig, offended.

He took no notice, distracted by the noisy drunks in the hall. He stormed after them. 'Fuck off, ya cunts!' I heard him bellow. That was the last I saw of them – and the last walkover I did in heels. I understood that no one was going to tell me what to do, only what *not* to do. I would have to find my own feet.

I don't think anyone really expected me to stay. Each night the working girls looked surprised to see me. I didn't have any idea that technically I was self-employed, that there were better places to strip or that sex workers were often unreliable, migratory birds. I had been schooled to stick out what I started. But I might not have, if it hadn't been for Jacinta.

When I left on Sunday morning, she smiled beatifically and said, 'Thank you for everything.' I thought it odd – until Monday, when I collected my pay. With her customary coldness she handed me a brown envelope marked 'Holly'. I waited until I was in my car before opening it to find two twenty-dollar notes. I stared at them uncomprehendingly. Where was the rest of my money? I got out of the Viva and climbed the stairs again. My heart was thumping so loudly with the fear of confrontation that I thought I might crack a rib.

Jacinta buzzed me in. 'Yes?'

'There's only forty dollars here,' I blurted. 'There's supposed to be a hundred and twenty.'

'Didn't Craig tell you?' Jacinta said, saccharine sweet. 'The first week, eighty dollars is deducted from your pay for training. From now on, you'll get forty dollars per shift.' Her demeanour was pure business, but her eyes gave her away. Jacinta was daring me to challenge her.

I stared back, unable to think of anything to say. I returned to my car and burst into tears. It was so unfair! Why would she do that? Then, thinking some more, I stopped crying and started getting angry. Paying for training hadn't been mentioned and I felt Craig had been straight with me. Jacinta, I suspected, had pocketed the money in the hope I'd go away.

Jacinta wasn't working on Thursday or Friday, but Craig wasn't around either. On Friday around midnight, just as I was tossing up between asking for his mobile number and leaving, he strode in and then out of the back room, evidently busy.

'Craig!' I hurried after him.

He stopped in the doorway. 'What is it?'

'I only got paid forty dollars this week. The rest was deducted for training.'

'Who told you that?'

'Jacinta.'

Craig's eyes narrowed. 'Leave it with me.'

On Monday I sweated all the way up the stairs, but it was Jacinta's day off. An unfamiliar receptionist handed me my envelope. I opened it in front of her. Inside was two hundred dollars in twenty-dollar notes. Two hundred dollars! That was more cash than I'd ever held. Until then, my relationship with money had been mostly *out* of my hands. My parents paid my living expenses, while KFC was my spending money. That cash was a tangible and multiple victory: over Jacinta, over the gymnastics coach who'd told me I wasn't good enough, over the tedium of university and the burden of my own meekness.

Two weeks in, and I thought I could smell independence wafting towards me on the cheap-perfumed, sexed-up breeze.

2.

MY THIRD FRIDAY NIGHT AT PLEASURES WAS quieter and colder than usual. I still hadn't performed a set by 11 p.m. Huddled backstage on a milk crate, I struggled to read *The Handmaid's Tale* in the low light. The windows rattled in the wind, while cigarette ash and bits of plaster eddied around my stilettoed feet. I was tiring of Pleasures – although technically I was getting paid to read.

Someone came into the back room. I put the book aside. Craig's diamond-encrusted digits yanked back the curtain. 'Get your gear together, you're gonna do a set around the road. You'll need three songs for this one.' He frowned. 'Where's your coat?'

'I didn't bring it,' I said.

He disappeared. Quickly I cued an extra tape. Craig came back carrying a long woollen coat belonging to one of the girls and bundled me up in it. Touched by the gesture, I shoved my tapes into the pockets and teetered after him. The streets were buzzing with packs of post-work drinkers: loud, leery and looking for something to do.

'Where are we going?' I asked, hurrying to keep pace with Craig's chunky stride.

'You're gonna love this place.' He grinned proudly. 'It's a real club, not like back there.'

Literally around the corner and up the road, among a row of old brick warehouses, a flashing neon sign lit up the night: 'Girls! Girls! Girls!' The muffled sound of 'Edge of Seventeen' drifted down from above.

Craig veered into a covered, outdoor stairwell. I clanged my way up after him. At the top, a bouncer with a white stripe in his dark hair was hunched over a hole-in-the-wall, chatting.

'Evening, Craig,' he said, straightening up and swinging open the door.

'Skunk.' Craig nodded curtly, so I did too.

We stopped just inside the doorway. Laser beams of coloured light sliced through the smoky darkness. The shallow, low-ceilinged room was packed with men. They stood shoulder to shoulder in front of the flashy glass and chrome bar down the back, or sat side by side at the small tables dotted around the phallic-shaped stage. The vibe was upbeat, potent yet surprisingly measured – perhaps because all eyes were on the stage. It ran lengthways down the centre of the room, fronted by a single pole made of clear Perspex and filled with pulsating golden lights. Near the top, like an angel on a Christmas tree, perched a leggy brunette in a silver-sequinned corset and G. She leant backwards until she was hanging upside down by her inner thighs. My mouth fell open. How did she do that?

The brunette unzipped her corset; it fell to the stage with a roar of approval. With bat-like precision she spied a man holding up a ten-dollar note. The girl righted herself nonchalantly, slid off the pole and sashayed to the edge of the stage. She crouched down, a thumb hooked into the front of her sparkly G. The man slid the note inside, his mouth in line with her generous breasts. The brunette winked and prowled on.

Wow, these girls got tipped! Then it dawned on me – these strippers were no entrée, they were the main course!

Even two waitresses stood watching the show, hips jutted. They wore black G's and cut-off tees with 'Rocking Rods' in script across the back. Who was Rod? Oh. I stifled a giggle. Perhaps sensing they were being watched, one turned around, saw Craig and whispered in the other's ear. They spun their trays to shoulder height and moved away.

'Come on.' Craig headed through the crowd to a DJ booth. Inside, perched on a stool was, well, a dwarf. He pulled his headphones off, scratched one ear and peered at Craig.

'This is Holly. Put her on next.'

Panic swept across the small man's face. 'Have you got any music?'

I nodded, the DJ thumbed behind him. We went into a boxy change room, palatial compared to Pleasures. A counter coated in make-up ran around three of the walls, which were mirrored and topped with bare bulbs like movie star dressing-rooms. Bags of glittery costumes were strewn about. I caught my first whiff of concentrated stripper scent: the tang of girl sweat, cheap perfume and stale air. It reeked of possibility. A dancer sat on an actual chair – no milk crates here – smoking. I recognised Lauren.

The DJ told her, 'Sorry, but the boss said to put Holly on next.' He scurried away with my tapes. I hung up my borrowed coat and glanced at Lauren. She looked at the floor.

'Give it up for *Tee-ah*!' yelled the DJ. The floor shook as the brunette emerged from a back passageway clutching her clothes, her olive skin glossy with sweat. She tossed her mane and gave me a blazing smile.

Reassured, I smiled back. Then I heard, 'Give a warm Rocking Rods welcome to *Hol-lyyy*!' 'Call Me' started. I hurried in the direction Tia had come from, towards a red neon archway that lit up the blackness.

I lurched onstage and into a blinding cloud of dry ice. Making for pole position, I held on until the fog cleared. Bobbing below me was a sea of faces, gazing up in adoration and desire and … was it subservience? This was awesome! I whirled around with a gleeful grin, the three songs a blur. Before I knew it I was back in the coat, tottering along the footpath sweaty and breathless, applause still ringing in my ears.

'You did good,' Craig said. 'Real good.'

Warmed by his praise, I laughed happily.

The following week, Craig rostered me on at Rocking Rods on Fridays and Saturdays, leaving me at Pleasures on Thursdays. At first, I waited for him to shift me across permanently. When I realised no one was queuing up to take my place I put down my newly stilettoed foot and announced I didn't want to work at Pleasures anymore.

Craig frowned. 'Can't you help us out for another week or two?'

'Can't one of the other girls?'

'Don't you start,' he said. Then he took in my expression. 'All right, all right.'

My backroom apprenticeship was over, but my real training was just beginning – and it's hard to hide a mistake when you're centrestage, spotlit and butt naked. Realising this, I applied myself studiously. There was a lot to remember.

Rocking Rods was open Tuesday to Saturday from 9 p.m. to 3 a.m. Around eight o'clock the bar manager, Nathan, would unlock the steel-reinforced front door. Nathan was a fleshy-lipped man who salivated when he spoke and oozed born-again Christian disapproval with every serve of overpriced, under-poured spirit. He was a stickler for rules and systems, aligning ashtrays, and chairs to tables, using the same inexplicable inner algorithm every night. By the time we dancers clanged up the stairs, he had switched on the overhead lights and the air-conditioning and the club would be whirring with half-hearted possibility, like a pinball machine in waiting.

Just before 9 p.m., Craig would rock up with the till floats, poke his head into the dressing-room and bark, 'Where's the midget?' Vince the DJ was always running late. He would hurry in the door moments before the club opened, breathless from having to take two steps for every one of ours. 'Who's up first?' he would pant, holding out his hands for that girl's tapes.

Four dancers were rostered on Tuesday and Wednesday, five on Thursday, and six on Friday and Saturday. First in the door was first onstage and the list rotated sequentially. Lauren was usually the first to arrive because her boyfriend Skunk worked on the door. She danced every night the club was open. I would often lug my gear backstage to find her in jeans and a t-shirt, simultaneously smoking a rollie and munching her way through a whole pizza.

'Hi!' I'd carol with the enthusiasm of the uninitiated.

'Hi,' she would reply sullenly.

At first I tried to be her friend and asked her all sorts of questions, but Lauren wasn't telling.

'What do you wanna know this stuff for?' she said at last, looking like she might punch me.

'I'm just asking, that's all,' I said quietly.

The only thing Lauren asked me was if I smoked. As I was puffing on a cigarette at the time, I thought it odd. I held it up.

'Weed,' she said.

'Ah. No.'

With that, Lauren and I went back to our silent pre-show face painting.

Star was more talkative. She was a 24-year-old hairdresser by day, stripper by night. She lived in a nearby warehouse with a group of artists, wore a long blonde wig over her dreads and danced solely to Transvision Vamp (much to Vince's annoyance). Soft-bellied with pert breasts and milky skin, Star minced around the stage in bondage-high stilettos looking like a naughty, sleep-deprived cherub. She would come straight from the salon in a velvet cape and patent Doc Martens, lugging an old suitcase crammed full of costumes. I liked Star; her sparkle reminded me of Sonia. The night Star ran her hands through my curls and said, 'Holly, you'd look like Marilyn if you went platinum, I can dye it for you,' I seriously considered it. Backstage, she was the one who asked me questions, nodding thoughtfully when I told her what I was studying, what my parents did and where I lived.

Shay, who went by her nickname, Mouse, was the only dancer who lived at home and that was because her mum 'needed a hand'. Mouse was as close to a dancer supervisor or 'house mum' as Rocking Rods ever got. Petite with scruffy brown hair, Mouse talked nonstop, pausing only to go onstage when she mouthed the words to the songs. Mouse didn't care what music Vince played. She dawdled around lip-syncing until her three songs were up and she could get back to fussing over the girls and the customers.

It was Mouse who showed me how to tie my stilettos on with bits of old stocking to stop them from flying off. She wound the stocking around the arch of my foot, crisscrossed and knotted it at my ankle then tucked the ends out of sight.

Mouse also showed me how to remove my G without revealing myself.

'You don't wanna get busted for indecent exposure,' she said.

I most definitely did not. 'How likely is that?'

Mouse said Lauren had been charged by an undercover cop at a now-defunct club. After that, I made sure I had my back to the wall when I went bottom up. And I cut off my tampon string when I had my period, as she suggested, so my own mousetail didn't dangle mid-show.

From Mouse I learnt who everyone was and how well they got along. As much as her gossip was the glue that bonded our motley crew, I suspected she was also responsible for creating some sticky situations, for she was confidante to both Jacinta – Craig's ex and part owner of Pleasures – and Tia, Craig's girlfriend.

Tia, the leggy brunette I'd seen perched up the pole, was the star of the show. And, like every good star, she emanated just the right amount of warmth, positivity and derision.

'You'll tone up quickly, just you wait,' she encouraged me, her green eyes shining. My bottom lip plummeted. I took to over-smiling around Tia like a groupie, watching from the sidelines while she pranced, high-kicked and side-split. Adding to my intrigue was the recurring thought of her straddling Craig.

At twenty-seven, Tia had been stripping for four years and had the flawless physique of a professional. She danced to Black Box, Paula Abdul and Stevie Nicks; her costumes were carefully assembled and meticulously hand-sequinned. My favourite was a black crushed-velvet dress worn with a magenta satin bolero jacket. Onstage, Tia was part flamenco dancer, part cowgirl. I tried to memorise her jaunty moves and seamless sequencing; although I was a head shorter, and heavier, I wanted to be just like her.

Lauren, Star, Mouse and Tia were the principal strippers. Several more sailed in on the weekends, including Violet, and Nadia and Sasha, a rumoured-to-be-couple. While Nadia was a flamboyant, haughty dancer, Sasha was the laziest stripper I ever saw. She would lope from pole to archway, grind left, grind right, flick her waist-length hair and lope on. In contrast I was constantly trying to bust out new moves and my thighs became black and blue from practising the pole. I covered the bruises with concealer as best I could.

But no matter how sore or tired my body, the moment I stepped onstage I was intoxicated by the thrill. As we girls weren't allowed to drink, this was as heady as it got. It was a phenomenal ego trip to be adored not just by boys my own age, but by all manner of men: old men, married men, single men, businessmen, labourers, locals and foreigners. Rocking Rods was a male melting pot of age, class and cultural diversity crammed under one roof; I'd never known anything like it. In the outside world I was frowned upon for wearing loud make-up and skimpy clothing, and flaunting my assets; in here, I was getting praised and paid for it! Like the Energizer bunny, I strode around the stage, feeling invincible. And Tia was right – with all that boinging, I dropped three kilos in two weeks.

We averaged six sets a night, which meant I needed a lot more music and costumes. Vince suggested songs he thought I'd like and he was often spot-on. Soon my cassette carrier was packed with M People and Jam & Spoon, but good costumes were harder to find – Christchurch wasn't exactly the showgirl capital of the world. Star suggested op-shopping: I found a white tasselled dress, shortened it and sewed the offcuts onto lingerie. Mouse recommended sex shops: among the rows of crotchless panties I discovered fluorescent G-string bikinis, which I wore with matching scrunchies and cut-off denim shorts. Sometimes costume sellers (and thieves hocking stolen goods) arrived unannounced. Their pieces were snapped up: I bought a red corset for forty dollars and sequinned it by hand.

My best outfit came about unexpectedly a month after I started at Rocking Rods, when I lugged my newly purchased vintage suitcase in the door to find Tia behind the bar.

'Craig forced her to choose,' whispered Mouse. 'Stripping or him.'

Tia adored the stage. How unfair for her – and for Nathan, who was instantly out of a job.

'Won't you miss it?' I asked Tia.

'Four years is long enough,' she said firmly, affixing a practised smile.

Her smile slipped the next night when she brought in her beautiful costumes to sell. I felt like a magpie, picking over the still-warm carcass of her former self. I bought her velvet dress and bolero jacket, but couldn't bring myself to wear them in front of her.

A week later Nathan was back and Tia was gone. She and Craig were over. If Craig was upset, he didn't show it.

At first I missed Tia's professional sparkle. I missed having someone to look up to. Then I began to wear her old clothes and added Black Box and Paula Abdul to my playlist. In Tia's absence, I got more tips.

Tips were a significant part of our income, as pay was fifty dollars a night. The first time I got tipped onstage, a man stood ringside with a ten-dollar bill folded lengthwise between his teeth; I drew back my lips and took it like a horse does a carrot. After that I kept one eye out for dosh and cavorted close to those offering it. Almost the only time we dancers spoke to the customers was when money changed hands.

In between sets, we were expected to don a G and cut-off tee and become drinks waitresses. One moment untouchable goddess, the next lowly servant, this archetypal duality added to our appeal – and ensured Craig didn't have to employ any waitstaff. Instead, dancers were paid fifty cents for every drink sold. Nathan initialled the orders in the little notebooks we carried in our tip jars; the total was added to our weekly pay, which I carefully checked. The drinks money and tips soon added up. I even slopped beer onto my tray so the men abandoned their coins and soggy paper notes. I changed quickly between sets and was soon snaring most of the drink orders. This upped my average amount to more than a hundred dollars per shift – no chump change compared to KFC.

Once home, I'd sit cross-legged on my bed, counting and separating my tips into piles of fives, tens and twenties. That it was possible to make this sort of money just by being naked astounded me. I couldn't believe more people didn't do it. And increasingly I wanted to tell everyone that I did.

For a month I had begged off partying, citing graveyard shifts at KFC. But Kim and Kate kept calling in on late-night chicken runs only to find I wasn't there. They were starting to think I didn't want to hang out with them anymore, which wasn't true. I decided to quit the rooster roster. Then I fessed up to my friends.

'Don't the guys gross you out?' Kim asked. This said after a house party when Kim got wasted on tequila and slept with the sleaziest member of our social circle.

'No,' I said truthfully. 'They're just watching.'

Instead of getting drunk and fucking for free, I was getting paid to parade around sober. Who was the fool?

According to Sonia, I was.

'I don't know how you can do it,' she said, repulsed. This confused me: I'd expected her approval. I tried not to care about what she thought.

Ben seemed amused then disinterested – not the response I'd hoped for either.

'I've met someone,' he said. I tried not to care about that as well.

The only person who did approve was Helen.

'Good on you, doll!' she said. 'If you can do it, why not?'

Then in December my parents dropped by unannounced while Helen was at work. Mum was appalled by the state of the flat, which wasn't bad by student standards. Gibson's food bowl was caked with jellymeat, the lawn was overgrown and there were dirty ashtrays in our smoke-free lounge. My parents didn't know that I smoked, let alone stripped. I wasn't about to enlighten them, not even when Mum said tightly, 'I think it's time Helen moved out.'

I protested, but her mind was made up. It was hard telling Helen.

The parental plan was for me to find a more suitable flatmate once university resumed. Meanwhile, I said I'd picked up extra shifts at the Cotswold Hotel and wouldn't be coming home for the holidays.

That summer was blissfully sweet. I spent my days lazing around the backyard naked, reading books and suntanning, putting on clothes at night to drive to the club and take them off again. Afterwards, I stayed up sequinning till dawn. My life was carefree and of my own making. Stripping was the dream job: I got paid to dance, get fit, wear fabulous costumes and make people feel good. Secretly I was rather proud of what I was doing.

One night in January, Dad came to Christchurch for business and slept on an airbed in the spare room. I tiptoed in at 4 a.m.

with a faceful of make-up, reeking of sweat and Impulse, my heart pounding. Dad stirred; we had a conversation in the dark about how busy work had been, which wasn't strictly a lie. Although I lacked the guts to tell my parents the truth, part of me wanted them to find out. That night, though, Dad didn't turn on the lights to see my garish make-up and I was kind of relieved.

My unreal summer continued and it was full of firsts. The first time I got tipped fifty dollars. The first time I made two hundred in one shift. The first time I saw Japanese businessmen butting out their cigarettes half-smoked. ('Why do they do that?' I asked Craig. 'To show they've got money,' he said.) The first time a customer — also Asian — offered to pay me for sex, whispering, 'Jiggy jiggy?' and making the international hand sign. Stunned, I could only shake my head. The first — and last — time I carried a teddy bear onstage and flounced around in a white sun frock and no knickers, realising too late that there was something awfully wrong when old men leapt up to slide me fives and tens.

And the first time I dyed my hair platinum. In her funky salon, Star brushed on a blue paste that made my scalp burn, wrapped my head in Glad Wrap, whacked on a hairdryer and gave me a knitting needle to scratch with. The result was incandescent white, with bonus head scabs.

'You look just like Marilyn,' Star declared.

Although unconvinced, I liked that people turned to stare at me. I looked like *someone*, even if no one knew who that someone was. Not until I bumped into Jacinta outside Pleasures — both of us wearing blue jeans and cream jumpers, she scowling silently — did I realise I'd recreated myself in her image.

Craig didn't mention the similarity but he loved the transformation. 'You're lapping up this shit, aren't you?' He chortled. 'Looks fucking great.'

It was going to be difficult justifying my new look to my parents, so I decided to minimise any potential conflict. At the end of summer when Kim and Kate again asked if I'd like to flat with them, I didn't hesitate. Then I told Mum and Dad I was moving out. To my surprise, they offered to keep paying my expenses. I couldn't refuse without causing them concern, so guiltily I accepted their generosity. Still, I felt I had won a significant battle in the cold war of independence.

I had high hopes for 1994. I had the freedom I'd craved, a well-paying job I loved and two years left on a degree that required little from me. It was time for the next challenge.

During Orientation Week I dropped into the office of the student newspaper, *Canta*. The editor was a left-wing feminist with a penchant for purple and a dislike of deodorant, but we bonded instantly over our love of the printed word. With the first issue hot off the press, Isabelle needed a sports editor, stat. She offered me the position on the spot. I would be responsible for filling two-to-three pages of copy each week. Unlike music or art, I knew sport. I said yes.

That year I said yes to pretty much everything. I stripped up to five nights a week, studied 'full time' and spent my free hours in the *Canta* office. I was often tired, but I was also nineteen: it was possible to stagger out of bed on four hours' sleep and feel buoyant by midday. After years of being told what to do, I was making up for lost time.

The only troubles I had, once again, were around my home life. My shoebox room grew stifling hot during the day, making it hard to sleep or study. And my ever-expanding wardrobe of costumes was out in the hall – a potential dress-up box for impromptu student parties. On weekends, I would often come home from the club to find a mate crashed out in my bed, too drunk to drive. On top of this, it was stressful asking my housemates to keep my secret. They worried about me too. I had taken to nuking myself Logie-bronze in the solarium, my fake nails were lacquered Revlon Red, and sometimes after work I went to the Palladium nightclub with the boys from the ice.

The United States Air Force had a base in Antarctica, accessed via Christchurch, and the servicemen – especially Bill, Chet and Randy – would call into Rocking Rods whenever they were in town. Most were married and some hadn't seen their wives and kids for months. They were like burly big brothers to us dancers, buying us bourbon and shedding light on why men were from Mars.

Then the youngest, Randy, took a shine to me. He was nineteen with bad acne, a blond crew cut and a tough-guy swagger that masked his sweet nature. I indulged him, listening to his stories, his dream of buying a farm in Minnesota. One day, he chartered a Cessna and took me flying. To say thank you, I invited him home for fish-and-chips and let him kiss me. But when I refused to sleep with him, Randy burst into tears. I didn't know what to do with a crying fly-boy; neither did my housemates. Thankfully he left without incident. Kim and Kate were still concerned, though. It was time to find somewhere else to live.

42

After a disastrous week in a six-bedroom, rat-infested dive, I practically begged two triathlete teachers college students to let me move into their Riccarton townhouse. Yes, I was a stripper, but I was also a sports-mad student. Fiona and Louise were doubtful, but my role at *Canta* got me across the line.

It proved uncomplicated living, for we three were seldom home. Most weekends as I was drifting off to sleep, I'd hear Fi and Lou heading out into the cold dawn to train. All of us squeezed every minute out of the day.

Life settled into a carefully compartmentalised routine: part stripper, part student, part writer. Then one afternoon in April, the home phone rang. It was Dad.

'How's the waitressing going?'

'Good,' I said casually.

'That's strange,' said Dad, 'because I just called into the Cotswold Hotel. They said you haven't worked there in months.'

I swallowed hard and thought fast. Not fast enough.

'We know what you're doing. You were seen.'

'By who?' I said defensively.

'It doesn't matter.' Dad's tone was measured, impenetrable. I tried to explain – it was a good club, it wasn't what he thought – but he cut me off. 'Your mother is waiting for your call.'

I sighed and thrummed my talons on the kitchen counter. Calling Mum was going to make me late for my sunbed appointment.

Mum answered the phone in a small, tremulous voice. 'Is it true?'

'Yes,' I said. She burst into tears.

I listened to her sob for a while, unmoved. I felt I hadn't received their support when I'd been miserable at boarding school.

And it wasn't as if I'd done anything serious like committing armed robbery or murder – though I seemed to be killing off everyone's perception of who I should be.

'*Why?*' she said at last. 'What did we do wrong?'

'God, Mum,' I said, 'this isn't about you.'

It had been my old next-door neighbour, in for Friday drinks. The club had been jam-packed; I wouldn't have noticed him. I was angry, but there was never going to be a good time or a right way to tell my parents.

At first they kept depositing money into my account then one day I noticed they had stopped. I felt relieved – I never had time to spend what I earned – and unexpectedly cut off. Determined to show Mum and Dad I could be both a stripper and a responsible adult, I continued to phone home but the conversations were stilted and filled with unspoken hurt. It became easier not to call.

3.

SIX LARGE TROPHIES WERE KEPT BEHIND THE bar at Rocking Rods. Five were Emmy-style winged goddesses, while the sixth towered a metre high and looked like a miniature Empire State Building. These were for the Miss Nude Canterbury competition, held annually whenever Craig felt like it – usually when patronage needed a boost.

One night in June, I arrived to find the trophies lined up on the bar, Nathan polishing them painstakingly. It had been decided: Miss Nude Canterbury 1994 would be held in three weeks.

The title, the trophies and the two-hundred-dollar prize were tempting for a girl who would never possess the right anatomy for a beauty pageant. (My butt was too big, my legs too short.) But I worried about exposure – or rather, overexposure. I imagined the competition on par with the real Miss Canterbury, complete with crown, paparazzi and girls from all over the region hotly contesting the title. Regretfully, I decided not to enter. Then Craig explained the terms – only his girls were eligible and entry was compulsory. 'And I expect you all to put in a bit of fucking effort.'

All dancers had to prepare a themed three-song show. I decided to make the most of my mop and impersonate Marilyn, sewing a white halter-neck dress and sequinning a matching bikini. My flatmates, skilled at darning polyprop underwear, gave me a hand. Satin gloves, gold sandals and paste jewellery completed the look. I rented *Gentlemen Prefer Blondes* on video and practised hip jutting, winking and pouting. My choreography was loose: lip-sync then strip off.

By competition night, I had become fixated on winning. My closest rival was going to be Misty, who had turned up at Rocking Rods in April with her boyfriend Glen. Since then, Misty had worked every day, even the day they got married. Glen didn't seem to work at all. Misty was a solid girl with jagged dark-blonde hair, an expressionless face and vacant grey eyes. Onstage, she moved like she was in water: slowly and with measured strength, as if battling a strong undertow. There were rumours the couple were 'using'; I didn't know what that meant but knew better than to ask. Fittingly, Misty wouldn't reveal the theme of her show, saying it was a surprise.

That night the club filled quickly with eager customers and excited parlour girls. But Mouse was still grumbling about having to enter, and Nadia and Sasha hadn't bothered to turn up.

Miss Nude Canterbury 1994 began with Craig jumping onstage and announcing the six contestants. In the first blow to my pageant fantasy, and counterintuitively, we were instructed to line up topless.

Then we each drew a number from a smelly hat procured from the old-timer in the front row to determine our order of appearance. I drew number four.

First up was Mouse. She sauntered onstage nude, wearing just a cowgirl hat, to 'You Can Leave Your Hat On'. Much to the bewilderment of the crowd she then proceeded to dress herself while two-stepping to 'Cotton Eye Joe', finishing as a fully clad cowgirl. I thought it clever and clapped loudly. The men didn't clap at all until Craig got up and yelled, 'Make some fucking *noiii-se*!' Perhaps the concept was too complicated.

Second was Lauren, who performed her usual rock-inspired numbers with her customary grace. This was in stark contrast to Demi, one of the girls from Pleasures who I had met on my first day. A stand-in for Violet and dancing third, she thrilled the crowd by wearing a glow-in-the-dark skeleton suit and breakdancing to 'You Can't Touch This'. During her final song, 'Gangsta's Paradise', Demi became unexpectedly shy. A working girl, she wasn't used to getting nude onstage.

Then it was my turn. I mouthed my way through 'Diamonds Are a Girl's Best Friend', exaggerating pouts and winks. During 'Material Girl', I started losing both my clothes and the concept. I was halfway through 'Candle in the Wind' before realising that Marilyn was technically dead by this point. The crowd didn't care but I left the stage clueless as to how I'd performed.

Star was up next. As expected, she stripped to a trilogy of Transvision Vamp.

Misty's was the last show of the night. AC/DC's 'She's Got the Jack' blasted out. Misty strode onstage wearing bondage-high stilettos, a tan pencil skirt and what looked like a real Nazi jacket, a Swastika on its sleeve. In one hand was a riding crop. An eerie silence gripped the room. Misty hauled an unsuspecting customer onstage, shoved the guy down on all fours and yanked off his pants. She whipped him softly at first, then harder. I wondered if *he* could get busted for indecent exposure, or if there was such a thing as an accessory to the charge. The guy hung his head and didn't move. The sight of his pale, welting flesh was disturbing. No one knew whether or not to applaud. It didn't matter: Misty hadn't just killed her competition – she'd massacred it.

Craig lifted the mood by declaring it time to announce the winner. We lined up topless a second time as the trophies for best butt, legs, chest, body and show were awarded. I was shocked by the blatant dissection of assets, but in a family-friendly gesture that stunned me even more, each dancer was awarded a trophy – Lauren won best body, Misty best show – except me. I was still trying to compute this when a massive bunch of lilies scurried onstage, Vince behind it.

'Second runner-up is ...' Craig paused. 'Lauren!'

Lauren took her flowers and murmured into the mic, 'Thanks.'

'First runner-up is ... Misty!' Craig handed Misty her bouquet and the mic.

'I'd like to thank my husband Glen for all his support,' said Misty, 'and Rocking Rods and Craig for giving me this opportunity.'

Of course she wouldn't advocate world peace, I thought, still wondering why I hadn't won anything.

'The winner of Miss Nude Canterbury 1994 is … *Holly*!' yelled Craig. Then he was kissing my cheek and slipping on a fringed red sash and handing me an enormous bouquet and the even bigger trophy. Startled, I just stood there. How could I have won without winning best butt, legs, chest, body or show? It didn't make sense.

Everyone was waiting for a response. I tried to kiss the runners-up, almost pin-cushioning Misty with my trophy. Then I waited for Craig to hand me the mic. Realising he wasn't going to I reached for it, but I hadn't thought of anything to say.

'I'd like to thank my flatmates for all their patient sequinning,' I said at last.

Craig frowned and snatched back the mic. 'Give Holly another round of applause!'

I smiled the way beauty pageant winners did on TV while Craig thanked the judges, whoever they were, then the audience. Then Saturday night resumed as normal.

At 3 a.m., I was halfway out the door with my trophy when Craig called out, '*Oi!* Bring that here.'

'I don't get to take it home?' I said disbelievingly.

'You've got your sash and your two hundred bucks, what more do you want?'

So I watched Nathan put it back behind the bar. There would be no inscription; there wasn't even a crown. I sensed the competition hadn't been a real contest – it felt self-serving, staged, even pre-determined. By what criteria, I wasn't sure. I drove home feeling unexpectedly cheated.

* * *

Over time I began to see the bigger picture, the different limbs of the Christchurch sex industry. Prostitution was still illegal, which meant investing in it – and improving workplace conditions – was risky business. I admired Craig's commitment. He was slowly building an empire that included Rocking Rods, Pleasures, and two other inner-city parlours – the upmarket Cherry's and the grungy Vixens.

It was through the parlours that bookings for outcall strips often came. On weekends, experienced strippers like Lauren would leave Rocking Rods for an hour or more with a driver, a ghetto blaster and the promise of an extra fifty dollars.

One Friday, Craig asked if I would do an outcall. I asked what it involved. He chuckled. 'What do you mean, what does it involve? Just take your kit off.'

Around 11 p.m., the driver collected me from the club in his battered Toyota Corolla. Ned was a hefty Caucasian in his late fifties. A man of few words, he had a piercing gaze – perhaps because he was a laser cutter by day. As he drove towards the poorer eastern suburbs, Ned spent as much time eyeing my breasts as he did the road. I sat stone-faced in the passenger seat sensing I'd made a very bad call. Perhaps misinterpreting my fear as stage fright, Ned fished a small pipe out from under his seat. He held it up. I shook my head.

'Can you hold the wheel?'

So I steered while he packed and lit the pipe. The car filled with the pungent aroma of hash.

We dawdled along the Avon River into Linwood, Ned making a few wrong turns through the sleepy streets. Then he pulled into a cul-de-sac lined with vehicles. Lights blazed and music thundered from one particular house. Ned took the ghetto blaster out of the boot regardless. I followed him to the open front door. In the hallway were two gangly boys in their late teens.

'Ssstrippershere!' one yelled, turning and crashing into the doorframe.

Someone twice as old but just as pissed greeted us with the cash. He said it was Scotty's twenty-first. In the lounge we found Scotty handcuffed to a kitchen chair wearing a pair of lucky clover boxer shorts. He looked at me like he'd just died and gone to a heaven he would never remember when he woke up in his own vomit. Surrounding him was a pack of mates in his likeness – and his nine-year-old brother, who was quickly shooed from the room.

AC/DC was turned off. Ned stumbled out of his stupor long enough to press play on the ghetto blaster. 'Call Me' sounded out. I began to gyrate; Scotty began to drool. I bounced around in his lap, not entirely sure what to do.

'Yorr prethhy,' he said.

Someone held out a cup of ice. 'Hey, put this down his pants!'

I plonked the ice down Scotty's boxers and bounced some more, feeling a sense of self-importance at all the attention. The boys made caveman noises and Ned stared off into space. Buzzing with adrenaline, free from club rules, I took off my G and grabbed my ankles. It was my first conscious flash. Scotty missed it: he was too busy defrosting his balls.

Then it was all over and I was shown into a bedroom with a single racing car bed and a poster of the All Blacks. I dressed, wondering where the nine-year-old was hiding.

As we headed back to the club I realised I had crossed a boundary: I had taken Holly into the outside world.

* * *

Holly went on plenty more excursions. For a while, I accepted every outcall offered. I stripped in broad daylight: in high-rise offices among middle-aged secretaries, balloons and plates of lamingtons. I stripped beneath the cover of darkness: cavorting among the cards at an illegal casino above a Chinese restaurant. I stripped for virgins and retirees, for groups of five and groups of fifty. I stripped when lively, tired, happy or sad. And I always stripped sober, though not always straight. Ned kept offering the pipe and occasionally I took it.

While stripping stoned made the unpredictable nature of outcalls easier to handle, I would wander back into the club with a goofy grin and little focus. Oblivious to drink orders, I made noticeably less money and felt unprofessional being out of it at work. The novelty soon wore off. As did the newness of doing outcalls: after a few months, I became tired of not knowing where we were going or what to expect. Usually it was a bunch of merry drunks in someone's living room, but not always.

One Friday afternoon Misty and I did an outcall in the boardroom of the local racecourse. It was packed with drunk, mouthy, middle-aged men.

'She's got a tidy arsehole,' one said matter-of-factly, 'I'd like to fuck that.'

I raised my eyebrows at Misty, wondering if we should continue. She kept dancing. Ned was gazing out the window.

The organiser leered over the table at Misty. 'I bet you taste good. How'd you like me to eat your cunt?'

Misty regarded the man with her usual blank stare. Slowly, she slid off her French knickers. Then she balled them up, cupped the back of the man's head and ever so nicely force-fed him until he gagged. That shut everyone up.

On the way home Misty asked Ned to make a detour so she could pick up something from a friend's house. Soon after emerging empty-handed, she insisted Ned pull over. We watched while she vomited neatly into a rubbish bin.

'Are you all right?' I asked as she got back in the car.

'I'm fine now. It was just something I ate,' she said.

Ned considered her in the rear-view mirror as he drove. I kept asking if she was okay and Misty kept assuring me she was. I couldn't understand how she could be fine one moment and so sick the next. Nor could I understand why the men had been nasty to us when we'd worked hard to give them a good show.

Infinitely more appreciative was a crew of warehouse workers who had purpose-built a stage two metres high. They forklifted me onto it while blasting 'Stairway to Heaven' on a primo sound system. I thrashed about happily for the full eight minutes while the men grinned like birthday boys. Afterwards Ned and I made an exception and accepted their generously poured Jack Daniels and Cokes. The organiser thanked me twice and I left with a warm glow, not just from the whiskey. I was appreciated; I had made a difference to the men's day. This working-class world had bucket-loads of heart, and this was where I began to have a real appreciation for blue-collar workers.

In contrast I began to hate the upper-middle-class outcalls. I remember one at a swanky twenty-first in a garden marquee, packed with smug private school kids necking Veuve and sucking cigars. It was the sort of place I expected to find Ben, who I hadn't seen in months. Fortunately I didn't. I did see several girls from the year above me at school, snickering, which caused me to cut the set short.

But it was the outcall for the cornflake guy that really got to me. On a midwinter full moon night, Ned and I were called out to a buck's party at a rundown two-storey house. A bonfire blazed in the backyard ringed by twenty guys as burly as rugby players. They had been drinking all day. Their fat, red-faced buck lay prone in the long grass, wearing a nappy. He was encrusted in what looked like sores but closer inspection revealed he had been coated in golden syrup and rolled in cornflakes.

There was no way I was going near him.

I skipped manically around the buck like a priestess performing a warped pagan ritual, both of us wearing white in the moonlight. The guys insisted I get 'real close' and got riled when I didn't. Even Ned was twitchy. I was just about to bolt when the buck spewed up all over himself. I swore I'd never do outcalls again, and I didn't.

* * *

At a failing pub in the city centre he'd renamed The Wild Stallion, Craig trialled lunchtime shows. All dancers had to work there every second Thursday and Friday. We did these two-hour, forty-dollar shifts begrudgingly: the midday start was a struggle, no one ever tipped and the place – a converted shopfront, long and narrow – was a dive. The Formica bar ran along one wall, the hastily built stage the other. The handful of regular drinkers seemed affronted by the stage. While we stripped topless, they sat with their backs to us, watching horseracing on TV. In between sets, we slouched on the couch in the front window, feeling stiff and wrung out.

The only thing wild about The Wild Stallion was the DJ. Travis smoked a lot of weed and ran the show in manic disorder. One Thursday he channelled a horseracing commentator. 'She'srunningherownracethisfilly,' he announced as I took off my bra, 'it'sHollybyanipple!' Tears of laughter streamed down my cheeks and for once our audience had turned around, but word got back to 'the boss'. No one was sorry when lunchtime shows at The Wild Stallion wound up.

Peepshows came next. Craig opened the first below Rocking Rods, the second beneath Vixens. Both doubled as sex shops, selling adult toys and videos. Like lolly stores, they had PVC strip curtains, enticing window displays and they took coins. Each booth was regulated by a timer fed by a fistful of loose change.

Parlour girls mostly worked the peepshows, but any dancer could roster on. At first, the thought of men jerking off while girls inserted lube-coated objects into their orifices appalled me. Then I became curious, especially after Star added a shift or two, shrugged and said she didn't mind getting paid to make herself come. So one night when Craig stuck his head into the dressing-room and asked for someone to work the next day I said I would.

'*You?*' he said. 'You're not fucking working there.'

'Why not?' I demanded.

'You're telling me you wanna show your cunt like that?'

'No,' I said, quietly relieved.

'Then drop it.'

Sometimes Craig was inexplicably protective. Not long after this he mentioned that a Japanese businessman had offered to pay five thousand dollars to have sex with me. Craig had refused.

'Why didn't you ask me?' I said angrily. Surely it was my decision? Five grand was a lot of money and the Japanese were always polite to my face. I might've done it.

'I did you a fucking favour!' Craig said, disgusted. 'Prostitution is selling your soul.'

I fell silent, figuring he of all people should know.

Although I was no longer shocked at the reality of prostitution, I had no desire to become a working girl. I stripped because I liked to dance, because I loved being onstage, because I enjoyed the freedom night work and good money provided.

Also, I didn't see any benefits to hooking, only the pitfalls. That winter, a young porn starlet from Sydney spent a week in Christchurch, working the parlours during the day and stripping at Rocking Rods at night. Angel was a size six with golden curls and cow-brown eyes. She began the week spirited and self-possessed, but by Thursday she had collapsed on the dressing-room floor, inconsolable. Nathan notified Craig, who came backstage and surveyed the crumpled figure we'd all been stepping around.

'What's going on?' said Craig. 'What's wrong?'

Angel lifted her head. 'I'm exhausted! I've fucked twelve fucking men today.'

'Then you've had a great fucking day, haven't you? Think of all the money you've made.' Craig tried to coax Angel to do a set, but she could barely walk. Sighing he said, 'Pack up your shit. I'll drive you home.'

We all watched Angel hobble out.

More resilient was fellow Australian porn star Sunny McKay, who toured soon after. Sunny arrived with back-up dancers, a choreographed routine and a husband. Barry was a kindly man who wore seventies-era suits and managed a strip club in Melbourne called The Men's Gallery.

'It's one of the best in the world,' he told me. 'Any time you feel like a holiday, luv, you let Craig know.'

I thanked Barry but had no plans to strip for longer than it took to become a journalist.

Indeed, carving out a career in the sex industry, deliberately or by default, seemed very far removed from the part-time act of taking off my clothes, which is why I distinctly remember picking up my pay one day from Pleasures. One of the working girls – a world-weary, forty-something bottle-blonde – observed my self-assuredness with a sad smile.

'This is a tempting industry,' she said quietly, 'but it can be very hard to get out of.'

I frowned. 'I can get out any time I choose.'

She handed over my pay packet with a wordless nod. I headed back down the stairs, wondering why she'd felt the need to warn me.

* * *

Since becoming Miss Nude Canterbury, my relationships with the other dancers had deteriorated. Craig's double standards hadn't helped. Nor had the Thai Cowboy, who would strut into Rocking Rods every month and fill his Stetson hatband with twenty-dollar notes. And on whose head would he place that crown? It used to be Tia's, now it was usually mine. In an instant, I would make more money than most dancers did in two nights.

Then Mouse fell pregnant and left, Nadia and Sasha quit, and Lauren's sister Nicole started full time. A bigger, louder, nastier version of Lauren, Nicole disliked me on sight. The first night we worked together, I tried to join in a backstage bitch about not being able to drink on the job.

'Who asked you?' Nicole demanded.

'Well, no one,' I said, startled.

'Then shut the fuck up.'

I'd only been in two fights in my life and both had ended with me face-planting concrete. I shut up.

Then I started finding my suitcase upended in the corner of the dressing-room. The first time I repacked it wordlessly. The second, I said in a wavering voice, 'Who did that?'

Nicole sniggered, Lauren too. Star looked on sympathetically as I gathered up my stuff. Soon the upending and the cold-shouldering were a nightly occurrence. I began to dread going to work. The night a dirty ashtray 'fell' into my suitcase, I phoned rival club Route 66 and arranged an interview.

Route 66 was a topless revue bar with male and female performers, that much I knew. Entering the airless music box, I was confronted by a muscly Ken-doll strutting around a low central stage. He wore steel caps and cut-off denim shorts, butt cheeks exposed. I wasn't sure I liked my men so buff, bronzed or hairless, but the hen's night ladies screaming stage-side certainly did.

I found the manager at the bar drinking a bloody mary. Sam was overweight, amicable and wore an ill-fitting suit. He said he'd heard of me and offered eighty dollars per shift, which sounded generous until I realised dancers didn't waitress. And even though the 'showgirls' – as Sam called them – were drop-dead gorgeous and their performances pop-video polished, there didn't seem to be any tipping going on. Also, the slicker, brighter atmosphere felt horribly exposing, as did the prevalence of women in the crowd. I knew all about girl talk: my antics would be public knowledge in no time.

Remembering Nicole's bullying, I agreed to start that weekend. Then I phoned Craig and quit.

'What?' he barked. 'Talk to me.'

'There's nothing to discuss.'

'Meet me for a coffee then. Don't you owe us that?'

Because *he* owed *me* a week's pay, we met at the pub opposite Pleasures.

'You can't leave,' said Craig after we'd sat down. 'You're our star performer.'

I sipped my long black and said nothing.

'What are they paying you?'

'It's not about the money.'

'Then what is it about?'

'It's been almost a year. It's time for a change, that's all.'

Craig eyeballed me; I eyeballed my coffee.

'Are the girls giving you a hard time?' he said sharply. I shook my head, but couldn't keep the misery off my face.

'I'll give you one hundred bucks a shift.'

One hundred! My eyes lifted; so did the corners of my mouth. I could put up with Nicole for that.

For a while, work did improve. Nicole must have been told to pull her head in because the bitchiness stopped. With Craig behind me, I felt less intimidated, more aware of my worth. That was until I glimpsed Misty's eighty-dollar-a-shift pay packet and realised other dancers had negotiated their wage too. I wasn't so in control, after all.

The unravelling feeling continued. One night after work my car wouldn't start so I caught a taxi home. The driver glanced at me in the rear-view mirror. 'Nice pics.'

'Huh?' I said.

'*The Picture* article.'

'I have no idea what you're talking about.'

He handed me a crumpled magazine and flicked on the inside light. 'Have a look. You're in there somewhere.'

Convinced he was mistaken, I looked anyway. And there I was. Three photos spread over two pages, all taken at Rocking Rods. Two of me onstage – one naked, one topless. The third in my waitering garb, a close-up from behind. 'Rear of the Year!' the heading proclaimed. It was undeniably me.

Beneath the flashing lights, my mind on the music, my eyes scouring ringside for tips, I knew I wouldn't have noticed the photographer. I also knew Craig must have condoned it.

At least the photos weren't bad. Just one was nude and my little runway stripe was all you could see. In fact, I looked pretty good, grasping the pole and pouting. But any thrill ended when I read: "'I love big cock," this luscious horn-bag confided.' I tossed the magazine aside, breathless with fury. I hadn't said *any* of this! How could people get away with writing such crap?

I wanted to sue Craig and every last person involved but a lawyer advised me to let it go. These types of lawsuits weren't easily won. They cost money and the only guaranteed outcome was unwanted publicity, which might affect my chances of becoming a serious journalist.

I was hopeful Craig might apologise or even offer compensation. In the face of my righteous indignation, he was dismissive. The photographer had been there to shoot Angel. Of course if I sued, he would have to let me go. And the photos were all right, weren't they? I conceded they were.

Craig chuckled. 'You're cute when you're angry.'

Around this time my Vauxhall Viva died and I tried to cheer myself up by blowing every last cent on a red Honda Prelude. Driving around with the sunroof open and the stereo pumping really was a blast, in spite of my residual fatigue.

Too tired to keep my worlds apart, I let them bleed into each other. I was often late to my Monday morning Middle Eastern politics lecture. One day I strode in wearing a pair of thigh-high boots and knew instantly I'd gone too far. The looks I received weren't adoring but horrified. I squirmed into a front-row seat and sweated out the hour, wishing I could disappear. That afternoon I went into a top salon in the city and told the first available hairdresser to cut off all my hair. He created me in his likeness – a golden version of his own short, dark crop. He told me I was beautiful and I felt beautiful, like a truer version of myself. When the salon closed we went back to his apartment and had wordless, unprotected sex. The next day I regretted all of it.

It didn't help that Craig hated my new look. 'What the fuck did you do that for?' he snapped. I said nothing because I had no idea.

After a week of making noticeably less money, I bought a white Cleopatra wig from Star. She tugged a cut-off stocking onto my head and affixed the wig with bobby pins. Cheap and synthetic, the ends caught in my mouth when I danced and became stained red. In fact the wig only exacerbated the mind-fuck. I felt like a caricature and started to become seriously confused about where Holly ended and Leigh began.

Increasingly, I sought refuge in the *Canta* office. The sports section improved and, some weeks, I was allocated extra pages. Under Isabelle's guidance I began writing for other sections of the paper too, including the arts.

When Manpower Australia came to town I arranged a review ticket, curious to learn how my nude brothers reconciled their public and private personas. The Palladium was packed with screaming middle-aged women, while I sat quietly up the back watching the performers' faces, trying to read their minds. Only once did a polished mask slip into white-eyed fear, when a hefty woman made an unsuccessful clean-and-jerk at Jamie Durie's G. Post-performance, Jamie spoke to me in between posing for Polaroids with women perched on his knee. Friendly, frank and clearly tired, he glossed over questions to do with personification. Short of ruining my limited press cred by confiding that I too was a stripper, I lacked the know-how to encourage more telling answers.

Nevertheless, that article saw me nominated for the Associated Student Press arts review of the year. The only nominee from *Canta*, I flew to Wellington with Isabelle for the awards night. Held at a Turkish restaurant, it basically consisted of eating kebabs, whingeing about the lack of student press funding and getting sloshed on carafes of cheap red. To my surprise, I won the arts review category (and a very cute snow dome).

Instead of returning to the hostel with the others, I found my way to Licks – Wellington's then only strip club – and talked the manager into letting me do a set. Some girl loaned me a dress and shoes. I made thirty-five bucks in tips and cruised out of there feeling like a rock star. In the morning I worried that word of my moonlighting would have reached the *Canta* office.

It hadn't. This was confirmed when I was interviewed for the editor's job for 1995. My plan was to get shortlisted, which would stand me in good stead for the following year when I'd finished my degree. In the interview the Student Union reps were adamant *Canta* start turning a profit and I made up some moneymaking suggestions that they liked. At nineteen, I was appointed the youngest-ever editor of the University of Canterbury student newspaper. No one was more astonished than me.

4.

THE TITLE OF MISS NUDE CANTERBURY HAD COME with an unofficial prize: a ride on Craig's Harley Davidson Fat Boy. For months he'd been asking me and for months I'd been saying no. Going out with my much older, bad-arse boss was not a good idea, however packaged. Still, the thought of blasting through Christchurch on a Harley thrilled the pants off me. I'd never been on a motorbike before and I was craving fun before the responsibility of *Canta*. One time couldn't hurt. So when Craig next sidled up to me and said, 'Tomorrow's gonna be a grouse day for a ride. Wanna come?' I surprised him by saying, 'Why not?'

Bang on 1 p.m. Sunday, Craig rumbled up the driveway. Cutting the engine on the sickest machine I'd ever seen, he tossed me some leathers. I kitted out and perched delicately at the far end of the pillion.

'You'll need to come closer than that!' he chuckled. 'Hold on tight, all right?'

I inched forward and wrapped my arms around his generous girth. Craig revved the throttle and wove out into the traffic, bound for the open road. The sun streamed down and the wind whipped at my skin. With potential disaster so close at hand, I felt keenly alive. Not unlike stripping. In the rear-view mirror, Craig caught sight of me – all teeth and slobber – and grinned back.

When he pulled into a manicured winery on the outskirts of town, I was almost sorry. But the disapproving yet envious glances of the white linen crowd made up for it. Ignoring them, we considered each other across a secluded picnic table. I lit a cigarette. Craig ordered a bottle of Moët and an antipasto platter. When the bubbles arrived, he toasted me. 'You're a hard nut to crack.'

I laughed and raised my glass, but didn't mention it was the first time I'd tried real champagne. Determined to keep pace, I was soon plastered.

Craig was entertaining, but he also asked a lot of questions, including my thoughts on the sex industry. I couldn't remember the last time someone significantly older had valued my opinion instead of telling me what to think. Champagne-loose, I blabbered along unchecked. I was having a great time.

So when we spilled in my front door at dusk, red-cheeked and merry, it wasn't hard to kiss Craig. Then, conscious my flatmates could appear at any moment and see me snogging a middle-aged biker, I gave him a playful shove. 'Go on, go. I'm not sleeping with you.' He strode off like a proud lion, knowing it was only a matter of time.

That December, Craig collected me at all hours in a Corvette, a Range Rover, even a Rolls-Royce. Aside from the Harley, these didn't impress me as much as Craig's enthusiasm for them. We would speed off to our next adventure – a spin around the Port Hills, a flutter at the casino or dinner at a top-notch restaurant. Everything was fun and I laughed – Craig made me laugh a lot.

Even working at Rocking Rods felt lighter. Now that the other dancers knew I was a regular fixture on the Fat Boy, they were much nicer to me. And when I finally slept with Craig, he proved as generous and playful a lover as he was a suitor. Against all good sense, I wanted to keep seeing him.

When Fi and Lou both accepted jobs up north, I decided to get my own place. There was a one-bedroom unit for rent nearby – quiet, spacious and seemingly secure. I wrote 'editor' on the application and was approved. Scrimping together rent and bond, I worked extra shifts to buy a second-hand fridge and washing machine, and picked up the keys just before Christmas.

Craig offered to help with the move. He arrived in a three-tonne truck driven by a morose Maori guy and the pair spent the early evening lugging furniture. They still hadn't finished by the time I needed to leave for work. Reluctantly, I gave Craig my keys and let him finish up.

I came home to an enormous Christmas tree sparkling in the corner of the lounge. Craig had also arranged my battered furniture, hung new curtains and stocked my fridge with champagne.

I dropped onto Fi's old couch and stared at the tree. Craig had done this for me, this beautiful gesture. But instead of joy, I felt an inexplicable sense of dread. I sat there for a long time, wondering if he was stifling my independence or if I was just being ungrateful. I went to bed still not knowing.

* * *

That summer Craig guided me around his multi-faceted world, which included his move to get into mainstream nightclubbing. Cruisers was on the first floor of a cavernous brick showroom on Manchester Street. On opening night, Craig's mates piled cash across the bar, but they might've scared away the few genuine punters, because no one stayed for long. The club sat empty. Two weeks on, even Craig's most loyal followers had stopped making polite noises about its potential. Cruisers had crashed and burned. So Craig did what he did best and turned it into a strip club.

Within days, a sprawling stage had been constructed out of plasterboard, painted black and fitted with rusty old poles. A new sign hung out front: 'The Flaming Phoenix'. I'd never heard of the mythical bird but begrudgingly agreed it sounded smoking hot. There were more punters that first night than the previous fortnight combined. I was happy for Craig – and relieved I didn't have to work there.

Then Craig shut down Rocking Rods. I could not believe it.

'It wasn't making money,' he explained. 'Some weeks, you pulled more outta there than I did.'

I couldn't believe that either. To my untrained eye, the boutique club had appeared consistently full.

The Flaming Phoenix was different from Rocking Rods because it catered to the masses. It also attracted roving packs of loud young tradies. These boys were cashed up and devoted to writing themselves off every weekend. They put money across the bar, but they didn't appreciate the finer points of striptease. Nor did they tip.

Worse was the pay rate. All dancers received fifty dollars per shift. When I complained, Craig said to wait until business picked up. The prima donna in me objected, but it was hard to argue with equal opportunity. There wasn't room for prima donnas at the Phoenix. There wasn't even a dressing-room. Backstage, dancers squeezed in between the bar and the fire escape, costumes and cosmetics piled onto beer kegs. Onstage, a single performer got lost in the vastness. Then Craig had the bright idea of having three girls stripping at once. He staggered the roster: one exited as another came on. With just six dancers, this meant three songs on, three songs off. I soon lost count of how many times I performed each night. We were all exhausted.

Between sets, there was barely time to change costumes, skol a free sugar hit from the bar and smoke a cigarette, let alone waitress for drinks. And Craig had hired a full-time waitress, a single mother desperate for dosh. Belinda was always one step ahead of me. I took to loitering backstage, smoking myself silly and lamenting the end of Rocking Rods.

One by one the old hands left: Lauren and Nicole went to Route 66; Star began hairdressing full time; Misty and Glen moved to Dunedin. Only I stayed, hopeful Craig would up my pay. With a new lease and just weeks before my editing salary began, I didn't know what else to do. I felt certain I'd burnt my bridges with Route 66 by not taking the job. Besides, Nicole was there, and it was too visible a club. I would be outed, fired from *Canta* before I'd even begun.

Now that I was to be editor, I'd swapped my Cleopatra bob for a long chestnut wig – a more serious disguise. Hurrying to get onstage one night I didn't pin it on properly. I was cavorting near the tip rail (a misnomer given no one ever did) when a sexagenarian gaped up at me, brows knotted. Puzzled, I turned to find road kill on the runway. My hands flew to my head. The cut-off stocking wavered like a Christmas hat. I scooped up the wig and shoved it back on with a carelessness that was only part fake.

Where had my rapture gone?

As the weeks passed, the only thing smoking hot about this phoenix was the cigarette lodged between my lips.

Meanwhile, the new girls were fresh out of school, enthusiastic and eager. They wore the same wondrous expression I'd worn only twelve months earlier. No wonder Craig hadn't upped my pay! Then I started to worry that if I kicked up a fuss or left the Phoenix it would be the end of us.

The truth was I liked being with Craig. I liked his Leo fierceness, his appetite for life, his lack of pretention. I liked that he was anti-establishment, that he didn't give a fuck. I didn't love him, but perhaps it wasn't that important. Perhaps age wasn't either. Craig was thirty-nine to my nineteen, but he didn't seem *old*. Could my fling have a future? I found myself wanting to prove my worth.

When Sonia's friend Jen, a cadet reporter at respected broadsheet *The Press*, asked me to be part of a series on ways students were putting themselves through university, I hesitated, wary of publicity. But it was an opportunity to portray striptease positively, perhaps to right *The Picture* wrong. I agreed, provided there were no photos and I could veto the copy.

'It'll be another black mark against the industry,' Craig warned. 'You wait and see.'

After I'd okayed the copy, Jen said the article might not run without a photo. Would I reconsider? The photographer assured my identity would be disguised. I agreed.

The in-house photo shoot – my first – was clumsy. Despite my wig, I felt overexposed, the costumes unflattering and tawdry under the studio lights. The image we chose – me from behind, wearing a sequinned dress, peeling off a long glove – was a mess of bondage meets cabaret. I left, wondering if I'd done the right thing.

The day the article came out, I sped-read it then broke into a cold sweat. I had been quoted as saying drug use was prevalent, which wasn't what I'd said at all. I phoned Jen and demanded an explanation. She said the subeditor had intervened to make it more interesting. It didn't matter that I demanded and got a retraction: the damage had been done.

'You don't get it, do you?' Craig said, once he'd calmed down. 'These girls don't do this because they're supporting kids or a drug habit or an abusive boyfriend. They do it because they don't fit into society, because they don't *belong*.'

This was a light-bulb moment. Was it the same for me? Had I been seeking somewhere I belonged? I thought I'd found it centrestage, but it hadn't lasted. Now the dancers wanted nothing to do with me, Craig was pissed off and my parents (who had recognised me from the photo) were deeply upset. I had been hoping to find my place in print, but my faith in the media had taken a serious knock. I didn't trust others to listen, and – more importantly – I didn't trust myself to get it right. I didn't seem to belong anywhere.

* * *

The more time I spent with Craig, the more disconnected I became from my own life. My flat was an expensive refuge, but I was hardly there other than to sleep. Occasionally, Craig stayed over. He would tug off his Johnny Rebels, pile his denim onto a chair and pass out. I'd watch him snore – his top lip curled into a soft snarl – and wonder how he'd come to be in my bed, this fat man with his faded tattoos and his conditional generosity. His phone would wake him at all hours and he was usually up and gone before me. His presence was so large and often demanding that his absence left a noticeable hole in my day or my plans.

Things were becoming semi-serious. I'd met his parents. He'd let me drive his Corvette. I'd accompanied him to the Tai Tapu auction where he'd bought a farmhouse bordered by willow trees and a bubbling stream. Craig promptly added two llamas, two Newfoundland dogs, and was given a Kunekune pig that slept on the living room floor.

I liked it on the farm. It was quiet, peaceful. It reminded me of my childhood – apart from the security gates, the crates of porn and the fleet of luxury cars on the lawn. Actually, farm and farm animals aside, it was nothing like my upbringing. This was why none of my friends had met Craig and certainly not my parents, who had greeted the news of our courtship with horrified silence. I thought it highly doubtful that anyone I knew would look past Craig's reputation and rough exterior.

In stark comparison, most of his friends had greeted me warmly. There was Tina, a fortyish fire-eater, who had a pet python and liked to critique German porn over breakfast; Fred, a fast-talking, chain-smoking professional thief with terminal cancer, who joked he'd soon be so thin the cameras couldn't catch him; and Peri, a retired retailer whose five ex-husbands had taken most of her money, and who gave Craig the Kunekune.

* * *

My new role at *Canta* didn't get off to a great start. Two days in, Craig said, 'Let's go to Queensland.'

I stared at him as if he were mad. 'I *can't*.'

'Of course you can. You're the boss. Can't someone cover you for a week?'

Liking this high-flier image, I arranged for the previous editor, Isabelle, to edit the second issue. I knew it was wrong, but I couldn't refuse Craig. We flew to Noosa and holed up in a five-star resort. He paid for it all.

By the time we were back the first issue of *Canta* had hit campus and a quarter of it was an indecipherable brown blur. To cut costs I had changed printers, but the files hadn't been formatted correctly. It was a 5500-copy disaster. That Isabelle hadn't picked up on it meant there was little chance I would have, but it was no consolation. I should have been there.

After that I set about producing the best newspaper I could. True to my word, *Canta* began turning a profit almost immediately. It didn't occur to me that perhaps student papers weren't about making money.

At first there was no time to strip and I struggled to pay my rent. I saw less of Craig too. It didn't last – I missed his spirit and spontaneity. And as much as I relished the creative challenge of planning a weekly paper, I yearned for the stage – for the physicality, the instant affirmation and the mind-numbing exhaustion. So every few Saturdays I squeezed in a shift.

One night I came home from the Phoenix to find my bedroom window had been jemmied open. Nothing was missing. A week later, I was in bed when whoever it was tried again.

'*Fuck off!*' I barked, in my best Craig impersonation. They ran away, but I was so shaken I spent a week on the farm.

Craig suggested I move in. He'd asked me before, now I said yes. Kim's brother took over my lease. The Maori guy and the truck came back, but this time Craig didn't help.

Shifting into the farmhouse felt like a good move. I loved walking the dogs in the evenings, cooking random hotpots with Craig, falling asleep to the dense quiet of the countryside.

Then after about ten days Craig turned to me. 'When are you going to clean the house?'

I thought he was joking. 'Most of it's your mess.'

Craig scowled. 'You're not paying rent. The least you can do is keep the place looking tidy.'

I scowled back. 'I'm not going to play housewife.'

'And I'm not going to live like a filthy fucking student! Is it too much to ask that you clean the place once in while? I pay all the fucking bills around here.'

'I'd rather pay my share,' I said.

'Well, that doesn't solve my problem, does it?'

We agreed that I would pay for a cleaner. I remember thinking at the time how well we had navigated that first intergenerational hurdle.

And about a month after that Craig barrelled through the door and announced, 'I'm not having you taking your kit off anymore.'

'What?' I laughed. 'That's not your decision to make.'

'Like fuck it isn't! You work for me, don't forget. I'm not having my girlfriend doing that shit.'

I stared at him, dumbfounded. 'Why didn't you say so before I moved in?'

'Why would you want to keep doing it when you don't have to?' Craig threw up his hands, baffled.

'Because I like it,' I said desperately, wondering if I still did. But I knew with certainty that I didn't like being told what to do.

'Look, why don't you give waitressing a go? Belinda is making twice as much as you girls. I'll fire her if you like.'

'I'm *not* a fucking waitress!'

I stormed out and sulked in the spare room. Remembering Tia, I saw I'd been a fool. I had thought it would be four years before Craig made any ultimatums.

I came out and made one of my own. 'I'll leave.'

'If you wanna fuck off, fuck off,' Craig shrugged. 'But you'll never strip in this town again.'

I believed him.

Stripping was a door I didn't want slammed shut. Perhaps I could talk Craig around. Besides, I was tired of moving and I was broke. I didn't want to ask my parents for help – to admit that I'd fucked up – when we'd hardly seen each other for a year. So I put pride aside and tried waitressing.

Craig was right: the first shift I made two hundred in tips alone, even with Belinda as competition. The dancers were literally working their arses off for a third of the money. But it wasn't just about the cash: I craved the limelight. I gazed up at the dancers with wistful longing just like the customers did.

The only guys there for the waitresses were the windswept Russian seamen in their cheap parkas. They ordered vodka by the bottle and drank it like water. The Russians didn't speak much English, but pressed tin badges of their ships – docked in Lyttelton Harbour – into my hand. They'd raise their glasses and with gaping smiles declare, 'Russia! Yah!' I'd smile back and treasure these keepsakes.

As winter closed in I pushed on, working six or seven days. Craig did too; his empire never slept. In the evenings, I would find him tallying take-sheets at the kitchen table, the dogs at his feet. He would churn down antacids and lurch out into the night, problem-solving with hot-headed ruthlessness. I admired Craig's ability to get the job done, but wondered if he had limits. Trying to keep up, I ignored my own.

One night at the Phoenix, I was carrying a glass of water through the crowd when a strapping man seized my wrist. I told him to let go. Instead, he held up my hand like a trophy, challenging me with his eyes. So I glassed him, before I knew what glassing was. His hands fled to his face. It seemed the room went very quiet. Then blood began pissing out between his fingers. My heart rate didn't rise. I walked out the back, sat on a keg and waited to feel something. That I never did shocked me most of all.

* * *

The year ticked by. I suspected I should leave Craig, I just didn't seem able to.

One afternoon he caught me pining over my suitcase of costumes. I was on my knees, admiring an exquisite rainbow-sequinned corset. He left the room and came back with a pair of scissors. 'It's either me or stripping, make up your fucking mind.'

'You can't mean it,' I said incredulously.

'I do mean it.'

Hesitantly, I took the scissors.

He stood over me. 'Come on!'

Several thoughts flashed through my mind. The first: he couldn't force me to love him. The second: I would never forgive him for this. The third: I had no choice.

Finally, I made a small cut. Repairable, perhaps?

'Faster!' barked Craig.

Another cut. The sequins tumbled like docked flowers. Tears streamed uselessly down my cheeks. I gave in, sliced and hacked at each hand-sewn creation until nothing was left intact. Then

I dropped the scissors. 'There. Are you happy now? Because I fucking hate you.' I wiped my nose on my sleeve and wouldn't look at Craig. Eventually, he walked out of the room.

Days later he apologised. It was a first. 'I was way outta line. I don't know what came over me.' His eyes were wet. I hugged him and said nothing.

Sometimes I wondered how it was for him being with someone he knew didn't love him, and I felt both guilty and sad.

Sometimes, though, he was pragmatic about it. 'If you play your cards right, you'll do well out of me. Look at Jacinta.' Jacinta had sold her share of Pleasures and started a pool hall with her new man.

'I'm not Jacinta,' I said. 'I don't want the same things she does.'

'You don't know what you want.'

He was right about that.

I began to doubt my dream to write for a living, especially when Craig called it 'childish'. I suspected the ambition he'd admired in me wasn't so attractive when it ran counter to his.

When my year editing *Canta* was over he suggested we go into business together. 'I need people I can trust. And I like having you around.' I knew this was his way of saying he cared for me. It was also a way of ensuring I stayed. I said I'd think about it.

Several times I packed my bags and slept on my friend Kim's couch. I never said why and she never asked. I always went back.

Was I a victim of domestic abuse? Surely not. After one heated argument in his Roller, when Craig wouldn't stop and let me out, I threw open the passenger door, narrowly missing a lamppost. Craig pulled over. 'You want me to belt you so you have a reason to leave. I won't fucking do it.' He was right again. By itself the emotional blackmail was too subtle to grasp – yet it continued.

I decided I had to fix what I could and started with my relationship with my parents. Mum and Dad's distress at my choices had eased to resignation. In January, they asked how I wanted to celebrate my twenty-first. Never big on milestones and thinking this one a little late, I still got that it was important we did something. We agreed on afternoon drinks at the winery Craig had first taken me to.

Craig had the sense not to come this time, in spite of me insisting he had to. 'I'd just be out of place. A fat old man.'

Sonia and her boyfriend Tom came. So did Kim and Kate. I put money on the bar, determined my fifteen or so school friends should have fun under parental supervision. In a quiet way we did.

Afterwards, I wrote stilted thankyou letters to my extended family, who had sent engraved silver bracelets and bangles. How little they knew me: I'd never liked silver jewellery. The pieces seemed childish compared to the gold and diamond rings Craig had bought me.

I decided to go into business with Craig, after all. We took on the ground floor of the Flaming Phoenix building and opened a pool hall. I gave Craig the travel money I'd saved for a trip to London – a trip that he reneged on – and he funded the rest. Initially I was excited by the project and by the prospect of making good money once we were licensed. Until then we ran it on the cheap, supplementing the pool tables with a hotdog stall on Friday and Saturday nights.

After several months, we were barely breaking even. I didn't know anything about running a business and was trying to finish my degree at the same time. Craig was too busy to help (he was being audited), and I began to suspect that one-upping Jacinta was his primary motivation for this venture. And I found it all so dull. Even his own mother told me, 'Running a pool hall isn't you.'

Not for the first time, I wasn't sure what was me anymore. But my dilemma seemed trivial compared to the problems of others. Misty had begun phoning Craig in distress. She wanted to leave Glen but couldn't do it, although Craig offered to help her out. The last time I saw her was outside The Flaming Phoenix one Friday around 10 p.m. She and Glen were visiting from Dunedin. I gave Misty a hotdog, which she couldn't stomach. She pointed out the second-hand Mercedes Glen had bought for her birthday; I didn't point out she'd paid for it.

'Maybe I should have a baby,' she said.

'Why don't you move here?' I asked gently.

Her vacant eyes filled with tears. 'I *can't.*'

Soon after, Misty hanged herself. The funeral was in Auckland, her hometown. We didn't go.

Then the young barman at the Phoenix was killed in a drink-driving accident. We went to that funeral, although we weren't welcome.

But it was a third death that changed everything. In late 1996, a man was killed in a bar brawl. An associate of Craig's – who we believed was innocent – was charged with manslaughter. In the weeks that followed, the police pulled out all stops to make the charges stick. At the pre-trial hearing, I watched a red-faced, stammering young officer glance at his superiors for assurance then give evidence I knew to be incorrect.

When Craig was subpoenaed for questioning, he grinned at me. 'I'm gonna make it as hard as possible for the cunts. Let's go on the run.'

'What? No,' I said.

'Go on! We'll be like a modern-day Bonnie and Clyde.'

Naturally such an image of glamour and rebellion appealed to me, and Craig's enthusiasm was infectious. While I didn't think there was any danger of a shoot out, I insisted on driving my own getaway car. Along with a couple of Craig's right-hand men, we travelled in convoy a couple of hundred kilometres west into the Southern Alps.

Being on the run wasn't as exciting as I'd anticipated. We spent most of it holed up in an alpine motel. Despite the glorious vista, Craig wouldn't let any of us go outside, which gave me plenty of time to think.

In two short years, I'd compromised my dreams and given up my independence for a man I didn't love and a lifestyle I wasn't fully committed to. Everyone else stuck in that smoke-filled motel room would give up their freedom unquestioningly. Was I prepared to sacrifice mine? On the third day I decided the fugitive life wasn't for me and headed home alone.

Craig followed a few days later. He was charged with perverting the course of justice and given a curfew for his troubles.

I already had one foot out the door when I heard the police had opposed my application for a liquor licence for the pool hall, arguing I was an unfit applicant on grounds of guilt by association.

The committee refused to grant the licence, effectively killing the pool hall.

With this decision I saw that the establishment was always going to win, regardless of whether or not they played fair. I didn't care enough to take them on. I was twenty-one, my whole life ahead of me. It was time to get out while I still could.

In early 1997, I walked away from Craig, from the pool hall, from the Christchurch sex industry. Kim offered me a room in her latest share house and Sonia's boyfriend Tom gave me a few shifts in a bottle shop. I was grateful for my friends' support, and relieved to have found the strength to move on.

Craig acted nonchalantly when I told him I was leaving. Realising I was serious, he held up his thick, capable hands and asked, 'What can I do to fix this?'

'Nothing,' I said quietly. It was beyond fixing.

I loaded up my car and left behind what wouldn't fit in. Possessions didn't matter anymore. Feeling like I had become one did.

Soon after, I began bartending at the Christchurch Clvb, an upmarket inner-city venue. When Craig found out he started turning up every night.

'What are you doing here?' I asked crossly.

'Me? Just having a drink,' he replied.

I couldn't tell if Craig was trying to intimidate me out of a job or convince me to return home. When I couldn't be swayed he stopped coming in.

* * *

Five guys tended bar with me at the Clvb. We worked twelve hours straight then drank till dawn. It was a relief to have little responsibility, to be able to act my age. My new buddy, Evan, had spent most of his student loan on Vintage classics and long lunches at the Park Royal. He chain-smoked Camels and could quote Dostoyevsky. He was housemates with the bar manager, Fletcher, a spunky, sports-mad 22-year-old, who was still in love with his Swedish ex-girlfriend. I'm not sure if that was the challenge, but one night after just enough wine, I propositioned Fletcher. 'Casual sex, no strings attached?'

'Sure.'

A month later I moved in.

5.

IN SPRING 1997, I ARRIVED IN MELBOURNE. I KNEW three things about the city: there was a couch with my name on it, there were penalty rates for hospitality work and there was a supposedly world-class strip club run by a guy called Barry.

I'd booked my three-month return ticket on a hunch. Back in Christchurch, Fletcher, Evan and I had decided we would move to London. But first I had to come up with five grand to apply for a UK working holiday visa. For the past six months I hadn't stopped partying with the boys for long enough to pay off my overdraft, let alone save. The boys both had full-time jobs, mine was part time. I needed a working holiday to pay for my working holiday.

Sonia and Tom had moved to Melbourne, so I knew that, unlike New Zealand, hospitality paid well. A stint of overseas work would look good on my fledgling CV. Then there was the small matter of my continued desire to strip. Saying a temporary goodbye to Fletcher, I packed my bags and put myself on a plane then a train.

Exiting at Richmond station, I sniffed the air, already tinged with jasmine, heady with possibility. Then I lugged my oversized suitcase along the bright, graffiti-coated backstreets, clutching a scrap of paper with Sonia and Tom's address scrawled on it.

Tom greeted me at the door with a warm hug and a cold beer. Sonia arrived home soon after, flustered from a long day at the printing factory where she worked.

'Leigh-Lou!' she said, planting a kiss on my forehead. 'It's so good to see you.'

I knew that whatever Melbourne dished up, I'd be okay.

That night they took me to Brunswick Street and I fell in love with Melbourne proper: the rattly green trams and vibrant shopfronts, the café culture spilling onto the street at all hours. I was determined to live close to Fitzroy's throbbing heart.

The next day we lunched at Bluetrain café in Southbank. I loved the colourful chaos: the mismatched tables and chairs and walls of tattered flyers; the t-shirted, tattooed waiters swirling trays of latte glasses; the frenetic kitchen pumping out food. I wanted to be one of those edgy, expressive people, working myself silly. A day later I was.

I was hired as a runner at Bluetrain for ten dollars an hour, speed-learning my macchiato from my babycino and getting barked at by underpaid, overworked waiters with a weakness for adrenal enhancers (although it was two days before they offered me speed). That first morning, I too sensed there wasn't time to sleep. There were dreams to be had, money to be made – and not like this. I was getting less per hour than in Christchurch. If I was going to save five grand before November, I needed to find that strip club, fast.

I had remembered Barry's offer but had forgotten the name of the club, yet I still walked through the front doors of The Men's Gallery. Thumbing through the Yellow Pages I saw there was another King Street club called Goldfingers. Not knowing the reference to James Bond, it sounded tacky and the fingers part creepy. I was prepared to delude myself a little too – The Men's Gallery sounded like an art gallery. I could consider myself a living work of art. Galleries were for viewing only: no fingers, gold or otherwise. Also, the sign on the deep-green building was understated, dignified. Simply 'The Men's Gallery' edged in a row of tiny bulbs; no flashing neon, no silhouettes of naked women. Craig would have been disappointed.

I strode up the red-carpeted steps, past the plastic palms and up to the reception booth. The receptionist – a classy blonde who looked like a real receptionist – radioed the day manager, Eddie. He emerged rubbing his bald, olive-skinned head and looking about as comfortable in shirtsleeves as a boxer.

'I'm looking for work,' I announced.

'Have you done this sort of thing before?' he asked, with a penetrating stare.

I was instantly wary: I knew an overly attentive boss when I saw one.

'Yeah,' I said dismissively.

Eddie was still staring. 'I'll show you around.'

To my surprise, the club was open during the day. Sade's 'Smooth Operator' played softly. I followed Eddie through the lounge bar, which was carpeted, low lit – and deserted. The décor was English gentleman's study meets Greek *plateia*: mahogany and brass, and frescoed colonnades with imitation ivy. Along the wall to our right, on either side of the shoebox bar, twelve pairs of green vinyl tub chairs faced each other. In front of the bar was the room's only podium, a diamond-shaped table built around a structural pillar. Replica oil paintings lined the walls. I was perplexed by one of a stately jersey cow – whatever turns you on, I guess.

We moseyed into the main bar, a low-ceilinged room with a lengthy bar lining the right-hand sidewall and a tiny kitchen at the far end. There were two podiums – one round, one triangular – each surrounded by a dozen chairs. On the triangular podium a dancer in a pink bikini sprawled on her belly, chatting to a customer who had pulled up a seat.

I asked Eddie how much the girls got paid.

He frowned. 'Thought you'd done this before?'

'Yeah, I danced in New Zealand,' I said.

'Table dancing?'

'Stage shows.' Runways or podiums, I didn't see the difference.

Eddie explained that the customers paid the girls, not the club. The tables or 'podiums' were a form of advertising, although a girl could strip during a podium set if she was paid to. The real money came from private dancing.

I absorbed this information with scepticism, but the venue looked luxurious and even though it was only mid-afternoon, there were at least twenty patrons lounging on Chesterfields to my left, sitting at the small tables dotted around, or playing pool down the back. There was a dignified hum to the place. I didn't see any 'private dancing' going on, though.

'Come have a look upstairs,' Eddie said.

Two wide wooden staircases led to the next level, one on either side of the entrance to the main bar. Eddie unclipped the nearest velvet cordon and I trailed him up to a colossal showroom that was closed during the day. It was bigger than all of The Flaming Phoenix. Its purpose seemed clear: drinking and watching. Two bars flanked the room and a stage lay in the centre like an enormous dog's bone, with a pole at either end. Beyond the stage, three glass-partitioned chambers held assorted couches and tub chairs.

But there was more: through a door at the other end of the showroom was a private dancing area, situated above the lounge bar. It consisted of four 'fantasy booths', a larger 'red room' and fifteen individual 'cubicles'. Each cubicle was enclosed on three sides by frosted glass and sported a single green armchair. It was a maze of possibility: I imagined on busy nights all of these chairs would be occupied.

'We're the best club in town,' Eddie said. It was a refrain I would hear wherever I went, but fortunately at The Men's Gallery it would prove true.

On the way out, we stopped in the lounge bar to watch two girls giving private dances in the tub chairs. These dances weren't very private or complicated and resembled mini-stage shows where you danced around the customer instead of the pole. Armchair aerobics instead of aerial acrobatics? I could do that.

Lastly Eddie showed me 'the boardroom', a function room next door to reception.

He said I would need to prove my age and work visa and sign a contract. This was a strip club first for me. We went into an adjacent office building where I sat among overflowing filing cabinets and skimmed the contract: no soliciting, no leaving the venue with patrons. The clause, 'the performer agrees to not act in any manner so as to bring the reputation of the venue into disrepute' amused me. Up until then, striptease and disrepute had gone hand in hand. Clearly this was a better class of club.

Then Eddie said he'd need a topless photo.

'What for?' I asked suspiciously.

'For our records.' He held up his hands. 'We've got three hundred girls on the books.'

Wow, three hundred! I doubted there were three hundred strippers in all of New Zealand. That sounded like a lot of competition.

Eddie waited expectantly. I removed my jacket, t-shirt and bra and stifled a nervous yawn while he dithered around taking a Polaroid. It felt embarrassingly clinical, like being examined by a medical intern.

'You can start whenever you like,' said Eddie, stapling the unsmiling photo onto my contract.

'Tonight?' I asked as I dressed. Watching, Eddie nodded. I made a point of shaking his hand before stumbling out into the sunshine.

At Spencer Street, I boarded the train to Richmond like a local. I'd been in the country three days and already had two jobs. Melbourne was shaping up to be a good move.

* * *

At 6 p.m., I returned for my first shift with the few costumes that had escaped the scissor slaughter and a bright, brittle smile. The same classy receptionist gave me a four-digit code for the dancers' entrance, hidden behind a fake-marble statue of Venus de Milo, complete with missing arms. I keyed in the code, opened the door and stepped onto a landing. The girls' entrance to the lounge bar was straight ahead. I turned left and descended into a vast open-plan dressing-room. At the foot of the stairs – overlooking six large mirrored booths – was the dance supervisor's desk. I'd soon learn this was command central, the point past which every dancer had to enter and exit, fess up to no-shows and try not to look shitfaced in six-inch stilettos at seven in the morning. Its commander was Carole, a forty-something single mother of two who had the body of a 25-year-old and a frankness that could silence a politician. Carole mastered the thankless task of coordinating all the dancers and their alter egos with fairness, nous and humour. That first night, though, I simply saw a woman with bobbed red hair, writing the podium roster while smoking a cigarette and screaming, 'Girls! Check your tables please!'

She saw me and grinned. 'Welcome aboard. What's your name?'

'Holly,' I said.

'Good, we don't have a Holly at the moment. Take a seat and putty up, I'll find someone to train you.'

I headed towards the second booth on the left. Like dividers in a half-dozen box of wine, the booths spanned the bowels of the building two across and three deep, and were encircled by a thoroughfare. Each booth had mirrored counters on three sides and chairs for ten dancers.

I took a seat next to one of at least thirty semi-nude, intimidatingly gorgeous girls. They looked like professionals. Many were alarmingly tall, with Vegas legs and manes of waist-length hair. There was a plethora of bottle blondes with orange-tinted skin, wearing string bikinis and fake nails in colours like hot pink and screeching peach. I felt like I'd stumbled onto the set of Australian *Baywatch*. How coveted was the stage name CJ? The topless blonde beside me was living proof Beach Volleyball Barbie existed. She was also my first exposure to fake breasts. They perched on her chest like halved grapefruit, ripe and immobile. I was torn between staring at her boobs and her equally set face, bright as a breakfast show host's.

'Hey babe,' she said, with a wink of what couldn't have been real lashes. 'I'm Harlow.' Her green eyes were mesmerising, catlike.

I forced my awestruck mouth to move. 'Hi, I'm Holly.'

'Where ya from?'

'New Zealand. And you?'

'Oh, I'm from Melbourne. My dad's Italian, but I'm an Aussie.' Harlow patted the white lace garter stretched around her bronzed thigh. A fifty and a hundred-dollar note were wrapped lengthwise and secured with a rubber band, like a lucky charm. 'You know what they say – green and gold all the way.' Her laugh was like the tinkling of tiny bells.

I laughed too, just a little nervous.

While Harlow put on a matching bikini and miniskirt in high-vis yellow, I began to resurrect my stripper face. It had been two years since I'd rimmed my eyes with black kohl and painted my lips scarlet. With locks no longer platinum but strawberry blonde, I hardly recognised myself. My black velvet dress was tighter than it used to be, my purple-and-black lingerie more boudoir than beach party. Fortunately, my under and outer things were colour-coordinated, as per house rules (no animal print or see-through). But no one else seemed to be wearing high heels tied on with cut-off stockings. Harlow had strapped her feet into a pair of six-inch white thermoplastic sandals, which most of the girls were walking around in as effortlessly as Nursemates. She told me these were Pleasers – $260 purpose-built platform stilettos from America. Pleasing to the eye perhaps, not to my feet or my wallet. My shoes seemed embarrassingly 1980s disco, but for now they would have to do.

Another of the Pamela Anderson wannabes popped her head into the booth. She brushed cheeks with Harlow, saving her hot-pink lipstick. Then she said, 'Holly? I'm Raine, I'll be training you tonight.'

Raine took me to reception, up the back stairs to the private rooms, and into the red room. Ten tub chairs were lined up in pairs around the periphery and artificial yuccas flowered in the sunless corners. Gilt-edged mirrors and prints of luscious maidens luxuriating in eighteenth-century nature hung on the womb-red walls.

Raine was one of the club's top showgirls and she resembled a rare breed of bird that looks peculiar up close and stationary but is extraordinary in flight. Of average height, she had a thin face, fine-boned limbs and buoyant breasts that threatened to pop out of a tiny turquoise halter-neck dress.

'Dances are ten dollars per three-minute song,' she said, with the assuredness of someone who had found their life's calling. 'Always get the money first, no excuses. Now, sit and I'll demonstrate.'

I sat.

'Spread your feet and put your hands up on the chair.'

I did, assuming the universal position of private-dancee, like sitting in an unrestrained electric chair. Before I knew it, Raine's bony knee was on my thigh, her buoyant assets in front of my face. She smelt like Hawaii, all coconut-y and floral.

'Take everything off within the first thirty seconds,' she said. I wondered with fear and fascination if she would. Instead, she arranged her body parts around mine in a set of geometric moves I hoped to remember, replicate and link. Each came with its own instruction: breasts were to be kept ten centimetres from a customer's face; a dancer's groin must be thirty centimetres from a customer's groin or face; a dancer could sit on the arm of a customer's chair, but not in their lap.

'You're allowed to do open leg work,' Raine added, which was a fancy way of saying I could flash my bits. I was relieved to hear this. In New Zealand, the threat of being arrested for indecent exposure had stilted the flow of my striptease. The thought of strangers staring at my vagina didn't really bother me. Getting touched – anywhere – did. Fortunately, customers weren't allowed to touch, except if a dancer placed a customer's hands on her hips and held them there during a private show, a move dubbed 'hold the baby'. Other moves included lying back in your chair and spreading your legs ('The Men's Gallery salute') and grinding the air above your customer's lap.

Raine then ran through the general house rules, which were plentiful and included a twenty-dollar fine if caught eating from the free happy hour buffet. Unlike in Christchurch, dancers could drink 'up on the floor'. We could also smoke, provided we were stationary. I wondered if this was to stop intoxicated girls in flammable apparel from setting fire to themselves or each other in transit, or if it was just considered trashy to approach a gentleman while fagging. We were not allowed to walk around the venue naked either. And we couldn't get down from a podium – even if our fifteen-minute set was over – until we were replaced by the next girl.

Raine checked her watch. 'Any questions?'

I thought as long and hard as my highly caffeinated brain would allow. 'What do you say to the customers?'

'Introduce yourself, ask how their night's going, then offer them a dance. If they don't want one, walk away.' She shrugged. Hustling 101 was over.

Thanking Raine, I returned to the dressing-room to buy a garter, check my podium roster, synchronise my watch to 'Gallery time' and finish getting my game on.

The club was packed with post-work drinkers. Planting myself beside a column in the main bar, I felt like an actor who'd stumbled onto the wrong set; no longer was I onstage, flouncing around in panty-less pantomime, but down with the masses. Perhaps if I stood still for long enough someone would ask me for a dance. No one did. They were too busy chatting up the sophisticates in the sandals, who sipped champagne and smoked cigarettes with VIP insolence. I watched the ever-moving Harlow whisk away yet another man for a private dance. She had a sniffer dog's nose for money. It was time for me to put my untrained snout to the test.

I approached the nearest balding, middle-aged man and flashed him the smile of a teenage gymnast. 'Hi, I'm Holly. Would you like to have a dance?'

'I've just arrived.' The man looked me up and down expressionlessly. 'Maybe later.'

'Okay,' I said, and returned to my post.

Two hours and two podium sets later – the first on table 1 in the lounge bar, the second on table 2 in the main bar – I still hadn't scored a dance. I was starting to panic when I saw Barry weaving towards me in a navy granddaddy suit.

'Barry!' I said.

He stopped with a harried frown.

'I'm Holly. I met you in New Zealand. I'm Craig's girlfriend. Well, ex-girlfriend.'

'Holly! Good to see you, luv,' Barry said warmly. If he didn't recognise me, he hid it well. He patted my shoulder. 'I'm a bit busy right now.'

I watched him disappear into the crowd, feeling momentarily comforted by the exchange.

The next time I saw Barry he was leaning against the bar, watching me tackling my third podium set, his expression puzzled. I hadn't been told that podium sets weren't mini stage-shows and I was running myself ragged, changing costumes before each set then offering up my best Paula Abdul impersonation. Barry caught sight of me high-kicking and after some quiet observation, approached the table.

'Holly, we don't dance like that here,' he said gently. 'You need to slow down. Watch what the other girls are doing.'

The other girls were moving as if through honey. The music had little relation to their movement, which was more languid wiggling than actual dancing. They looked detached, bored even. This was called playing hard to get, and it was necessary, even though our nudity was a sure thing. I hadn't twigged that no one was paying me to channel a cheerleader or provide a fashion show, though I had thought it unusual when Harlow remarked, 'You're getting changed *again*?' Unfortunately, what I had succeeded in doing was advertising my wardrobe and someone downstairs had stolen all my costumes. At the sight of my empty backpack my eyes filled with tears. I realised the other girls had padlocks on their bags. Ashamed at how stupid I was, I said nothing to Carole. Those costumes never resurfaced.

Wearing my one remaining outfit – a silver slip and bikini – I returned to the floor with renewed determination. Remembering Barry's words, I tried not to try so hard.

My first private dance was with a mild, middle-aged Maori man, one of the club's regulars. Every club has them and some dance only with the new girls, a kind of civic duty to the uncoordinated poor.

'You're a New Zealander,' the man said with a genuine smile. 'How long have you been here?'

'It's my first night,' I confessed.

'Come on,' he said, 'Let's have a dance.'

I grinned with relief. It was far from the seductive smile I'd learn to perfect. The man reached for my hand as I bobbed along beside him into the lounge bar. This took me by surprise. I glanced around furtively. Was handholding allowed? I didn't want to hold his rough, callused hand, but I didn't want to offend him either. At least not before I'd got the money.

He gave me ten dollars and I began to dance in the triangle formed by his feet. Being in close proximity to a stranger making bedroom eyes at me had a curious effect. My instinct was to bolt, but I didn't. (Private dancing is as natural as smoking cigarettes: it feels toxic, but you persevere, hopeful of learning why everyone else looks like they're enjoying it.) Just thirty centimetres separated our chairs. I managed to disrobe without tripping over and even remembered to lie back and spread my legs. Ta-da! I finished feeling rather proud of myself.

My customer was frowning. 'That wasn't a good dance. You didn't come close enough.'

I screwed up my nose. 'I'm not *allowed* to come any closer. There's a regulation thirty-centimetre gap –'

'Watch what she's doing.' He indicated the dancer beside us, who was kneeling between her customer's legs and stroking his chest, gazing up at him adoringly. Her guy was slack-jawed with wonder. She was a good actor, this girl. I wasn't going to do that for ten dollars. It didn't occur to me she might've been paid a lot more.

Watch. It was good advice – and the second time it had been given to me on my first night – but I was in too much of a hurry to make money. Dressing quickly, I thanked the man and rushed away.

By 1 a.m., I'd managed twelve private dances. I'd stripped for middle-aged men in polo shirts, young guys in t-shirts, corporates in suits and loosened ties. With each dance, the desire to flee had lessened. But now exhaustion was setting in. It was bad timing: the club was peaking.

The showroom had opened at 10 p.m., when security guards in penguin black-and-whites unclipped the cordons and stood aside as the customers rushed to secure front-row seats. Unlike the podiums downstairs, they could sit around the stage without having to buy a dance. Overwhelmed by the busyness of the showroom, I continued to work the main bar.

Now, though, my next podium set was on the showroom stage. I waited for Raine to finish her Spanish-inspired show, choreographed to Latin music. All that was left of her technicolour dream-dress were arm ruffles, which fanned out as she spun the length of the stage with giddy precision. My old shows were trite compared to this; any thoughts I'd had of resurrecting them vanished. As Raine exited the stage like a miracle descending, I stomped my way on, the last of five dancers. Every seat around the stage was occupied, the showroom a heaving mass of several hundred men and all of them staring. Like a possum in headlights, I tried to get my bearings.

Around me, the other girls began to get podium dances. I hadn't yet had a podium dance and watched out of the corner of my eye as they writhed on their hands and knees, splaying themselves centimetres from their customers' faces. The stage lights lit up every fold and follicle. For some reason, it reminded me of a rotisserie. It was a visual devouring, a fantastic all-you-can-eat flesh roasting for the sexually starved. And it unnerved me. It was one thing to twirl around a pole nude, quite another to get down on all fours and moon a room. I tried not to encourage anyone by making eye contact.

Predictably, a wizened old man peering up at me held out a ten-dollar note. Horrified by both his blatant need and what others might think of me if I stripped for him, I pretended not to notice. He began to wave the money. Gritting my teeth, I took it and got naked. As I spread my legs, he leant forward – loading, unloading his false teeth. Bubbles of spit formed in the toothless gaps. Revulsion rose up inside me. I hadn't signed up to be a geriatric service provider – I couldn't, wouldn't, do this. Pride forced me to finish and dress before bumbling offstage, headed for the girls room then the safety of the wide-open street.

A burly security guard with a thinning flattop blocked my way down the stairs to the main bar. 'Where do you think you're going?'

'Home!' I blurted out, pushing past him. I couldn't have known that G. I. – head of security – played this trick on all the new girls. I thought he'd seen me walk offstage. He must have radioed Carole, because I was in my civvies, packing up what remained of my stuff when she found me.

'Were you planning on telling me or were you just going to walk out?' she demanded.

'I was going to tell you, of course!' I said truthfully.

She didn't believe me. 'If you're going, go.'

I went, my chest corseted with emotion. Not until I was in the back of a taxi, speeding towards Richmond, could I breathe properly. Then the night slid off me in hot, angry tears.

With the light of day, I suspected I'd overreacted. This was confirmed by another gruelling shift at Bluetrain where I failed to keep up, prompting the barista to offer me speed (which I refused) and the manager to scoff, 'At this rate, you'll never make waitress.'

For ten dollars an hour? At that rate, I didn't want to 'make waitress'. Not when I could make ten dollars in three minutes. That night, I phoned the Gallery and asked Carole if I could try again.

'Sorry I freaked out,' I said. 'It was just so busy.'

'Why didn't you say so, instead of storming out?'

'I don't know,' I admitted.

Carole suggested I roster on Monday night, when the club would be quieter and the showroom wasn't open. It was sound advice. With my psyche sufficiently numbed by round one, my second night went much more smoothly. I even managed a podium dance without losing it. It helped that the early week crowd were more docile, less drunk. They actually planned on going to work the next day. By Wednesday night I could moon a room with ease. I wasn't sure how I'd manage on Saturday nights – rumoured to be longer, later and much busier – but I knew I wouldn't walk out again. I gave Bluetrain a week's notice and quit my day job.

* * *

The Men's Gallery was open seven days a week, from midday on weekdays and 6 p.m. on weekends. It closed as late as 8 a.m., crowd depending. This was potentially a sixteen-hours-a-day window of opportunity. I needed to make two hundred and fifty dollars a night, four nights a week, to pay off my debt and save five grand. This was achievable on early weeknights, but dancers were supposed to work a minimum of one weekday night plus Friday or Saturday. Initially Carole didn't push me to work weekends, so I worked from Monday to Thursday.

From that first Friday I had learnt that while weekends were busier they weren't necessarily better. With more dancers rostered on there was greater competition, and with the showroom open, the customers were sidetracked from private dancing by the antics on the main stage. These included not only individual shows, but also 'top forties' and 'mega-privates'.

'What's that?' I asked Carole anxiously, the first time I saw 'T40 1.00' beside my name on the podium roster.

'Cattle class,' she said with a grin.

At 1 a.m., I had to line up with approximately thirty other bikini-clad dancers and wait for the MC, Stanley, to introduce us. Stanley was a perpetually dieting former radio announcer who spruiked Herbalife and kept the show going with his bustling efficiency. He held out a hand to help us onto the stage, then around we paraded, smiling inanely.

'Make some *noiiiissse* for our *Top Forty* girls!' Stanley bellowed, neglecting to mention that the parade was randomly rostered and there weren't forty of us. Round and round we trotted to the parade theme song, a nasty remake of Dead or Alive's 'You Spin Me Round'. How fast we circuited depended on how many stimulants the lead girl had consumed. Some nights were a dizzy orbit, others a slow stagger.

Carole had handed each of the Top Forty girls a raffle ticket to give to the next person we stripped for. They would go into the draw to win a gold membership to The Men's Gallery. At first I doled out the tickets. Many guys stashed their lucky number as if it were a Wonka Golden Ticket to a lifetime supply of free pussy-perving. As time wore on, though, I would find the flimsy squares crumpled in my garter and had to remind myself to be more diligent. I was denying some pervert a golden opportunity, which, depending on how you saw it, was either good or bad for business.

The second stage-filler was the mega-private, a one-song panty-free pick 'n' mix. Six chairs were put onstage and the first people to fill them received a random girl – with dress, without bikini – to perform the antithesis of a private dance. Usually, Stanley waited until every seat was occupied before he announced that it cost ten dollars. Occasionally, someone would refuse to pay and jump down, leaving the rejected dancer to trail offstage, silently screaming, 'I'm not worth ten bucks?'

Sometimes another beaver eager would scramble up and save the night. Mega-privates were popular and the only opportunity for crowd participation, even if it was enforced. The show would not start until the seats were filled. Then on and on it went, longer than any ten-dollar private dance ever did. Afterwards we were encouraged to escort our customer offstage as if celebrating a sacred rite of passage, but really just to ensure the guy didn't stay up there.

The first guy I did a mega-private for was the mad scientist. He looked like Einstein and bopped along in his chair, gangly limbs perilously close to knocking me over, grinning like an imbecile. I thought he wasn't all there until I realised he was literally having the time of his life. Who was I to stop him? Megas were a bargain. I grinned back, entertained by me entertaining him entertaining me.

Still, I preferred the early weeknights when there wasn't as much hype or running around and shifts were shorter. When the showroom was open the showgirls were rostered off first, which was great for the queens of the night but meant longer shifts for us worker bees. That first Friday, my last podium was at 5.30 a.m., almost twelve hours after I'd started. There were also fewer rules to remember midweek. I never thought to ask what would happen if I broke the rules though suspected, like boarding school, I'd be asked to leave.

* * *

Sonia wasn't too thrilled I was stripping again. She said nothing, but observed me with worried eyes. Before I outstayed my welcome, I found a cheap room in a rundown two-storey terrace house in Fitzroy, sharing with Dan, a drama student, and Gemma, a nanny. My room was airy, overlooked Nicholson Street and came with a bonus not-too-foetid mattress.

The day I moved in was the Brunswick Street Festival. Dan came home with tabs of acid, which we took on impulse, before tramming to the Dali bar. 'Short trip or long trip?' the driver asked routinely. It was hilarious! I rolled around in the aisle until Dan hauled me off the tram, still shaking with laughter. After partying until 3 a.m., it was imperative I phoned Fletcher back in Christchurch to share how mind-blowing it was, cutting open glow-sticks and Jackson Pollock-ing my bedroom wall. Fletch tried but failed to appreciate my first trip.

Once the acid had worn off I set about finding what some strip club patrons patronisingly refer to as 'a real job' – preferably one less demanding than my 'surreal' job. I found what I was looking for at the Hotel Grand Chancellor. It had been recently renovated, except for its back bar and bottle shop. The bar even had its own entrance via a Chinatown car park. It was dingy and vaguely depressing, but it meant I could put 'international hotel chain' on my CV, and it excused me from working weekends at the Gallery. Thursday afternoons and Friday and Saturday nights, I put on black-and-whites and poured cheap liquor for a handful of melancholic barflies, most of whom administered deceased estates for the State Trustees Office. Gazing out at the swaying red lanterns of Chinatown, listening to passing laughter, this was when I missed Fletcher the most. On weekends I'd walk home with a container of Peking duck, unhooked from the window of a nearby restaurant and chopped up by an unsmiling man with a cleaver. I was always glad when my shifts at the Grand Chancellor were done for another week.

At The Men's Gallery I never counted down the minutes. There was a completely different sense of time, a dream-like chaos, like being suspended by a sideshow ride. As the madness spun around me – none of it real, but all of it believable – I was forced to hold my centre or be swept away.

Routinely, I arrived at work at 5 p.m. and seldom left before 3 a.m. I rarely drank and kept my mind on the money. Back then, the club was swimming with it: it was tossed around generously and fanned from garters like man-made flowers. Sometimes Harlow's garter was so full she emptied it into her locker partway through the night. While I saw the big money, I didn't see how to get it. It didn't occur to me to up-sell (KFC had failed me there) or to ask a customer if he'd like to extend a dance. I wasn't aware of the false promises made, of the men who handed out hundreds regardless of the number of songs. I didn't realise that not every girl adhered to time.

Instead, I worked honestly and I worked hard. That glittery enclave became my version of the all-American dream. From one of the dressmakers who came in hawking costumes, I bought a stars-and-stripes bikini and a short white halter-neck dress; from a Chinese shoe seller at the Victoria Market, I bought a pair of red platform stilettos reminiscent of Minnie Mouse. Following Harlow's lead, I coated myself in self-developing tan and turned Malibu orange. Every night, I stayed until I had reached my target amount. Remarkably, I almost always made it – to the dollar. I didn't question why this might be. I simply ticked it off, went to bed, got up and did it all over again.

I got used to falling asleep to the sound of the birds waking and the first tram of the day rattling by. In the afternoons I'd zombie-stagger down to Brunswick Street for breakfast. I would sit outside, order black coffee and muesli with fruit and yogurt, smoke a few cigarettes, watch the street and write. The words flowed out of me, a blend of documentation, narrative and angst. I tried to make sense of my first foray into the industry and subsequent relationship with Craig, something I hadn't allowed myself to do for the past six months because I'd been too drunk.

While I saw how dominating Craig had been, I didn't understand why I'd put up with it. After boarding school I was used to controlled environments, to feeling powerless. That wasn't reason enough. Nor did it explain my fascination with stripping.

Was I making a mistake, veering into the world of the great undressed a second time? I had no problem getting nude for a living, but private dancing took more from me than I'd known I had, more than stage shows ever did. It was innately exhausting. How could that be right? I reassured myself that whether wrong or right, this was a three-month detour before getting back on track.

6.

AT THE GALLERY, I KNEW FEW DANCERS' ALTER egos or stage names, let alone their true selves or real names. The girls weren't bitchy, but they weren't friendly either. Mostly, like me, they were money fixated. Unlike me, they were super-confident, with attention-deficit-disorder-like demands on holding centrestage. Too shy to ask, I wondered why they'd become strippers, what they thought of the customers, and how they unified their work and home lives. Up on the floor I watched them; down in the dressing-room I eavesdropped.

One night I was reapplying lipstick while two dancers – Trixie and Skye – sat nearby, smoking. Trixie was a thirty-something single mum who personified Marie Antoinette with her Baroque wig, white shoes and cutting humour; Skye was an aloof ex-gymnast who walked on her hands during podium sets, as if to locate the angle where the world still spun on its rightful axis. Trixie was addressing her cigarette – 'You don't own me, you scrap of paper, you *weed*' – when Melissa, a ballet teacher and circus performer, sat down heavily beside her with a sigh. 'I'm so sick of guys who say, "Why do you do this?" Because I make five times what you make, you dumb fuck.'

'I say, "Because I enjoy it,"' said Skye.

'No, no, no!' Trixie waved her cigarette. 'Don't justify yourself! When guys say that, I believe what they're really asking is, "What am *I* doing here?" Put it back on them. Say, "Well, why are you here, you sick pervert? If you have such a low opinion of me, don't lower yourself to my standards. Go!"' She flapped her hands. '"Rise above me."'

'You actually say that?' asked Melissa.

'I say all sorts of things,' said Trixie airily.

Skye laughed. 'Carole told her that she can't say what she says to the guys, it's too crass.'

'Oh they love it.' Trixie butted out her cigarette and stood up. 'When I finish a private dance, I say, "Since I'm a pussycat, do you mind if I spray you?"' She cocked her leg and made a pissing sound, laughed and flopped back into her chair.

Melissa smiled despite herself. 'I am so over the guys who ask for extras. I ask them for a dance and they say, "What can you do for me?" A simple yes or no will do.'

'I tell them they have to come and see what's on offer first,' said Skye. 'Get a dance out of them then say extras are a million an hour, cash up front.'

'No!' Trixie shook her head. 'One-up them! Tell them you're gonna fuck them senseless.'

'But I'm not, am I?' Melissa said.

'Financially, you might.' Trixie's smile was warm, but her eyes were cold.

Melissa looked away. 'A guy just told me he hadn't been in a brothel for thirty years. I said, "Well, you're not in one now, honey, are you?" He said, "One and the same."' She rolled her eyes.

Trixie leant forward. 'The men who come here want to be told what to do. Make the most of it, manipulate the fuck out of them.'

I wondered if Trixie was right. I doubted I could do that, even if I knew how. It didn't seem fair.

Other conversations left me astonished by some girls' priorities. Desiree kept everyone updated on the progress of her $2500 hair extensions, which were being specially grown in Russia. After affixing someone else's hair to her head, she planned on getting breast implants. So did Bambi, who had stuck a picture of the boobs she wanted onto a photo of herself and taped it to the mirror. As DD-day inched closer, I'd catch Bambi eyeing the picture and murmuring, 'They're fucking massive. I'm worried I'm going too big.'

Mostly, though, the dressing-room banter left me thinking Aussie girls were more willing to crack a joke and have a laugh than us Kiwis. They played hard, but they worked hard too. Some owned businesses; others were married with children. These dancers blew apart my small-town stereotype of what it meant to be a wife and a mother, and I admired them for it.

One night I asked Harlow to tell me her story. She was thirty-one, married with two young children. She had been stripping for less than a year. As a shop assistant, she had scrimped to pay the mortgage. Now she was fast-tracking the payments and had her sights set on a second property. Before and after every shift, no matter how tired she was, Harlow said she parked outside her 'dream house' in upmarket Brighton to remind herself what she was working towards.

'They probably think I'm a stalker,' she laughed.

'Is it for sale?' I asked.

'No, but one day it will be. Everything's for sale, babe.'

I wondered what I was selling. There was a large chunk of my brain that didn't want to acknowledge that, for some men, I was a sexual fantasy. (I was so naive, I'd been shocked to learn that the pole was a phallic symbol.) Most men sat immobile during a private dance, as per house rules, but some bolted for the toilets afterwards. It grossed me out to think that they might be jerking off. Others asked why I stripped, what turned me on, and if I fucked for money. Like Melissa, I found these questions annoying and irrelevant. I just wanted to dance and to be admired.

Once, a young insurance broker asked me how much I charged for sex. I said I didn't do that.

'Why not?' he asked.

'Because prostitution is selling your soul,' I said, parroting Craig. The broker frowned and let it go.

Another night I asked a middle-aged Turkish man how long he'd like me to dance for.

'For eternity and beyond!' he declared.

'It's ten or twenty dollars,' I said.

'I have two thousand. What does that get me?'

'You get to watch me dance for a very long time.'

'That's it?' He threw up his hands. 'We start with twenty.'

My dress was on the floor when he said, 'I have a lesbian friend. I give you two thousand, you meet her.'

I scowled. 'I'm not meeting your friend. If I wanted to meet women, I'd do it on my own time.'

'So you like women? It is a possibility then.'

'No, it's not a possibility. You can't pay me to meet your friend.'

'You'll meet her for free?'

I spread my legs to shut him up. It worked until after the dance when he offered to buy me a drink.

'Look, you paid me to dance, that's it. Finished.'

Stunned, he watched me walk away. While it wasn't surprising I didn't get much repeat custom, I wanted the men to understand what was on offer and what wasn't.

This attitude was partly what attracted my first regular, John. The night we met, he was perched on a stool in the main bar, observing the centre podium over the rim of his champagne glass. He was a slim man with muddy-brown hair who, back then, wore dress shorts with knee socks and a semi-studious expression. Usually I boycotted the shorts-wearers, abhorring unavoidable skin-on-skin contact, but as I sashayed past John smiled at me. I stopped automatically. 'Hi, I'm Holly.'

'I know. I've seen you somewhere before.'

'I don't think so.'

'Yes, I saw you dance in Christchurch. I was there for a meteorological conference.' He chuckled. 'You're rather memorable. Your hair was white, but your name was Holly then too.'

There was no point denying it. Nodding, I held out my hand.

'John.' He shook it. 'Let's see if you're as good as I remember.'

Apparently I was: John would go on to become my most loyal regular. We would know each other a whopping fifteen years. John liked New Zealand (he and his wife went tramping there), he found me amusing (he didn't like 'fake girls') and he thought I was beautiful. Perhaps most importantly, I was willing to strip for ten dollars. I'd recently discovered some girls refused to and was slowly starting to wise up.

Another trick of the trade was setting your own price. In the packed showroom one night, Harlow grabbed my hand – I was the nearest available dancer – and marched me over to meet four Japanese men, impeccably attired in expensive suits.

'This is my beautiful friend, Holly,' she said. I smiled brightly. The men nodded approvingly. We went into the red room and Harlow did the talking.

'It's fifty dollars each girl,' she said, straight up, all smiles. Unhesitatingly, the men paid. After two songs, she asked if they'd like to continue. They'd like. I was paid one hundred bucks for fifteen minutes of smile-lacquered bopping. On my own I lacked the gumption to be so forthright.

Sitting on my mattress, sorting the cash into colour-coded piles, I saw that by setting a goal I had inadvertently capped my earnings, when I could potentially come away with far more. Finally, I was grasping how the game got played. But in ten days Fletcher was arriving for the Melbourne Cup, and then we were heading back to Christchurch and on to London.

I was torn. It wasn't much of a life I'd created – I hardly saw my housemates, while Sonia and Tom had left Melbourne soon after I'd arrived – but I had stripper fever. I was chasing the dollar, yearning for just a few more days, weeks or months to earn a bigger and better lump sum.

* * *

I had become used to navigating the usual industry come-ons: the amateur photographers looking for life models, the middle-aged men seeking young secretaries, the gallant 'you're too good for this' rescue talk. And the invitations of hotel-room romps – because what every stripper wants, after being paid to feign sexual arousal for twelve hours, is to do the deed for free with a drunken man (or two) she doesn't know. Strippers are the *least* likely ladies to find this offer appealing. I blamed the minuscule percentage that gave us a bad rap. Then I became part of that percentage.

It was a Wednesday night in late October, around 2 a.m. I had just finished a private dance and was casing the main bar for another when the spectacle at table 3 caught my eye. A rotund man in shirtsleeves was prancing around the podium, directing a topless dancer reclining on her elbows. It was The Maestro: a weekly weirdo and master of grandiose hand signals, with dubious musical ability. He gesticulated like a conductor and the dancer scissored her legs open and closed, a silly grin etched on her pretty face. His was set in a theatrical frown of concentration. Despite his flamboyance, The Maestro had the bearing of a judge or a politician. I never did find out if he was.

'What's he doing?' an incredulous voice asked.

I turned to look up at the tall, solidly built man standing beside me. His boyishly handsome face was tanned, his receding hair spiky and sun-bleached.

'That's The Maestro,' I said. 'That's what he does.'

'The *Maestro*?' The man shook his head. 'You girls let him do that?'

'Some do, some don't. He pays very well.'

The Spice Girls were belting out 'Wannabe' and The Maestro had upped the tempo accordingly. His cheeks were flushed and his fringe had fallen into his eyes. Pirouetting nimbly, he stabbed at the air – the signal for the dancer to remove her G. She unclipped it with her legs spread wide.

The man beside me grinned. 'He's not shy, is he?'

I laughed. 'No, he's not.'

The song ended and The Maestro pulled a wad of cash from his shirt pocket, peeled off ten notes and threw the money into the air, showering the naked girl. She squealed with exaggerated delight.

'I don't know who to be more embarrassed for, him or the girl,' said the man. 'Do you do that?'

'No,' I said. Whenever The Maestro canvassed the podiums I turned away.

'Why not?'

'I don't know,' I admitted. 'It doesn't feel right. I don't like anyone telling me what to do in a dance.'

'Fair enough.' The man held out his hand. 'I'm Darren.'

I took it. 'Holly.'

'Would you like a drink, Holly?'

I hesitated.

'I'll pay you for your time.'

'Okay.' I had been rostered off podiums and had almost made my target. It couldn't hurt to relax a little.

I found a table while Darren ordered. He wore dark-green suit pants, his shirtsleeves rolled up, his tie loosened. Putting a gin and tonic and a fifty-dollar note in front of me, he sat down. I tucked the money into my garter. A bemused grin swept up to crease the corners of his warm brown eyes.

'You're not from around here, are you? What are you *doing* here?'

I grinned back. 'Working! What are you doing here?'

'I'm out with some guys from the office. They're around somewhere, probably having a dance.' He offered me a cigarette. I accepted, bent my head to the extended flame. 'So, where are you from?'

'New Zealand.' I told him I'd come to Melbourne to save up to go travelling, that I had a boyfriend back home. Darren was from Brisbane, a sales manager for a building company, thirty-four, married, no kids. Aided by the alcohol, the conversation flowed effortlessly. When he slid another fifty across the table, I took it, but I would have stayed anyway. His charm and good humour was very welcome, and I was tired of being alone.

'It's three o'clock, I should go,' he said. 'I've got an early start in the morning.' Darren looked at me searchingly. 'Unless you want to go for a drink when you finish?' He reached across the table and toyed with my fingers. I didn't move my hand.

'Technically, I'm finished.' I swallowed hard, pushing all thoughts of Fletcher aside. 'But I can't leave with you.'

We agreed to meet at the sports bar in the casino in thirty minutes. Darren gave me one last lingering look, shrugged into his suit jacket and left. I went down to the girls room and got changed, feeling only slightly guilty. Monogamy had always seemed worth pursuing, but somehow unrealistic.

Despite the hour, the casino was packed. Foggy with gin, I lost my bearings and it was 4 a.m. by the time I found Darren, hunched over a fresh bourbon and Coke.

'I'm sorry,' I said breathlessly, 'I got lost.'

'I thought you'd changed your mind.' He looked at me oddly. He'd sobered up and I realised how slutty my make-up must have looked under the bright lights. I wished I'd thought to wipe it off.

'I'll get you a drink,' he said flatly.

We drank and smoked in awkward silence. This wasn't what I'd expected. Had I misread him? Getting laid no longer appeared to be on the cards – or the table.

Darren stubbed out his cigarette. 'I should go. Come on, we'll share a taxi. I'll drop you home.'

We walked out to the taxi rank in silence. The young Indian driver didn't know where Swanston Street was, and I didn't know how to get home from where we were, so Darren pored over the Melways with the meter running. Once he had directed the driver, he placed a hand on my knee and gazed out the window. I stared fixedly ahead, not knowing how to respond. I liked him; I thought he'd liked me.

The sky was lightening when the driver stopped outside my house. I turned to face Darren uncertainly. He leant over and kissed my cheek. 'Good night, Holly.'

'Good night.'

I got out and watched the taxi speed away. Darren's rejection stung. I went to bed, vowing not to let it bother me.

But the next afternoon at my day job, among the last-will-and-testament talk in the back bar at the Grand Chancellor, I couldn't stop thinking about what had happened – or rather, hadn't happened. That evening at the club, as I moved from one soulless encounter to the next, I forced myself not to look for Darren. If he came back in, I would ignore him.

Around 3 a.m., I saw him standing at the bar and bounded over, grinning uncontrollably. He grinned back, drunk.

'Did you find your hotel all right?' I asked.

'Forty-five dollars later! That guy was hopeless.'

We stood staring at each other.

'Would you like a drink?' he said.

Once again, Darren paid me to talk. Once again, he took my hand and asked me to meet him later. This time I suggested we leave together. I removed my make-up and oddly, not even G. I. on the door noticed us getting into a taxi together. We returned to the casino and sat quietly, me in my hospitality black-and-whites, he in his green suit. Darren fidgeted with his wedding band and wouldn't look at me. This had been his idea, and it was simple enough. When he offered me another drink, I said, 'How about in your hotel room?'

Finally he met my eyes. 'Let's go then.'

In the foyer I waited behind a potted plant while he retrieved the key. Wordlessly we rode the lift to the fourteenth floor. He ushered me into his small room, tastefully decorated in beige. I went to the window, admired the city lights and waited for Darren to make the next move. What he did was make me a gin and tonic, hand me the TV remote and yawn.

'I'm going to take a shower,' he said.

I sat on the bed and sipped at my drink, wondering if I should join him. Then I heard the water being turned off. He emerged with a towel around his waist, his skin bronzed by the Queensland sun.

He brushed past me. 'All yours.'

When I came out in a matching towel, Darren was in bed watching the news. I dropped the towel. He kept staring at the TV. Embarrassed, I slid under the covers and began stroking his chest.

He sighed and muted the TV. 'I suppose we have to go through with this now.'

Stunned, I withdrew my hand. 'Not if you don't want to.' My voice was small.

Darren touched my arm. 'Holly, you're welcome to stay, but I've really got to get some sleep. I've got an important presentation in the morning.' He flicked off the bedside lamp. By the glow of the TV I saw he had shut his eyes.

I knew I should leave, but I was too tired, too deflated to move. The sheets felt crisp and clean against my damp skin. I thought of my shabby room with its mattress on the floor. Sleeping here beside Darren was better than sleeping there alone. Besides, why should I make this easy for him? He had inconvenienced me enough. I turned off the TV, rolled over and let sleep take me.

I woke with Darren at the end of the bed, knotting his tie. I tried to read his eyes, but he began checking papers in his briefcase.

'You're welcome to let yourself out in a few hours,' he said, looking at me at last.

I shook my head, got up and dressed. He wasn't going to offer me an explanation; I wasn't going to ask for one. No stripper likes being played at her own game.

In the elevator, Darren handed me his business card. *What for?* I thought. *Why would I contact you?* But I slipped the card into my backpack.

Outside the morning sun was glassy and bright. There was one taxi alongside the hotel. Darren kissed my cheek. 'Take care, Holly.' Then he was gone.

Blinking back tears, I dawdled towards Flinders Street station. Loneliness combined with weeks of adoring propositions and Darren's two rejections cut deep. I didn't understand his behaviour but it had exposed an emptiness in me I hadn't known was there. Acknowledging it hurt.

* * *

I finished up at The Men's Gallery the night before Fletcher flew in. Leaving was as simple as not rostering on. Aside from management, the only person I told was Harlow. She sealed my departure with an air-kiss. Then she winked. 'You'll be back.'

I wondered if I would. I kept my costumes, thick with Jean Paul Gaultier Classique, but binned my shoes on the way out. I tried to locate a sense of victory or remorse at leaving, but I just felt numb.

The next day in the taxi from the airport Fletcher drew me suffocatingly close, chatting nonstop. I had booked us into a hotel on Flinders Lane, a twelfth-storey suite with a glittering view across the Yarra. I'd wanted to see the city lights again, this time with the guy I was supposed to be with. But instead of surrendering, I roamed the room as edgy as a caged tiger. After months of having strangers in close proximity, my nervous system was stuck on red alert.

'All you've done since I got here is chain smoke,' Fletch accused, as I wiggled out of his embrace to light up yet another cigarette.

'I'm just really tired,' I said.

So we did what we'd always done: we got drunk. We got so drunk that we were too hungover to go to the Melbourne Cup. I wore my specially bought hat with a tracksuit to the nearest TAB, watched the race, lost ten bucks and crawled back to bed. After a few days, though, things seemed to have righted themselves and we flew back to Christchurch, excited about what London had to offer.

* * *

Four months later I was back at Melbourne's Victoria Market, searching for the Chinese shoe seller and another pair of candy-apple-red pumps. Fletcher, Evan and I had got our UK working holiday visas, then – at Fletch's suggestion – had postponed going to London until after the English winter. We'd flown to Sydney, spending six weeks and most of our savings backpacking up Australia's east coast. We'd stopped in Surfers Paradise with high hopes of finding hospitality jobs, but it was the low season. I could've stripped, but in Queensland the guys could touch from the waist up. Eww. I'd proposed we go to Melbourne for work. Reluctantly, Fletcher and Evan agreed.

Within a week the boys had more waitering shifts than they could handle and I was back at The Men's Gallery. (Harlow greeted me without a hint of surprise.) We stayed at a busy backpackers hostel half a block from the club, and while the hostel was clean and modern, its after-hours entrance was on Little Bourke Street, opposite Tunnel nightclub, renowned for its late-night brawls. No longer was the creative hub of Fitzroy my backyard but the drunken thoroughfare of King Street.

Those ten weeks were trying for all three of us. They were especially difficult for Fletcher, who had left behind a well-paying bar manager's job with potential for career advancement, only to be dogging his way up the Melbourne food chain. My good-time boyfriend was irritable, and unhappy his girlfriend was stripping for strangers less than a block away. (I wondered if any man would find this arrangement acceptable.) Increasingly, I stayed at work not for the money but because I didn't want to go home. When I did we'd end up arguing in hissed whispers. No one won these fights; several times we almost called it quits. It was only Evan's quiet humour that kept us on track for London.

* * *

At least once a week Carole would shout: 'Girls! Who wants to go to Santa Fe?' Perhaps it was my need for space that made me put my hand up, because usually we pretended we hadn't heard her.

Santa Fe Gold was the sister strip club to The Men's Gallery, located in the Portland Hotel on Russell Street. Reputedly danker, mankier and less lucrative, its strippers were increasingly not showing up for shifts. This wasn't an enticing carrot to dangle before committed Men's Gallery bunnies.

Santa Fe conscription was for the new girls and I was no longer a newbie. But that night Carole bundled me into a taxi with two grumbling novices. We were dropped out the front of a cream stucco building that looked a bit like a Mexican drug lord compound.

True to rumour, Santa Fe Gold *was* smaller and shabbier than The Men's Gallery, with one recessed stage and two private dancing annexes. It was worn around the edges – like your local, the difference being that the punters could have a private dance with their pot instead of a parma. I scanned the curtained corners, half-expecting to see the last-will-and-testament crew, whose offices were just up the street.

Santa Fe was also friendlier than the Gallery. The girls acknowledged my presence, asking my name and if I'd danced before, then invited me to quaff shots at the bar with the regulars. Politely, I declined.

This was blue-collar country. I employed my factory-style approach and as the evening conveyor-belted by, discovered the guys agreed to dances without stalling or ego-tripping me. Unlike the white-collar boys, they didn't try to impress me with their latest business venture or what car they drove – or try to expense-account my dances. They just grinned appreciatively while I got my tits out and threw me bucket-loads of compliments. And they were generous: it wasn't unusual to be handed a fifty straight up. I liked these guys – what wasn't to like? That Tuesday, I made more money than usual and with less effort. There were fewer podium sets, the club closed at 3 a.m. and Gallery dancers had a priority finish.

Why not switch clubs? Well, while the men made me feel like royalty, there *was* a disturbing seediness to the place. It reminded me too much of Pleasures. I also detected a hard drug culture that wasn't evident at the Gallery. In hindsight, it was unsurprising: Russell Street in the late nineties was heroin central. No dancer, least of all a user, likes an out-of-towner flying in and stealing her take.

So I compromised: at the Gallery from Monday to Wednesday and Santa Fe on Friday and Saturday nights. When the Gallery girls asked if Santa Fe was any good I said I preferred it because of the early finishes. At the Russell Street venue, I kept to myself, worked hard and tried not to poach anyone's regulars. For a couple of months, I had the best of both clubs, even if I wasn't having a great time.

Occasionally, unexpected lightness crept into the dark spaces of the night. One Saturday around 5 p.m., I was standing outside Santa Fe with the other early birds, waiting for management to let us in, when a softly spoken man with John Lennon glasses and a greying ponytail stopped to ask if we could use a masseur. Basically, he was suggesting that *we* should pay *him* to let *him* touch *us*. It was the stripper-world equivalent of trying to scale Everest. But there was something genuine about this man and someone more influential than I saw it, because soon George and his massage table were set up in the girls room. George was a true healer, as well as a saver of stiff soles, and just one of the many amazing people I'd meet through the industry over the years.

Meanwhile, Fletcher had expressed an interest in seeing where my sexual energy was spent. I didn't know what he'd make of my work, but I wanted him to understand it, so he and I ventured into the Gallery together one evening. Not much silenced Fletch, but that night he said little. Disdainfully, he watched the girls on the podiums going through their daily grind.

'They look bored and unhappy,' he said at last. 'There's no way I'd pay one of them to dance for me.'

On one hand, this is what every girl wants to hear from her guy. On the other, as I was 'one of them', it was unsettling. Back at the hostel I felt like Fletcher hadn't understood what it was I did. It was a big ask, given I didn't fully comprehend it myself. Luckily, my travel fund was complete. I binned my shoes and vowed to get a 'real job'. When we three finally boarded the plane to London, it wasn't a day too soon.

7.

I DIDN'T MUCH LIKE ENGLAND AND I CLOSE TO hated London. Fletcher, Evan and I had been living there for nearly a year, in an ex-council flat in Shepherds Bush. With the Aussie dollar almost three to the pound, our savings had long since gone.

As the months had slipped by, the city's dour grittiness had become familiar. I grew accustomed to the Tube turning my snot black, to our two-bedroom flat sleeping five, to the train drivers at our local pub slagging off their wives. The culture of misery was almost comforting.

The point of coming to London had been to travel, but I'd only managed two weeks in Greece and a few weekends away – the latest being to Paris with Evan. In seductive Montmartre I'd loitered under the slow-turning lights of the Moulin Rouge windmill, fantasising about busting out of petticoats and drinking absinthe with Toulouse-Lautrec.

In reality, most of my time was spent in a staid office block on the right side of Lambeth North earning £250 a week. I was the press office manager of the BSE Inquiry – a government investigation into mad cow disease – sending out witness statements by newswire and filtering calls from scientists convinced they'd found the cause of prion protein mutation. As the hearings had wound down, the press office quietened and I went stir crazy. It was time to quit my straight job and get back to stripping.

I just assumed strip clubs in London would be more lucrative than those in Melbourne or at least on par. At Santa Fe Gold, one of the girls had raved about the Windmill. I knew the stripper grapevine was prone to exaggeration, but so far it hadn't been wrong. So I dug out my American flag bikini and phoned up for an interview.

The Windmill is London's oldest strip club. Situated in the heart of Soho, it began life as a theatre in the 1930s and became scandalous when manager Vivian Van Damm – inspired by the Moulin Rouge and *Les Folies Bergère* – introduced nude girls into its line-up. The Windmill was as close to dancing at the Moulin Rouge as I was going to get.

The afternoon of my interview a cold tailwind, dank with the smell of piss and rotting garbage, blustered me along Greater Windmill Street towards the old brick-fronted theatre. I was ushered down a dark corridor ripe with mildew into the dressing-room, where the boss and his son cranked up the lights, asked me to strip to my knickers then critiqued me as if I wasn't there.

'She's a bit fat,' said the son, who had a perpetual sniff, an untucked shirt and bedroom hair.

True, I was a little out of shape from sitting at a desk all day, but nothing a layer of fake tan wouldn't fix. I wished I'd thought to buy a bottle. And a wig. After dying my hair brown, only to have it turn green, I'd shaved my head. I was now more Julie Andrews than Pamela Anderson. At least I'd made up my face.

'She's not fat! She's wholesome,' said the father, who wore tweed and sported an impeccable grey moustache. He winked at me. I gave him my best stripper smile. He held up his hands. 'See! We need more like her. How old are you, luv?'

'Twenty-four,' I said truthfully.

I was hired. I soon discovered this meant that *I'd* be paying *them* for the privilege of working there. The Windmill had a house fee: forty pounds per shift, with the first night free. I received this news rather unhappily as I was given the grand tour, which wasn't very grand. The club had retained the original theatre façade and arranged chairs and tables around the old stage. All 'shows' would be done in this room – there were no private dancing cubicles or fantasy booths. It certainly wasn't The Men's Gallery, but I tried to keep an open mind.

I turned up for my first shift in a short white singlet dress, the American bikini and a black fembot wig – the West African hairdresser on the corner of our street didn't stock blonde. The dressing-room was already full to overflowing, with dancers getting changed in the fusty corridor. I squeezed into the room, found myself a spot and began to get ready.

The girls were lovely. Seriously. They were chatty, happy and welcoming, including a beautiful blonde fellow Kiwi who had just spent six weeks travelling in China.

Up on the floor, the club was empty. There wasn't one customer. I bought myself a vodka and listened to Cherie, a French newbie who had generously offered to explain the rules. A few customers came in while she talked and were dive-bombed by the hungriest girls. Two climbed up onstage and began to strip off.

'Hang on, what are they doing?' I asked Cherie.

'Private shows,' she said.

'That's not a private show,' I said with a wry laugh. The whole room was watching.

That was because the Windmill wasn't licensed for offstage nudity. Girls took to the stage to dance for their customer, maintaining eye contact as they wiggled alongside other 'private' dancers like a school of fish. The whole thing was antiquated and ridiculous.

As the evening wore on it clicked that this was a hostess club: the serious money was getting booked to drink, and I didn't work like that. I heard a guy come in off the street and argue with management that his credit card had been overcharged the week before. They didn't believe him. I suspected it probably had.

The first night back is always the hardest and my Motown garb only compounded the culture shock, but I knew that the Windmill wasn't for me. Still, I forced myself to try to get a dance. After my third rejection offered to fly me to the Seychelles for the weekend if I gave him a hand job in the toilets, I stumbled backstage with a choked-up throat. The house mum was nowhere to be seen. A tired-looking blonde in a leopard print bikini was yelling, 'Anyone got haemorrhoid cream?'

I stared at her in shock, unaware it disguised bags under the eyes. She glowered at me. I burst into tears.

'I can't do this,' I sniffed. 'The men are nasty and there's no private booths! It's *horrible.*'

The blonde took the cream from an outstretched hand and turned away. 'You'll get used to it,' she said, sounding personally insulted. 'Every club in London is the same.'

My heart sank. She looked like she'd been around long enough to know.

That weekend I lay on the couch wondering how to pay my rent.

Fletcher was less fatalistic. 'Don't take her word for it,' he said. 'You don't know that every club is the same.' He was right, of course.

For Your Eyes Only was a half-hour walk from the nearest tube station in the middle of an industrial estate. The exterior resembled an old Tudor mansion in a field of asphalt, but the insides of this northwest London man-cave were thankfully familiar. For starters, the house mum Robyn was a Kiwi, a Wairarapa farm girl not much older than me. The main room was spacious and softly lit, two-tiered in an L-shape around a purpose-built stage with an assortment of banquettes and big tables, much like a 200-seater family restaurant. There was also a VIP room, all glass-and-brass with spongy sofas. The place smelt like Brasso and lemon table wax. Like good clean fun.

'How close can I get in a private dance?' I asked, sounding like the dirty girl I wasn't.

There was an arm's length rule, which seemed workable, and dances were ten pounds per three minutes. Additionally, every girl performed a two-song stage set, dictated by a rotating roster, stripping topless to the music of her choice.

'What songs would you like to audition to?' Robyn asked. My mouth fell open. I'd never had to audition before. For a moment, I thought she meant I'd be giving her a private dance, but she was switching on the stage lights. It seemed appropriate to go country with some Shania Twain. This time, I'd bought the fake tan and left the wig at home. I took to the pole in my pseudo-American ensemble and tried to ignore Robyn sitting pokerfaced in the front row with her clipboard – although I wondered if growing up on a farm had unintentionally prepared her for this meat market. Round and round I went, gyrating and grinding. My moves were a little stiff, but really, it was just like riding a bike. I panted offstage with raised eyebrows and received a businesslike nod.

We got down to details. The club was open from Monday to Saturday, 8 p.m. to 3 a.m. Long dresses were worn before 11 p.m., themed costumes from 11 to 1 a.m. and dancer's preference for the last two hours. It was all sounding good until Robyn said there was a sixty-five-pound house fee – forty-five on quiet nights – and new girls were not exempt. Thursdays had been 'a little slow'. Robyn suggested starting the following night when there was a greater chance the club would be busy.

So I did. Less than twenty-four hours later, I was back with a hastily bought long red dress, the stars and stripes bikini, a blonde fembot wig and a bellyful of nervous enthusiasm. In the small change-room I squeezed in between a refined Canadian who looked like Princess Di and whose stage name was, predictably, Diana; and Jamie, a pert dancer from Essex with a freckled chest and scraggly blonde hair, who announced into the mirror – 'I'm gonna make five hundred tonight.' This was encouraging, my wigs and dress alone owed me one hundred pounds. Robyn asked me what I wanted to be called. I realised I'd outgrown Holly – she sounded too young and naive. I introduced myself as Sabrina, a homage to my former admin assistant at the BSE Inquiry who raced home early every Wednesday to catch *Sabrina, the Teenage Witch*.

Robyn was a little pissed about my wig. 'You weren't wearing that when we hired you,' she remarked. Wigs had been big in Melbourne. Not so, I was discovering, in London. Clubs favoured a more natural, classier look. Bodily additions were subtle: hair extensions instead of wigs, highlights instead of block colour, French-tips instead of hot-pink talons. Skin was sun-kissed instead of heavily tanned. No bling dangling from bronzed belly buttons. Even garters were discreetly wound around wrists or ankles. Still, I knew emulating Barbie was safer than going bareheaded.

Out on the floor, I joined the thirty-odd dancers sitting around, smoking and sipping champagne, simultaneously relaxing and gearing up, while a handful of customers, with the barely concealed edginess of the unwittingly trapped, succumbed to the persistence of the girls who reached them first. I made sure I was one of those girls. Fortunately, the first man I danced for fell in love with my flouncy blonde hair. He was a round, middle-aged Indian, mild mannered and appreciative. I tried not to make bodily contact as I slam-dunked the air with my butt. It wasn't hard to gaze hungrily into his eyes for a full three minutes: I was still fifty-five quid in the red.

After that I whirled around the room, approaching every Ben Sherman–clad man until I realised I was fast running out of options and needed to slow the fuck down. There was no place to hide, no loitering in the dressing-room allowed. I went back and sat with the girls and sussed out the best place to buy Pleaser stilettos – my very own Cinderella slippers. There was a lot of anxious sitting around before 11 p.m. Dancers kept one eye out for potential moolah at all times and unabashedly leapt up mid-conversation if they spied an opening. Diana, I noticed, was very popular. Jamie didn't even bother to remove her G during a dance; she left it stretched around her ankles for a quick exit. It wasn't a good look, but then no one was looking at her feet.

After 11 p.m. the club swirled giddily for four hours – no time to pee, costume changes in under a minute – until the closing track (yes, 'For Your Eyes Only') began and those girls still on the floor scurried to secure one last dance before the house lights came up. Backstage, it was a weary, silent derobing as extensions were unclipped, false eyelashes peeled off and sweat-soaked garters shoved into handbags. I felt like I'd been at stripper boot camp; I could barely bend over to unbuckle my shoes.

Still, I had ninety pounds in my hand and I figured I could double it once I knew what I was doing. Two nights and I'd be earning more than a five-day week at the Inquiry. It was far from Jamie's super-ambitious target (which she'd failed to achieve), but I was on my way.

* * *

With a six-inch pair of Pleaser Adore stilettos, it didn't take me long to find my feet. For Your Eyes Only was run with a straightforward, impersonal efficiency that reflected the harshness of big city life. If a customer wasn't having dances, he was asked to leave. It was confusing, the first time I saw a man being escorted out for doing nothing, but I approved of the rule. It declared that our time was money and what we offered was a service, not a substitute lounge room. There were no 'seagulls' hovering for a free glimpse of pussy, no barflies gazing bleary-eyed at the stage like a TV. Or worse, gazing at the TV instead of the stage.

Here, the customers were almost always seated. It was a system of subtle dominance that began with them being shown to their table by a hostess and continued with table service only. The bar was out back, invisible from the floor, which meant that the only reason a guy had for getting out of his chair was to go to the toilet. It was like being on board a jumbo jet with the seatbelt sign switched on, except all the airhostesses wanted to take their clothes off. Being seated also ensured a customer's face was in line with a dancer's breasts when she approached. Clearly, this system had been well thought out by a man who knew men.

I don't know who that man was, but our manager was an Eastern European man called Sergei, who had an air of ruthless thuggery undisguised by his suit. This commanded my instant respect, as did his good sense to leave the handling of the girls to Robyn. One of the few times I spoke with Sergei was when a customer refused to pay up, claiming he didn't have any money. A burly security guard was sent out of the shadows and onto the floor, and my ten pounds materialised as if by magic.

Unlike at The Men's Gallery, payment for dances was made after the event. This rule seemed excessively polite and was too ambiguous for my liking. Management guaranteed to retrieve payment for the first song; after that, you were on your own. Consequently, I never danced for more than two songs without being paid.

This rule left both dancers and customers open to being taken advantage of. It wasn't unusual for a guy to refuse a dance and a girl to begin anyway – Jamie did this a lot. Sometimes an argument ensued, though usually the guy conceded. Perhaps it's hard to say no when a pint-sized blonde with a no-nonsense smile is bullying you.

Another dancer who got away with this was Anna, a busty Czech dominatrix, who wore PVC and played down her ability to speak English. 'Zit up,' she would command, prodding stammering Hugh Grant lookalikes with her riding crop. They seldom refused.

For me, even on the nights when I thought I'd end up owing the house, I needed verbal confirmation to begin a dance. A 'maybe later' was met by me ruminating out loud on whatever came to mind – why there was no bush in Shepherds Bush or what the Queen's corgis might be called – until the man realised I wasn't going away without getting a dance. Sometimes I left empty-handed, but not without a fight. I couldn't afford to just walk away. Few dancers could.

For the first two to three hours we worked to pay back the house, after which we only had three or four hours to make money for ourselves. Dancers often outnumbered customers so, despite my co-workers' initial friendliness, I anticipated our relations would be cool at best, a backstabbing bitch-fight at worst. Remarkably it was the opposite. Battlelines had been predetermined by gender: united, we stood; divided, they sat. No one had the energy for insider conflict.

As we waited for the enemy ranks to swell, we shared cigarettes and stories of our lives and loves as much as tips or tools of the trade. There were dancers from all over the world – Russians, Brazilians, Canadians, Australians, Romanians – and they had followed the scent of cash from Iceland to Ibiza, Okinawa to Ontario. They knew the best clubs in Roppongi, Tokyo; they knew that Guam was quiet right now. They could say 'no touching' or 'very sexy man' in five or six languages. Some had stripped for most of their lives, like 36-year-old Imogen from the US, who told me, 'I'm grateful for every day I have left in this industry. I've had the most amazing ride.' Others were on a gap year – or a gap decade. Regardless of how long they'd been doing this, though, like strippers the world over, their alter egos fell into three distinct types: princess, whore and girl next door.

The A-listers were princesses: classy and intimidatingly gorgeous, with names like Victoria, Chelsea and Diana. Naturally elegant, they wore gowns in silver, turquoise or pale pink, with diamante sandals. They were public-school-girl articulate and it was understood that men would pay handsomely for moments of their time. The sports cars in the car park belonged to the A-listers, as did the bouquets of flowers left to wilt in the dressing-room.

The whores oozed sex appeal and wore patent leather stilettos, suspender belts and animal print. They included two Brazilian sisters (who never waxed, anywhere) and Foxy Roxy, a raven-haired, hard-drinking, thirty-something mother-of-two with a filthy mouth and a Pilates-sculpted body. It was the whores who filled their faux-leather Filofaxes with photo-shoots for lingerie catalogues and B-grade video clips, and aspired to be page 3 girls.

Then there were the real whores. A couple of the Eastern European girls would spend hours talking with carefully selected customers. I wondered how they could afford to waste so much time, then realised they offered an afterhours service. I accepted this without judgement, however soliciting couldn't be disguised for long and management soon moved these girls and others like them on. Pretending to be available was one thing, actually being available was another.

Most of us, though, were the girl next door – students and travellers, immigrants and single mothers. We were the ones most likely to hear the tired line: 'What's a nice girl like you doing in a place like this?' Ella was the only stripper I ever met who'd had a breast reduction. She was a hearty Danish gal dating one of the Bros brothers. Suzy, beautiful and black, wore a maid's outfit and set back the civil rights movement with her 'let little Suzy look after big daddy' routine. She also had a law degree. Juliette was a trained dancer from Canada, who infused the room with her sultry jazz-inspired performances.

And then there was Larissa. She was onstage the first time I saw her, dancing to 'Bittersweet Symphony' in a floor-length fishtail dress, patterned deep blue like the ocean. She slid off the dress to reveal long, lean limbs and pendulous breasts, tattoos inked on her hips and shoulders. Her hair was a mess of waist-length red curls and she was completely, unabashedly lost in the music.

I was enthralled. When she finally slipped into the seat beside me and bummed a cigarette, I discovered she was every bit the gypsy she appeared to be. She'd started stripping in Tokyo when she was supposed to be teaching English. She'd been to Africa, caught malaria and nearly lost her mind during the treatment. She wanted to move to Australia, but had fallen in love with an older man who had commitments, a son. Her life seemed to be this wild, crazy, never-ending ride and I wanted a life like hers.

In contrast, my daily regime was strict, self-regulated and revolved around work. I calculated everything I did in relation to how much energy I'd have left for shaking my money-maker. From the moment I woke up on a workday, I was acutely aware of being sixty-five pounds in debt. The fear of not making money, of potentially *owing* the house, was ever-present. So too was the possibility of fast cash for travel. It was a teetering seesaw of inner turmoil I rode out as best I could. The easiest way of calming your nervous system if you're not partial to putting illegal substances up your nose? Work even more.

* * *

London had accentuated how different Fletcher and I were: I wasn't interested in getting pissed and watching rugby at Antipodean watering holes; he wasn't interested in backpacking around the almost-dry Middle East. So we did the sort of thing you do when you're in denial: we planned a road trip around Europe, giving ourselves four months to save. He focused on portering at the Sheraton and I dived back into hustle-town.

Dancers' rosters were put up a month in advance and it was compulsory to work at least two Mondays. Soon I was working four nights a week, paying my former wage in house fees. The weekends were busier, but making money was capped by 3 a.m. closing. No matter how hard I worked, there wasn't time to do more than thirty dances a night, and I often did less.

I seldom remembered a face and never a name on any given night. I kept track of them by where they sat – Mr Table 3, second-on-the-right. Investing time in building up regulars wasn't a risk I could afford to take.

One Wednesday night I got talking to a guy from Christchurch. We knew the same places, but not the same people. I danced for him and thought nothing more of it. Some weeks later, Fletcher mentioned an old school friend wanted to meet up for dinner. He was good-looking, charming and charismatic – and vaguely familiar. 'I know you from somewhere,' he agreed. Afterwards, I remembered I had danced for him. As a customer, his attributes didn't count: he was a three-minute transaction I sought to honour as best I could. I simply never saw *him*.

In my defence, it didn't help that For Your Eyes Only attracted a generic type of Englishman: clean-cut, proper and mostly polite. Sometimes when I got naked, younger customers grew embarrassed, reddening or fixing their eyes on my face, so I didn't think it unusual when one night a guy blushed wildly when I removed my G. Impressed by my ability to shock the boy, I batted my fake lashes at him and licked my lips. He chewed on his and stared at the floor.

'Excuse me,' he said finally, 'I think you've got something stuck … down there.'

I ducked my head between my legs. Snagged on my pubic hair was a snowflake of toilet paper, glowing nuclear-white under the UV lights. It was the stripper equivalent of having food stuck in your teeth.

'Oops,' I said brightly. 'Do you mind if I ...?'

He waved me away and I darted out back, glad the dance had been a prepaid gift from his brother. While I wasn't as mortified as he was, I avoided that table for the rest of the night.

There were other, more positive firsts. Culturally enlightening ones. Like the first time I danced for a black guy.

'Damn girl, you got back,' he said.

'Huh?' I turned to look over my shoulder at him.

'Your butt is damn fine. That all yours?'

'Just me and a little bit of KFC,' I said, not realising he was talking about implants. In London I would get asked a lot if my butt was real.

'You're too much, girl,' he said. 'Work it for me.'

I worked it gladly, grinding at the air like a peppershaker. I made a mental note to approach more men of colour.

'I reckon you were black in a past life,' he murmured appreciatively in a voice like molten lead.

There were unexpected treats in the humdrum of table-dance land. When in town a Bollywood film producer would reserve the large table at the top of the stairs, arriving with an entourage of gorgeous young actors, each one latte-skinned and sculpted to perfection. They were like modern-day pirates with billowing white shirts, colourful headscarfs and large gold hoop earrings. A dancer was allocated to each rising star then we'd rotate with every song, like some bizarre lazy Susan. My face got hot under the gentle gaze of those lush-lashed young men and I'd giggle and forget what fantasy island I'd been shipwrecked upon.

Occasionally, a celebrity would come into the club. I never knew how to behave when this happened, whether to acknowledge their fame or ignore it. The night Rod Stewart came in wearing a canary yellow shirt, white jeans and matching zip-up flats, I blurted out, 'Ooh, I like your shirt.' Afterwards, I was too embarrassed to trail him into the VIP room where his party was swiftly relocated. (Incidentally, the VIP room was open to anyone willing to pay for the privilege.) Rod stayed almost till close; reportedly, he had become enamoured with an Aussie dancer who looked like Rachel Hunter. The next night, I arrived to find Sergei coordinating a tell-all between the dancer and a crew from tabloid newspaper *The Sun*. Tacky. That wasn't something a top club like Stringfellows would have done.

After a few months I lost the wig. Short hair was fashionable and Englishmen loved my blonde crop. I bought a royal-blue dress that accentuated my hair and an army outfit that exposed my butt for theme time. Boot camp became booty camp; I could legitimately start commanding privates. This was fun – serious fun.

With just nine months left on my visa, I wanted to save as much as possible. I gave up junk food, lost weight and toned up. Dinner became Campbell's soup, a small treat a Milky Way. I stopped drinking outside of work and rationed my cigarettes. On days off, I'd go running around Hammersmith. Workdays, I would wander through Holland Park to Notting Hill, browsing the bookshops. I became fascinated with the Vietnam War and read every book available; the dream of being a war correspondent hadn't totally died. When not at the Sheraton, Fletcher was about during the day, but increasingly we avoided each other. One time there were rumours of infidelity on his part and I was shocked at how hurt I was by them. I didn't believe his denials.

Fletch and I soldiered on and in September took off for five weeks around France, Switzerland and Italy, meeting up with friends of his along the way. To my delight, one was an art history buff. Marcus and I stayed on in Florence to explore the hidden wonders of that ancient city while the others travelled on to Rome. Wandering Florence's marbled streets with Marcus, downing espressos on two hours' sleep and deconstructing Masaccio's frescoes at sunset over sticky glasses of *limoncello* all signalled that my relationship with Fletcher was over. A month later, it was.

A fling wasn't a good idea, especially not a drunken fling during the Rugby World Cup, but I waited until then to launch myself across the table of a pub in Notting Hill and into Marcus's lap. We trudged the streets for four hours looking for a cheap room – four hours that were offered up like an intervention – but I couldn't stop myself.

Marcus returned to New Zealand and Fletcher moved out soon after. His friends had become mine and I lost every one of them except for Evan. (I was grateful for and humbled by Evan's reluctance to take sides.) So I did what I could do, what I would do again and again during personal crises: I filled the void with hard work and fast cash.

Stripping gave my restless mind a focus, and it offered me a chance to reinvent myself. In all that was new, I was comforted by what was old. By the bright lights, the aching face and feet, the compliments and the laughs, the sweaty money. At the club, I could shelve my infidelity. Perhaps, even, find a sense of belonging.

* * *

I decided to tell my parents I was 'dancing' again, but this time I emailed them with the news. It was my father who replied: *Just the other day, we were saying it seemed you were finally over your stint in the sex industry, but apparently not. You are very talented and could do anything you put your mind to.*

I sat in the internet café – suddenly oblivious to Hammersmith Road behind me, to the whiff of the Jamaicans' reefer wafting in through the door – and stared at the screen. The *sex industry*? Table dancing was *entertainment*, quite distinct from selling sex. I wasn't fucking fat truckers in some dingy backstreet bordello! I was simply getting my groove on, nude, for anyone willing to pay to watch.

I told my mother this in person when the loneliness and the dismal London winter became too much and I flew to New Zealand for a break.

'I've been to Amsterdam, Leigh,' she said, not looking at me. 'I know what it is you do.'

I had been to Amsterdam too and thought what they did was nothing like what I did. I had walked the lanes of the red-light district with mounting horror, seeing girl after girl boxed into life-size dollhouses. Some of the prostitutes were young; some were used up; most looked bored. They had nowhere to hide, yet no one saw them. Did they want to be seen? I couldn't tell. One old Goth turned her back on me. Another was young, incredibly pretty, with white candyfloss hair. A hungry goldfish, her model legs in their matchbox-red shoes too long for the space. She smiled at me like she wanted me. I knew she did not.

It wasn't what these girls did or what I imagined they did that most bothered me, although disappointingly it bothered me plenty. It was the judgemental eyes of the rubberneckers – tourists like me, who robbed the girls of what power they had.

Yet I still couldn't comprehend why my stripping evoked a similar response in my mother. Neither of us seemed able to deal with the issue – or appreciate the other's viewpoint. It was easier not to talk about it. So we didn't.

* * *

In the month I'd been away my London bases had begun to break down. I returned to find that Evan was moving in with his girlfriend and had applied for sponsorship, while For Your Eyes Only was unexpectedly quiet. Partly, it was because American strip club chain Spearmint Rhino had opened on Tottenham Court Road and (rumour had it) let you touch the girls. I greeted the news with dismay. I wasn't prepared to get groped for any amount of money. That was the line I simply wouldn't cross, the line that to my mind differentiated 'entertainer' from 'sex worker'.

Core dancers began to jump ship: the Brazilian sisters left, reportedly to work at Stringfellows; Roxy went to Venus. I considered trying another club – Secrets or Venus perhaps; I knew I wasn't model-gorgeous enough for Stringfellows – but they might be worse, and For Your Eyes Only might not take me back. With two months left on my visa, I opted to tough it out.

One drink a night turned into several. I began making promises I had no intention of keeping, and often couldn't quantify: yes, I would come *extra* close; yes, *of course* it would be the best dance they'd ever had. Although I never left owing the house, more than once I made only fifty pounds.

After an especially slow night, Larissa burst into tears. As we formed a consolatory stripper huddle around her, she held up a twenty-pound note. 'Twenty fucking quid! The measure of my worth.' She laughed at the irony as the tears slid down her cheeks.

Something in me snapped then. I looked from Larissa's proud face into the mirror at my own, baby-wiped clean, lined and blotchy and white. My eyelids were puffy and red from an allergy to the eyelash glue, my eyes glassy and empty. I didn't care about sticking out the visa anymore, I needed to get out of London while I still recognised myself. The very next day I booked a ticket to Cairo.

I had lasted a year at For Your Eyes Only. It gave me five months' travel in total, including two very soulful months in the Middle East. Nights sleeping under the stars in wadis in Jordan and days roaming the jostling alleys of old Jerusalem made me feel so at home – the culture and the landscape so familiar – I couldn't help but wonder if I had lived there in a past life. Being covered from head to toe in a former incarnation might explain why I kept wanting to take my clothes off in this one.

I left my headscarves in Istanbul and flew to New Zealand with three thousand dollars and no clue of what to do next. Two thousand went on a road trip to catch up with old friends –

including Sonia, who had broken up with Tom, had a new partner, and had just given birth to their first child. That trip made it clear: I wasn't ready to settle down.

So I did what felt like the logical next step. I bought a one-way ticket to Melbourne, booked into the backpackers and boarded another plane. I had five hundred bucks to my name. For the first time in years, I was completely on my own.

Two

JULIETTE AND JASMINE

8.

THE DAY I HAD PLANNED TO RESUME STRIPPING, I woke up at the backpackers with a faceful of bedbug bites. I felt like a right skank. It was three days before the nasty red welts had subsided enough to be concealed. By then, I was down to two hundred dollars and was desperate to get nude.

It was a Wednesday. As soon as The Men's Galley opened, I called and asked if I could roster back on. The receptionist said I'd been gone too long and would have to undergo a 'compulsory retraining session'. She told me to meet Raine – the club's former top showgirl – in the foyer at 5 p.m.

Arriving early, I waited impatiently on the casting couch, dressed in a t-shirt, jeans and thongs. With me were two first-timers from Frankston, a depressed outer suburb of Melbourne and a breeding ground for nubile strippers. They wore low-slung velour tracksuits that exposed matching Playboy bunny tramp-stamps. One was chewing gum. She squeezed my thigh. 'I'm *so* excited! Hopefully the guys are hot. That'd really piss my boyfriend off.'

I gave her a tight-lipped smile. Two years in England had cultivated the snob in me.

Raine finally arrived at twenty past, sporting a sizeable baby bump. Ever the showgirl, she had teamed it with four-inch stilettos, a black jersey dress and leggings. In the face of her glamour, my superiority faded. Grasping for recognition, I flip-flopped along at her elbow as she led us up the backstairs, into the showroom.

'Wow, you're pregnant,' I said, disbelievingly. Plastic-perfect flesh just wasn't made for procreating.

'Well,' said Raine with a sideways glance, 'you can't always flash your gash for cash.'

We filed into the red room where Raine explained the house rules, which hadn't changed. The new girls asked a lot of questions along the lines of, 'What do you say if someone wants to pay you for sex?' and 'Has a guy ever vomited on you?' To the latter, Raine gave an offhand shrug. 'Once. Industry hazard. If you're a builder, sooner or later you're going to fall off the ladder.' She looked to me for moral support. I shrugged too, but said nothing. I've always believed that if you hustle a guy who's so drunk he could mistake you for a public toilet then you deserve what's coming to you.

One of the new girls asked Raine to demonstrate a few moves. She obliged, her belly giving new measure to the regulation thirty-centimetre gap between a performer and a customer's groin. When she lay back and splayed her legs in 'The Men's Gallery salute', it was disconcertingly close to birthing. I was relieved when she told us to go and start getting ready.

Down in the girls room, I found Carole presiding over the dance supervisor's desk, puffing on the ever-present fag.

'Welcome back, what's your name again?' she said.

'It was Holly,' I said.

'We already have a Holly. You'll have to pick something else.'

Feeling a pointless surge of possessiveness, I thought fast. Sabrina was too pretentious.

'Juliette?'

'Juliette it is.'

I'd named myself after a sultry Canadian dancer I'd worked with in London, unaware of the Shakespearean overtones (or that my first name was in there, too).

The first dancer I saw was Harlow. She was snapping domestic instructions into her mobile, presumably to her husband. While she looked as breathtaking as ever, there was a new coldness in her eyes and sharpness to her tone.

'How are you, babe?' she asked evenly as she hung up, as if we'd seen each other yesterday. Time had a way of vaporising in stripperville. 'Guess what? I got the house.' Harlow's dream house in Brighton had come on the market and she'd bought it at auction. Watching her fasten her garter and head resolutely towards the stairs, I wondered at what cost.

While I spied a few more familiar faces, no one else said hello and I said hello to no one. Up on the floor nothing much appeared to have changed; thankfully, the club was still busy midweek. I slotted back into the routine with a metaphorical skin hardened by the London hustle and actual toes permanently disfigured by my grown-up stripper shoes. It was a relief to be able to go down to the girls room, put my feet up and smoke a cigarette without management yelling, 'Get your arse out on the floor!' as Sergei had done in London.

Around 11 p.m., I was doing exactly that when Carole stomped down the dressing-room stairs, dragging one of the Frankston newbies by the elbow. They disappeared into the costume room, the door slamming behind them. I got up and loitered nearby, expressing unusual interest in a bowl of rubber bands.

'What the fuck were you thinking?' I heard Carole say.

'Look, it's okay, he respected me totally,' the girl said.

'What part of "no touching" don't you understand, you little twerp? Pack up your shit, you're fired.'

I hurried back to my booth. The girl emerged looking livid and began scooping her belongings into her bag. Later, I would learn she'd been kissing a customer. Word was if security hadn't called Carole, the girl would've fucked him then and there. I wondered if her sidekick would stick around. She didn't.

The girls' motivations were perplexing, but once I'd made enough money for rent and bond I began to question my own. Despite the memory of the London nights when I'd yearned to be where the cash flowed, I just couldn't bring myself to work more than three nights a week. Three nights was plenty to live off. Stripping had always been the vehicle to get me someplace else, and this time I wasn't sure where or what that was.

* * *

I found a room in a three-bedroom house in Richmond sharing with two guys. James was a politics major and ran marathons; John worked in insurance and spent weekends getting wasted at iconic live venue The Tote. Neither was interested in the fact I took my clothes off for a living.

What else to do? At first I roamed the streets, observing the lives of others. Then I took up yoga classes at a nearby gym. I had tried yoga once before – with Sonia, my first weekend in Melbourne. I'd had three hours' sleep and had panted and trembled through the weird positions, convinced I was going to pass out. But afterwards I'd felt euphoric. Now I went every Monday and I did find a fleeting sense of peace, although never the all-encompassing, transcendental bliss of that first class.

My purposelessness remained, ramped up by the fact that I didn't know anyone. I had only the girls I worked with – and I didn't really know them, only their alter egos – so I was thrilled to learn that Sonia's ex, Tom, was back in town. We met for a drink and discovered that we lived around the corner from each other. Soon we were catching up several times a week. I officially had one friend.

Next, I tried for entry-level positions in media but after two months I hadn't got one interview. It was time to do that one-year postgraduate journalism diploma I'd always intended to do. To be accepted, I was going to need a normal job on my CV.

The 2000 Olympics were held in Sydney that September. Instead of flying interstate to derobe, I found a gig covering the coverage as a media monitor. I had high hopes; I even bought a suit. What a waste. Media monitoring would go down as one of the most boring jobs I've ever had. For two weeks from 6 a.m. to 2 p.m., I transcribed radio shows for twelve dollars an hour, keeping an ear out for information potentially floggable to big business. When the Olympics finished and the media monitors kept me on part time, I traded my suit for my birthday suit at the club in the afternoons, from midday until 7 p.m.

Day shift attracted a different clientele. In my experience, men who spend sunlit hours in a girlie bar are generally avoiding something, and when they're skiving off work or unemployed, they're tight with their money. These placid gents expected a lengthy chat before considering a dance. I actually had to pretend to be interested in them as people! London had taught me how to do this, but I was by no means a master of it. Nor was I prepared to marriage-counsel or get drunk at 2 p.m. But with as few as five guys in the venue at any one time, a degree of playing along was required.

This slippery slide of make-believe continued into the dance itself. Back then, The Men's Gallery was still considered a no-touch club, but the day girls bent and broke this rule long before the night girls did. Customers had always been permitted to hold a dancer's hips during a dance, but at her discretion. I'd never allowed it – there were so many customers I didn't need to. But on my first dayshift, one man after another reached for my hips. Annoyed, I brushed their hands away. 'You can't touch,' I said haughtily. They looked surprised, then pissed off. 'The other girls let me,' they said. 'Why won't you?'

It was a fair question and, looking around, I knew that the correct answer wasn't, 'Because I don't want your filthy hands on me, you emotionally fucked-up voyeur.' I saw that if I was to make any money I would have to permit 'holding the baby'.

Some men's touch was neutral, neither giving nor taking from the experience. Others made my skin crawl. Usually these men were needy, greedy cheapskates. I made a mental note to avoid them: their money wasn't worth what the experience took from me. While I never liked the contact, I wanted to like the men, even respect them, so I could continue respecting myself. I began to look for common ground in our conversations, making the effort to humanise these walking wallets. I also learnt how to create intimacy without being physically intimate – to dance closer, to hold eye contact, to try to stay mentally present. This reduced the men's need to touch. My box of tricks was expanding: I was becoming a better private dancer.

* * *

It took a special kind of girl to choose dayshifts over night, to nursemaid emotionally dependent men for less moolah. Generally I found the day girls to be more giving, less fixated on time and money. With only eight to ten of us working each shift we were a close-knit sisterhood, and I appreciated the camaraderie. We crammed small talk into the half-hour we had to get ready, while up on the floor we shared ciggies and swapped tables when someone had to catch the last train. They were day girls for many reasons: some travelled from regional Victoria, others couldn't cope with big crowds, still others wanted to spend evenings and weekends with their boyfriends, husbands or families. Some were simply early birds. Was it possible they were more in tune with the natural rhythms of life?

Then there was Amber. She had a repertoire of farm animal noises she brought out on request. The first time I was doing a private dance alongside her, she spread her legs and began barking like a dog. Amber's farm animal men responded in kind, converting the lounge bar into a warped menagerie, a kind of call-and-response between star-crossed sheepdogs. This irked me. My job of creating a believable illusion was made that much harder when the couple beside me were barking mad.

More irritating were the dancers who offered up breasts to mouths, soft skin to eager fingers. I learned to turn a blind eye to anomalies, to what I saw unfolding in the corners of the lounge bar.

The best way to approach dayshift was to treat it like a slow-paced night. From midday to 2 p.m. and from 5 to 7 p.m., I got serious. I'd invested in a long ash-blonde wig, twisted up in a chignon, figuring at least some of the office absentees were fantasising about their secretaries. I didn't sit with customers for long enough to cultivate a crop of mid-afternoon spenders, but I did meet some lovely men during happy hour. These men would stay loyal as labradors after I had crossed back to nights.

They included Kevin, a meter reader for Origin Energy who often smelled of pollen from people's front gardens. Kevin was short, round and eternally cheerful. The first time I offered him a dance, he said solemnly, 'If you promise to do the right thing by me, I'll do the right thing by you.'

'Okay,' I replied. To my mind the right thing wasn't groping me, which would have been grounds for instant dismissal.

But what Kevin wanted was common courtesy: for me to look happy to see him, to ask how he was, not to rip him off. That this didn't go without saying saddened me. In return, he would do his utmost to make me feel good.

'How are you?' I would ask.

'All the better for seeing you,' he would reply, smiling eyes sinking into cherub cheeks. He'd reach for my hand and off we'd go into the private dance area. He'd extend his stumpy arms; I'd place them on my hips, do the Mr Whippy and ask after Essendon's chances, because Kevin usually dropped by when the Bombers were playing a home game. He could be found camped at the bar, surrounded by dancers, the beautiful and the not so beautiful, for Kevin discriminated more on personality than looks. He also had an excellent memory. Kevin danced with me every time he came in, unless he'd spent his allocated amount. If that was the case I went to the top of his dance card next time.

Every Friday around 6 p.m., my first and favourite regular, Weatherman John, would arrive. (His wife dropped him off on her way to classical concerts.) John would straddle the changeover from dayshift to night, confident he was getting the best of both worlds. We'd talk bushwalking before I stripped off and he peered at my vagina like a man hypnotised. His eyes would glaze over and a hungry smile would creep up his face. Fascinated by my ability to produce this reaction simply by opening my legs, I'd resist the urge to quip, 'Don't fall in.'

Also on Fridays was Christopher, a bespectacled undergrad engineer and amateur glamour photographer. I'd taken a short course in photography in London, so I could talk shutter speeds and f-stops before striking a pose. I never made light of what may well have been an excuse for Christopher's weekly voyeurism – I wanted him to keep paying me.

While day pay never came close to night, it was more than double my media monitor's wage. And I was dressed and out the door by 7 p.m., in time for dinner with Tom. After several months, our friendship was evolving. One night over a second bottle of wine, he smiled at me playfully. 'So when are you going to sleep with me?' he said.

I actually laughed. Up until then, I hadn't considered it. As the ex-partner of my former best friend, I hadn't seen Tom outside that role. After mulling it over, however, I saw no good reason not to: Tom was considerate, funny, a fabulous cook, and completely unfazed by my work. We soon fell into an easy routine that was as much about shared history, companionship and good times as it was about romance.

That spring I rarely slept five hours a night. While being brain-dead made both my menial jobs easier to tolerate, I couldn't keep it up indefinitely. I quit media monitoring the week the University of Canterbury offered me a place in its journalism programme. Then I went back to no-touch nightshift. Once Tom had accepted I would be returning to New Zealand in the new year – a prospect that filled me with a sense of inevitability – I stripped with renewed vigour. Every dollar would count as a full-time student.

As spring gave way to summer, Melbourne – and the club – grew festive. The AFL grand final was followed by buck's nights, the Spring Racing Carnival and Christmas parties. The frivolity began at 6 p.m. and rolled on well into the night.

It wasn't all light and laughter. Barry, The Men's Gallery manager, was diagnosed with terminal cancer not long after his wife had a stroke. He stayed at the club for as long as he could, and it was distressing watching him fade away. And Harlow suffered an agonising wait after her ten-year-old son stepped on a syringe on the way home from school. At work, she remained unflappably bright and social. When the good news came through I told her I didn't know how she'd kept it together.

'I *had* to keep it together,' said Harlow. 'Falling apart wasn't going to help anyone.'

I was challenged in a far less serious way when one night, while performing a podium set, I saw Darren walk in. Three years on and my emotions still ran the gauntlet, settling on righteous indignation. He was with two other suits and they carried their beers to a table near my podium. Darren had gained weight, lost hair. Comparatively, I was fitter than before.

Darren glanced up and saw me. My gaze was unapologetically direct. He regarded me thoughtfully, his expression unreadable. I tossed my head and spun away, moving languorously to illustrate what he'd missed out on. After my set, I couldn't resist approaching the group.

I touched his colleague's arm. 'Hello, I'm Juliette.'

'Juliette, I'm Phil,' the man said with a smile that said he liked what he saw. 'This is Tristan and Darren.'

I eyeballed Darren. 'Yes, I know. We've met before.'

'I don't think so.' Darren turned away.

'Oh.' I chuckled. 'I could have sworn … My mistake.'

Phil slipped fifty dollars into my hand. 'Take him for a dance, will you? It's his birthday.'

'Happy birthday,' I murmured sweetly.

Darren lifted his hands. 'No thanks, Phil, I'm fine.' He turned to me. 'It's not my birthday.'

'Just go, mate,' said Phil. Darren looked pained. I realised Phil was probably his boss.

I cupped Darren's elbow. 'Come on, let's go.'

In the private area, I sat like a therapist with legs crossed, hands in lap. 'So, how's life?'

Darren ran a hand through his hair. 'I thought you'd left.'

I shrugged. He smiled sympathetically. I realised he pitied me for still being there – for *still stripping* – and wanted to laugh. 'How's Queensland?'

'I live in Perth now. I got a transfer.' Darren reached for my hand. Surprised, I let him. He no longer wore his wedding ring. He stared at my metallic-blue nails, which I'd painted on a whim. 'These look awful, Holly.'

I pulled my hand away. 'It's Juliette now. How's your wife?'

'We're separated.'

'When?'

'Two years ago. Not that it's any of your business.'

At last, I understood. I had intended to make him squirm, but the urge had gone. If only he'd said something.

'I'm sorry,' I said.

'Thanks, but it was for the best.' Darren's eyes softened. 'Are you still with your boyfriend?'

I shook my head. 'He stayed in London.'

We held eyes. I leant over, kissed his cheek and stood up. 'It was nice seeing you.'

'The conductor – does he still come in?'

I frowned. 'The Maestro? Yes, sometimes.'

I didn't tell Darren I'd danced for The Maestro. I didn't enjoy it, but I figured out what bothered me about him. It was as if the maestro were a puppeteer, pulling all the strings.

Darren stood up and grinned at last – that captivating, cheeky grin. 'That guy was weird.'

'He was manipulative,' I said, and walked away.

Darren stayed for about an hour. Occasionally, I glanced across, wondering how he was. Part of me cared and part of me didn't; while I had offered up my real self, he had never revealed himself to me.

After that night, Darren came in from time to time, but we never acknowledged each other again.

* * *

The week before university began I flew to Wellington for Sonia's wedding. Tom wasn't invited, but Sonia had asked me to be her bridesmaid. From the moment I arrived, though, it was clear she wasn't cool with me hooking up with her ex. We had never discussed it and now wasn't the time, but the occasion did make me realise I didn't believe in marriage as an institution. Feelings changed – it was crazy to promise to love someone forever. That weekend Sonia and I tried to be happy for each other, but we both knew we had grown far apart. I left for Christchurch hoping I hadn't outgrown it too.

Another school friend, Kim, was renting a one-bedroom flat, one of four in a tumbledown two-storey manor – the sort of cheap, inner-city dwelling plentiful before the earthquakes. Conveniently, the rear flat was for lease and three days later it was mine. My parents arrived with household necessities; friends of Tom's donated a couch. A mate of Dad's sold me his Mini Clubman for five hundred bucks. My parents' support was wordless but resolute, as if I was a wayward child finally finding my feet. Was I?

Within a week I had submerged myself in my studies, hunching over Dad's old computer seven days a week, my fingers swollen with chilblains. During the day it was colder inside the flat than out.

From February to June, I returned to Melbourne as often as I could, to strip and to see Tom. We had agreed to stay together and in the middle of winter Tom quit his job as a wine rep and moved to Christchurch. His brave decision made me uneasy, although I never said so. Tom's relocation signified a commitment I wasn't ready to make – to him or to the city. I wasn't sure where I would end up after journalism school, but I hoped it wouldn't be Christchurch. After London and Melbourne it felt even more conservative.

On top of this, employment was scarce. While I'd been living on my savings, plus a student allowance and loan, Tom needed a job. Eventually he found work in a café. It was hard for him, as we'd both known it would be.

And it was disconcerting for me being back where I had started stripping. There were too many reminders – especially when I began writing for *The Press*. I spent two months interning on the education section, whizzing out to schools for interviews and liaising with photographers. The last time I'd set foot inside that building had been the photo shoot for the ill-fated student stripper article. The photographer was now pictures editor. If he remembered me, he never said. In fact, if anyone on staff recognised me from my former life, they kept quiet.

The Press was then housed in a Gothic-style building in Cathedral Square. Behind it was Vixens, one of Craig's parlours and peepshows. I often walked past the red-lit doorway, fully expecting – almost hoping – to bump into him. But I never saw him. In the newsroom there was talk of bankruptcy and tax evasion, but there was little coverage of it. The fight to rid Christchurch of Craig's sex-stamp had waned.

Craig wasn't the only memory haunting me. As the year dragged on I interviewed artists, musicians and community leaders. Increasingly, I didn't want to write about them: I wanted to *be* one of them. Where had that loud-mouthed rebel with an ill-defined cause gone? When university finished, I'd had close to seventy articles published – a surprisingly easy, almost joyless feat. Had pursuing the old dream been a mistake? I didn't know.

Routinely, I sent my CV to *The Press* and was relieved to find no permanent positions available. But they offered me a month of casual work and I had no good reason not to take it. I was to be their Christmas writer. Joy!

Partway into the faux cheer, my grandfather died. His death followed that of my first boyfriend Ben's mother, who had been such a support through some tough teenage moments. I'd also been watching my brother assist his ex-girlfriend through treatment for breast cancer. All this slammed home the stark realisation that life wasn't forever and I'd better start living it.

But how?

Just before Christmas, Tom and I were running around Hagley Park – something we'd started doing to improve our moods. This particular day, Tom told me about his boss's son, who had just cycled from London to New Zealand on a budget of six dollars a day.

'I'd love to do something like that,' Tom panted wistfully.

'We *could* do it,' I countered. '*Let's* do it.'

'Are you serious?' he said.

I thought of my grandfather, bedridden for months. 'Why not?'

By the time we arrived home it had been decided. We were going to cycle from London to New Zealand! How would we fund this pedal-powered half-circumnavigation of the globe? The most obvious answer was return to Australia.

Just after we'd booked our tickets, *The Press* offered me a full-time job. It was a dream opportunity for a rookie reporter, a last-minute 'Are you sure you want to give up a career in media to get naked in public?' fate-tempter. I *was* sure. I was going back to Melbourne not just to strip, but to create a life I believed in.

9.

IF TOM AND I WERE GOING TO TURN OUR CYCLING dream into a reality, we each needed to save fifteen thousand dollars. While Tom worked vintage at a winery in South Australia, I was back in the strippersphere. A year on, The Men's Gallery was quieter, especially midweek. Possibly it was fallout from the GST – introduced in Australia in 2000 – and changes to fringe benefits tax. The price of dances had also doubled to twenty dollars per song, an overdue increase that initially made them harder to sell. I needed to find a way of being mega-watt brilliant from dusk till dawn. So I gave up drinking and smoking and took up yoga.

The effects of daily yoga were subtle but profound. Astonishingly, I could strip for fifty hours a week and still feel fresh. Being sober and smoke-free helped, of course, as did living in Brighton with ex-workmates from the Christchurch Clvb. Brett and Cheryl's bayside pad was perfect for a night owl, with soundproofing and block-out curtains. With yoga I became more at ease in my body. The mental chatter lessened and I discovered I actually *liked* my stripper self. The guilt I'd been carrying for pursuing such a socially unacceptable occupation disappeared. I even felt *grateful* for the opportunity, for physically being able to strip.

As a likely result of all this there was an openness to my modus operandi that hadn't been there before. I tried not to judge the customers – to treat each person equally and not to assume who would spend. In a place that prized appearances I'd learnt the hard way they could be deceiving: the dirty-looking old man could be a real sweetheart, the youth in the crumpled t-shirt a cashed-up computer whiz. (I'll admit my motivation may have been suspect, but the lesson was there all the same.) Instead of being purely goal fixated, I began to embrace the process. Sometimes I sensed intuitively who to approach, other times customers were drawn to me and revealed baffling connections.

One night, two young men – Luke and Guy – sat down at my podium. Guy was from Adelaide. Learning I was from New Zealand, he said, 'I've been there! My dad and I did a house swap when I was little.'

I shivered. When I was eleven, our neighbours had swapped houses with a chiropractor from Adelaide and his twelve-year-old son, Guy. Guy had been a sunny, sophisticated boy and I had shown him my tree house and introduced him to my pet goats. Unlike the boys next door – my only playmates within a five-kilometre radius – Guy had been happy to play with a girl. When he'd left I'd been quietly devastated. I still had the goodbye note he'd written.

In fact, I'd come across it just the week before, rifling through a box of stuff I'd had shipped to Melbourne.

'Hey, is your dad a chiropractor?' I asked, my heart pounding.

Guy's eyes widened. 'How'd you know?'

I confessed I'd been the girl next door. We stared at each other in disbelief while Luke murmured, 'That's fucking trippy, man.' It *was* trippy. I couldn't figure out the odds of that ever happening, or what it might perhaps mean, if anything.

It *didn't* mean that I was going to sleep with him. Guy kept saying, 'You're really hot. Who would've thought?' Sure, I was no longer a buck-toothed, eleven-year-old tomboy, but Guy's inability to see past my appearance was disappointing, even given where we were.

Guy said he worked for a brewery; I said I'd given up drinking. He asked for my number anyway. I gave it, but warned him I had a boyfriend. The next day Guy called three times, which was my sign not to keep in touch.

Another night, a larger-than-life American asked me for a dance. He was exceptionally tall, well built and preppy. I asked what brought him to Australia. He stared at me, taken aback. 'I'm here for work. I'm a motivational speaker.'

'Wow.' I'd never met a motivational speaker before. 'Are you any good?'

'Well, I made several million dollars last year.'

I nodded, intrigued by how he measured success. Who was this man? Would he extend the dance? He could certainly afford to.

He didn't.

Several weeks later I was watching a movie with my housemate Cheryl when the man came onscreen.

'Hey, I've danced for that guy!' I exclaimed.

Cheryl's eyes widened. 'No way! His personal coaching collection revolutionised my life.'

'His what?'

'I have all the DVDs! I can loan them to you.'

'No thanks,' I said. My yoga DVD was challenge enough. That my own personal development was a by-product of chasing the dollar didn't occur to me. But a famous motivational speaker in a strip club seemed proof that what I did wasn't totally unacceptable.

So was getting a rental application approved after daring to put 'table dancer' under 'employment'. When Tom returned to Melbourne in May we signed a one-year lease on a beautifully renovated terrace house in Fitzroy. Then we booked tickets to London for the following July and continued working and saving. Tom began waitering in a nearby food store and I changed my shifts so we both had Sundays and Mondays off. On these days Tom usually gave dinner parties that went long into the night. He loved cooking and our table would be piled high with tagines and cassoulets, French and Italian wines. While I liked his friends, increasingly I struggled with the drunken banter. It felt like work, only I wasn't getting paid. At the end of the wiggling week, all I wanted to do was sink into the bath with a book. Still, it was important to make an effort.

Soon I was drinking and smoking again.

And soon after that, my yoga practice slipped away. Although the discipline had been so beneficial, it was easier to start the day making love or eating. I would often crawl out of bed to find a Spanish omelette browning, a pot of coffee brewing. 'Morning, sweetie,' Tom would say, planting a kiss on my lips. 'Hungry?' I'd tuck in and vow to practise afterwards, but hardly ever did.

* * *

Without yoga I resumed my old way of working but with slightly greater awareness. Because I was stripping five nights a week, I rarely felt disconnected from my role as I had done in the past. My fight-or-flight mechanism was set to fight, my nervous system hot-wired to the proximity of strangers. I relied on instinct, noticing who glanced my way, who looked relaxed, who was spending. I was also more non-discriminatory: I approached the busloads of reserved, middle-aged Chinese tourists; the joyful Indian students; the lonely men; the amped party boys; the distinguished businessmen; the nervous couples and the occasional wide-eyed girl. Even so, I *always* kept an eye out for my bread-and-butter customer: the middle-aged, mild-mannered, moneyed, respectful irregular strip club visitor – preferably solid enough for me to balance on without wobbling. Gilbert was the perfect example of this.

Early one Wednesday I spotted him at the bar. He reminded me of the actor Ralph Fiennes. I approached at an amble, measured to disguise my true intent and to accentuate my new blue-sequinned, mermaid-esque ensemble.

'Hello.' I gazed up from beneath my phenomenal fake lashes.

'Hello,' he said, faintly bemused. I held out my hand. He took it. His palm was rough, but not too rough. We exchanged names.

'Are you English?' he asked.

'I danced in London.'

'An international entertainer ...' Gilbert's eyes flicked to my padded cleavage.

Gotcha, I thought, but smiled deferentially. An extra moment of small talk could mean the difference between a twenty-dollar and a fifty-dollar dance. 'Where are you from, Gilbert?'

'The Hunter Valley. I'm here for work.'

'What do you do?'

'I'm a winemaker.' Gilbert was ogling my breasts now. 'Would you like to dance for me?'

I led him into the lounge bar and outlined the options: twenty for a song, fifty for three or one hundred for six – mentioning the last option increased the chances he'd spend fifty. He did.

'All you need to do is keep your hands here,' I patted the arms of his chair, 'and enjoy.'

'Prepare for lift-off,' said Gilbert, and I realised he was a bit nervous.

I placed my knee on his thigh and my hands on his shoulders to establish a sense of intimacy. He sighed, his warm breath hitting my throat, not unpleasantly. I turned and untied my long, wraparound skirt.

'Very nice,' Gilbert murmured. 'You must work out.'

'A little,' I said. Translation: I strip ten hours a night.

I arched back in my chair, knees drifting apart. Rolling upright, I locked eyes with this stranger I was pretending to be – and conversely was being – familiar with. Then I pushed my breasts together to unhook the front clasp of my bra. It came away with my hands. His eyes on mine, Gilbert missed it.

'Oh,' he said, realising.

I stood and cupped my breasts above his mouth, mindful of the regulation ten-centimetre gap. A virtual gift.

'You're beautiful,' Gilbert murmured into my hair.

As the next song began, I lay back and spread my legs, hinting at what was to come. Thankfully, he didn't notice my mouth fall open as a cockroach skittered across the wall. I drew my G up and over bent knees. Then I dropped it in feigned carelessness, stood up and turned around.

My knees on my chair, my feet on Gilbert's knees, I lifted one stiletto, liking the line of my leg as I twisted to look at him, as if to connect, but really, I was just checking his fingers weren't reaching for my pussy. Mine was a routine move – Gilbert wasn't that sort of man.

The third song was teen band Hanson's 'MMMBop'. I did what I could. When it ended I brushed my cheek against Gilbert's. 'Would you like to continue?'

'No, thank you, I enjoyed that very much.'

I moved aside so Gilbert could stand up. He smiled, a decent smile. 'When I'm next in Melbourne, I'll come back and hopefully you'll be here.'

I nodded. Maybe he would, maybe he wouldn't. The supporting cast varied nightly in the theatre of the undressed.

The lead roles remained the same, though. At 6 p.m. weekdays, I'd find Phil, an ex-Vietnam vet, propped at the bar with his back to the wall. Phil was the gatekeeper between worlds. 'Here we are again, Juliette,' he would say, as if we'd both turned up for another tour of duty. I never saw Phil have a dance.

Lecherous Graham – a barrister who tried to recruit girls for private parties – might appear any day of the week. He would stand at the bar and breathe an afternoon's worth of red wine down the cleavage of any girl daft enough to listen to him. Some girls tried to play Lecherous Graham at his own game. They would agree to party if he had a dance first, but Lecherous Graham only ever relinquished a twenty and only after a lengthy closing argument. He might have been a horrible drunk, but he wasn't a fool.

Bill, reputedly a B&D expert, was harder to get away from. A silver fox, he would arrive after 1 a.m., order a Scotch and wait. When approached, he would control the conversation, making it almost impossible to ask him for a dance without making it sound like you wanted to remove one of his kidneys with a blunt kitchen knife. Chatting with Bill was complicated choreography, but he always had at least one fifty-dollar dance. The key was finding the 'in'. Some nights it would elude me, other nights I'd outwit him. But I always knew he had the upper hand.

Most Fridays during happy hour, Harry would come in with a crony or two. Harry was a semi-retired businessman who'd peaked in the eighties. He would tell me what far-flung destination he'd just returned from – St Tropez or London or Singapore – offer me cigarettes and champagne (which I always declined), wax lyrical about his oil business days (in case I'd forgotten) then introduce me to his colleagues ('now you remember Bob') before whisking me away (usually while I was talking to someone else) for a twenty-dollar dance. Once I realised I could just excuse myself, Harry stopped making me edgy. Besides, he preferred to approach me for a dance – he liked being the deal-clincher.

I revealed more of myself to Liam, because I didn't strip for him. Liam was my age, skinny with sparkly eyes and spiky hair. He came in early weeknights. Whenever I found myself trying too hard, I would seek him out and he'd flick me a twenty and a cigarette. If Liam was in a good mood, he'd crack bad one-liners. 'Take five, Fluffy,' he might say. (He called me Fluffy because of my hair.) 'No, take twenty.'

His passion was music, his reality real estate. He suffered from food intolerances and smoked too much. Then he fell for a bolshy Russian dancer, even though he knew better. We talked through all of it. Liam respected my time and valued my opinion, and chatting with him made me feel less robotic. Which generally resulted in more dances, as did being seen to be busy.

As the months passed, I built up a stable of regulars. Most danced with other girls as well and weren't big spenders, but I appreciated their loyalty. My two most loyal were Weatherman John and Kevin from Origin Energy.

I was also fond of Ralph, even though he talked nonstop. A bachelor in his mid-fifties, he worked in an appliance store and carefully monitored his Men's Gallery outings. There was no getting away from Ralph. He'd bound over, sandy comb-over flying. 'Juliette! It's so good to see you,' he would say, eyes shining. 'I'll have a dance, of course.' And he'd make a beeline for the private area.

Dancing for Ralph meant perching naked on the arm of his chair while, in a breathless rush, he might say something like: 'I didn't think I was going to make it in before nine tonight. I missed the tram and then it was twenty minutes till the next one. I had planned on going to Red Rooster, but by the time I got there it was closed, so I had to go Pancake Parlour instead. That was all right, I could use my seniors card, it only cost twenty dollars forty-five for a cheese and potato pancake with extra bacon. Of course, it doesn't really matter if I don't get here by nine, it's only seven-dollars fifty to get in, but with my gold membership it's free before then. I was lucky to get that, don't you think?' I would nod, smile and murmur agreeably.

Ralph struck me as someone who had been passed over his whole life, even though he played by the rules. He never tried to touch; he simply appreciated having a beautiful naked girl's attention for as long as he could afford it. And sometimes, when he could afford it, he'd have two. Occasionally Harlow and I would double dance for Ralph. We'd perch on opposite arms of his chair while he peered up from within a sea of boobs and beamed. For just a moment, he'd be speechless.

* * *

I had been back at The Men's Gallery for about six months when I met Peter, the owner. Peter was a rarity among strip club bosses: he almost never came into the venue and I only met him the once. Now that Spearmint Rhino was shouldering its way into the Melbourne market, Peter wanted to talk to girls who had worked overseas about turning the Gallery into 'more of a hostess club'.

Peter floated the idea of dancers receiving a percentage of the take on bottles of champagne. I was against it: boozing for a living wasn't my cup of tea and chitchat was hard to place a dollar value on. The Gallery's strength had always been its performances and its open-door policy. But the club – and therefore Peter – didn't profit directly from these.

Instead, a house fee of twenty dollars per shift was introduced. Apparently this was to cover tea and coffee supplies, and sandwiches on weekends, which made for some expensive International Roast and Sunblest; no one was buying the explanation. Yes, the fee was a token amount, but it marked the fact that Gallery girls were now a secondary source of revenue. After London, I knew exactly which direction we were headed in.

The only dancers exempt from house fees were showgirls on the nights they performed. Until then, there had been no real incentive to become a showgirl, apart from having pull with management. Most performed for the love of it. I was already tempted to try out and the house fee clinched it. I began watching the stars to see if I had what it took.

Diamond was the best showgirl, with the prized 1 a.m. timeslot. A tall, ex-jazz dancer with F-cup implants, platinum hair and Vegas legs, she had four routines: cop, air force pilot, genie and French maid. Diamond could side-split and dangle from the pole by one ankle. She demanded applause, refusing to undress until the crowd roared. This was a risk: most strip club patrons are too busy ogling anatomy to care for choreography. But Diamond had the boobs to back it up. And titles. And autographed posters. She'd hold these up while the guys reached out and cried, '*Me-me-meeeeee!*' like a classroom of five-year-olds. Diamond would then pussy-kiss the rolled-up posters and toss them into the crowd, before exiting the stage with an elaborate bow.

Bonnie was a very cute pint-sized blonde who performed a nurse show. Bonnie had the 4.30 a.m. timeslot. By then, most patrons were munted and many dancers well on their way. Bonnie crawled around on her hands and knees. She also encouraged participation in her undressing, as if she couldn't manage it herself. Once nude, she would roll the length of the stage with her legs splayed like a horizontal whirling dervish. So she was no trained dancer. Who cared?

While my pole tricks were rusty and basic at best, I could confidently undress myself. I announced I'd like to do a show.

'About bloody time,' said Carole. 'I'll get Raine to help you.'

Post-baby, Raine was back as dancer trainer, but I refused the offer, preferring to create the show myself. I decided to wear black and strip to songs featuring the word 'black' in the title. A lace skirt, gypsy top and G were duly hand-sequinned. Every Friday for a month, I rehearsed in the showroom before my shift.

One night, Carole asked, 'What's your theme?'

'Sort of French boudoir,' I said. By then I'd realised I could do with some help, but was too proud to ask for it. Instead, I added fishnet stockings and a feather boa for clarity.

On the fourth Friday, Raine watched as I writhed around onstage, clutching the boa like a blanky. Afterwards, she approved my six-minute offering with a thin smile. New performers premiered on Thursdays when the showroom was quietest. The following Thursday at 10.15 p.m, I waited beside the DJ console, fidgeting and suppressing the urge to pee. It was five years since I'd first walked through the front doors of The Men's Gallery and at twenty-seven I was no longer a hick novice, but my palms were so damp I was certain I'd slide right off the pole.

Carole appeared beside me, clipboard in hand. 'Just remember to take off *all* your clothes,' she said. I stared at her blankly. She laughed. 'Some first-timers have been known to forget.'

I wiped my hands on the boa. The crowd was alarmingly large, my costume already generating some interest. Showgirls got noticed. Suddenly I didn't want to get noticed. What if I'd overestimated my abilities, if I forgot to undress?

Stanley cut short my second-guessing. 'Ready, baby?'

I nodded unsurely. He lowered the music. 'Gentlemen, it's sshoww-time!'

A busboy darted onstage to wipe the poles. Too soon the opening chords of 'Black Betty' started. Amid a cloud of lace and feathers, I teetered up the steps and onto the enormous stage. While Ram Jam jammed, I pirouetted madly, grinning at everyone and no one.

Overly conscious of Carole's advice, I didn't forget to take off my clothes – instead I stripped way too early. Halfway through the last song, 'Black Velvet', I was already nude and out of moves. To kill time, I flossed myself with the boa, causing feathers to litter the stage. Then I gave a Stanley pointed look to call me off. He mistook it as a cry for applause and bellowed at the crowd, 'I can't heeaaar yoouu!'

This caused the mad scientist – already bopping in the front row – to imitate a seizure. His hair was a bird's nest, quivering in line with my toes. In a trance-like moment of self-sabotage, I was tempted to step into it.

Stanley called me off in time. He demanded applause and it came, most vigorously from Carole. 'Yay, Juliette!' she cheered as I streaked past. 'Good show, well done.'

In the tiny showgirl dressing-room near the private rooms, I stood panting and plucking feathers out of my crotch. My fake tan was scummy with sweat; one stocking was down to my knee. But I had become a showgirl! I glanced up at the posters of feature performers past and present – Miss Nude Victoria, Miss Erotica Australia, Miss Nude World. They stared down with glittering eyes and glossy smiles. I grinned back disbelievingly.

After several months and two more routines – army and cat – it was still hard to believe I was a queen of the night.

As well as added respect, being a showgirl came with extra practical privileges too: a locker, an early finish (useful on a slow night) and the option of working the floor in costume. I almost never did this – partly because I struggled to reconcile my showy hyperactivity with my increasingly sensual private dance persona. And also because my costumes were embarrassingly grubby. Washing ruined the sequins, so I baby-wiped them clean instead. Baby-wipes didn't remove fake tan stains, making my G's a hybrid of dirty-looking, clean-smelling nappy. As I wasn't specialising in adult diaper fetishism it was better to go downstairs and get changed.

One night a customer offered to buy my cat panties; primly, I told him they weren't for sale. Later in the girls room I regretted my lack of entrepreneurship when Diamond rushed down the stairs in her French maid outfit, yelling, 'A guy wants to buy my panties for a hundred! Quick, who's got an old pair? I'll go you halves.'

As disgusting as it was imagining these men using our G's as face masks, at least they offered to pay. Every few weeks a dancer would storm into the girls room, cursing the lowlife who had swiped her knickers out from under her nose. I took care where I left my underwear.

Now that I was a showgirl, I began replacing short dresses and string bikinis with sequinned bras and floor-length skirts in dazzling reds, purples and blues. I learnt to show off my narrow waist and toned arms, hide my strong thighs and accentuate the in-between. I'd stopped wearing wigs and my hair had grown into a strawberry-blonde bob, adding substance to the glamour somehow. My Le Tan in Le Can was meticulously applied, my long nails lacquered OPI Rosy Future, my eye make-up a subtly smudged combo of MAC Perverted Pearl, Night Owl and Smut. After eight years of stripping I had joined the elite.

The customers knew it too. 'Was that you up there?' some would say with awe. 'You were amazing!' Others would queue patiently to have a private with me. I knew it wasn't because I was better than any other dancer; it was just the perception that I was. Becoming a showgirl had been a good move.

So I put my hand up to do functions too. These private parties — usually buck's nights — were held in 'the boardroom'. The boardroom had a polished mahogany table and frescoed colonnades with tethering rings, making it a fantastic fusion of corporate nirvana meets Greek dungeon. Again, my timing was spot on. Functions were especially popular in spring and summer and the Gallery was actively promoting them — and building 'the VIP room', which was only bigger, not more exclusive.

Just like my days of outcalls in Christchurch with Ned, I never quite knew what would greet me in a function but the guys were now on my turf. They were told the rules upfront — no touching, no photos, no verbal abuse – and warned that if anyone misbehaved they'd all be escorted out.

Because new girls went first, I would usually find the buck in a chair up on the table, waiting expectantly. It was a precursor to the altar and a little like an arranged marriage: if neither of us liked the other, we still had to go through with it – only it was for twenty minutes, not for life. I had two seconds to make a solid first impression, spot the troublemakers and take charge. If the guys and I didn't gel, time crawled by like a maimed snail.

Playing party games helped. These included 'fish'. I would slip the buck's watch inside my G and shuffle backwards while he tried to retrieve it with his teeth. Astonishingly, many guys were shy about face-planting my Red Door–scented crotch, perhaps because 'fish' bent the no-touch rule. Still, it was a crowd pleaser until the day I realised too late the buck had no teeth.

Another game was 'walk the dog'. I'd borrow two belts, choker the buck and lead him around on his hands and knees. 'This, boys, is what marriage is all about,' I'd titter, before whipping him playfully. I gleaned some pleasure from the buck's submission, but refused to belt him as hard as his mates usually encouraged. He was there to celebrate, not to be cured of potential infidelity. 'Walk the dog' was popular, but not as popular as dressing the buck up in my clothes. I never figured that one out.

Some nights simply stripping was enough. Most guys rated enthusiasm above boxes of tricks, which was fortunate because mine didn't extend as far as tucking my ankles behind my head and spinning like an upside-down turtle – unlike Bonnie. With me, what the guys saw was pretty much what they got.

Groups could make requests, but some weren't feasible, such as 'only Asian girls with massive tits'. Carole would roll her eyes and holler, 'Whose got big boobs and looks Asian? Melody?' And Melody – who was part Filipino, with implants – would snicker. 'What, and ruin my chances of a gazillion privates?' As functions grew in popularity, some Saturdays there were as many as fifteen. Carole would hunch over the roster with the function sheets fanned out, coordinating seventy girls and fourteen hours down to the minute. On these nights if the guys expected a busty Korean and I sauntered in they were going to be disappointed.

Functions might've been half the reward for double the exertion of a private dance, but they were guaranteed cash and the chance to impress. Many guys would recognise or request me as a result. It was good for business – and satisfying to know that even on the nights when I'd been a zombie stripper, I'd managed to brighten someone else's day.

10.

S TRIPTEASE IS REFRESHINGLY ANTI-TALL-POPPY –
the nude sisterhood celebrates its alphas, drawing them near
just in case glamour rubs off like glitter. The shinier I became
the more dancers acknowledged me, sharing trade secrets such
as 'I always make more when I've got my period, don't you?' (I
did) or 'Watch out for the filthy pig at table 2' (I would). On any
given night, there were at least ten sisters I could exchange the
international stripper greeting 'hey babe' with, and another ten I
knew well enough to talk to. Mostly, these girls were like me –
full-timers who had worked in the industry for years and who had
made it work for them.

Girls like Harlow, who had separated from her husband and was
enjoying an affair with a famous married cricketer. Harlow couldn't
help but show me his barrage of explicit texts. 'He's reckless,' she

said, clearly delighted to be the hunted for a change. But Harlow could play the game better than most. Even then I suspected the high-flying spinner might've met his match.

Bonnie was the pint-sized blonde I'd watched rolling around onstage in a nurse's uniform. She worked weekends while her parents minded her three-year-old daughter. I would arrive to find Bonnie in the second booth, topless before a cornucopia of costumes, cosmetics, hair rollers, baby-wipes, fake tan, tampons, cigarettes, coins and keys. There was nothing that Bonnie didn't have and she would give you anything you needed. 'Hello sweet-cheeks,' she would say, sipping a champagne with raspberry. 'Sorry! I'll make some room.' And I would admire her daughter's latest drawing taped to the mirror while Bonnie cleared me a spot. Most nights she dithered around in the dressing-room till late, but you'd always find her on the floor at 6 a.m. with a sympathetic ear. I never saw Bonnie eat, ever. At thirty-one, her body was compact, but it mapped her history: she had a decade-old boob job and scars from knee surgery.

Diamond also sat in the second booth. She would arrive at 8 p.m. ready to go, fake-tanned to her jaw like a body stocking. 'How are we, girls?' she'd sing out, walloping her enormous suitcase onto the bench. Five minutes later she would be dressed and up on the floor.

Diamond simply adored being the centre of attention. 'I'm one of seven – I had to go to extremes to stand out,' she once told me. Originally from the Gold Coast, Diamond had been raised in the Church of the Latter Day Saints. She was known for her quip: 'I used to say "Mormon" now I say "More men!"' Then she'd whoop and throw one perfectly manicured hand into the air.

At twenty-five, Diamond had more energy than a kindergarten of kids on candy. She was also the hardest working, most professional stripper I ever met. She had twice toured the United States, where some clubs let international dancers work under the table, but try as she might, she couldn't strip in Las Vegas without police clearance. In an unsuccessful stunt she'd even barrelled up to the cop shop in her police costume to beg for a sheriff's card. 'Look at me,' she'd said. 'I belong here! Vegas is my spiritual home.'

Jade and her best mate Tiffany had also worked in the States. Tiffany was a sophisticated brunette in her late twenties, model material. Jade was a fellow Kiwi, a Xena the Warrior Princess lookalike who had been stripping since she was sixteen. Now thirty-two, she lived in the country with her husband Simon in an off-the-grid house they'd built themselves. Three nights a week, Jade stayed in Melbourne with Tiffany.

For six years the girls had travelled to New York. The last trip had coincided with September 11. 'I knew I had to come home and be with Si where I belonged, so I strapped all of my money to my body and went straight to the airport,' Jade told me. 'They patted me down and found the cash round my ankles. I fessed up and showed them the rest so they didn't cavity search me because I had an E inside me in a tampon, I'd been taking so many to get through I was scared I'd flip out on the plane without one.' She had been allowed to keep the cash but had been temporarily banned from returning to the US.

I was full of admiration for Jade. She was into all sorts of things and talked about reincarnation, crystals and plant medicine the way some dancers talked about shopping. Inspired, I experimented with ear candling, colon therapy, foot patches and juice detoxing. Jade got me thinking that it *was* possible for stripping and spirituality to coexist.

Together with Carole and Stanley, these girls became my on-set family, like a weird sit-com that just kept rolling. We traded pole tricks and make-up tips, lamented the rise in house fees (now thirty dollars) and debated the use of rugs – bathmat-sized pieces of fake fur used to protect your kneecaps on the podiums. Tiffany was pro-protection; I cast mine aside after Weatherman John said I looked like I was 'clutching a comforter'. And while we aired boyfriend woes, sat around naked and peed with the door open, we almost never caught up outside of work. That would have fried our vampire-like alter egos. So it was a rare, treasured thing when a stripper friendship evolved into a real, multi-dimensional one, like Jade and Tiffany's.

There were few girls I didn't like but Dakota was one of them. She was a bully and wouldn't take no for an answer. If a customer refused a dance, she would grab his wrist and march him into the private area, or pick up his drink and walk away with it. To my annoyance, the men nearly always paid up. They complained, but rarely to the club. 'I feel violated,' one told me. 'I'm leaving and I won't be coming back.' Thankfully Dakota moved on after six months.

Other dancers flitted in for a weekend, a week or a month. Once a girl was on the books, all she had to do was text her roster on a Monday and wait for it to be confirmed. A jazz singer stripped between gigs; a doctor from Sydney flew down between shifts in Emergency. A psychic medium raised enough money to start a magazine; a budding entrepreneur began a line of ethical bottled water. These girls made me realise that I didn't have to dumb down my conversation to make money. They made me proud to call myself a table dancer.

Still, I was selective who I told. 'What do you do for work?' is a conversation opener, like the weather. It's also a stripper stumbling block. I hated lying (and the casino can only have so many hostesses in its high-roller room). I had discovered that most people viewed stripping from opposing polarities: acclaim or disdain. No one's eyes ever glazed over when I told them what I did. While I wanted to be accepted, I didn't want to be the centre of attention on my days off.

* * *

The Men's Gallery had become a familiar, cosy enclave. Most nights, there was nowhere I would rather be, nothing I would rather be doing. The ritual of transformation and the scripted methodology of working the floor became second nature. I walked tall, my muscles taut, my skin radiant with fake tan and sweat. It was a perpetual cycle, moving from one man to another, from one dance to the next. Sometimes stripping felt like sport, like being in the zone: my attention focused on a tangible goal, my body pushed to the max, the reward instantaneous. I was well paid and adored. In the dressing-room mirror I saw an assertive, glamorous young woman, comfortable in her role, settled in her place.

Juliette was me, of course, but I wasn't her. She was confident and articulate; I was hesitant and unsure. She made time for people;

I was dismissive. It wasn't surprising I wanted to stay in her stilettos long after I'd saved my travel money.

Stripping became the opportunity to pay off my student loan, then to put away for a rainy day. By January 2003 it didn't matter what I was saving for: I *had* to work. I told myself that most people worked a five-day week, that I might never get this opportunity again. But it went deeper than this. Inside the club my past faded and my future didn't matter: I was an immortal goddess. I didn't have to stop and think about the rest of my life: if I had, it might've paled by comparison.

Tom and I motivated each other by continuing to work fifty-hour weeks. Though frustrated by in-house politics at the food store, Tom opted to stick it out. He needed every shift to save his half of our travel fund. There was never any question we would contribute equally: Tom wouldn't have had it any other way, while I wasn't about to become one of those strippers who 'supported' her boyfriend.

It was miraculous neither of us got sick, because we *never* rested. Two mornings a week, Tom and I took pottery classes; on Monday nights, I studied photography. Every second day, I hauled my stiff body out for a run. Most nights I walked to work. I even rollerbladed in on Saturdays for a while. It loosened my muscles, but I wasn't very good. G.I. would reach out and catch me as I hurtled towards the front door. After rolling up with bloody knees one too many times I gave it away. With the cycle trip just four months away, I told myself I couldn't afford to get injured.

Tom and I had slowly stockpiled the items we would need and our spare room was stacked with panniers, windproof vests, waterproof jackets, maps, tools and tyres. We'd also started taking test trips. Once a month on Saturdays I finished at 2 a.m. (exceptions were made now that I was a showgirl). Tom and I would pick a town in country Victoria – Woodend or Stony Point or Portarlington – rise early on a Sunday and cycle there for the night. At dusk, we'd wobble up the main street with shaky legs, sloppy grins and the growing realisation that we just might be able to pull the whole thing off.

Yet as our departure date nudged ever closer, the less I wanted to leave. Two months out I quit smoking and began to question everything. Did I really want to ride off into the sunset? I was in the prime of my so-called career: I had the respect of management, an established clientele, a girl posse and enough money for a house deposit. I was sitting pretty. And, most importantly, I *belonged*.

Did I belong with Tom? While I loved him, I wasn't in love with him. That hadn't bothered me when we'd first hooked up. Two years on, we were talking about buying property together after the cycle trip. (We even had matching windproof vests, like middle-aged tourists.) Should I be making life plans with someone I wasn't in love with? Weren't we both deserving of more?

At the club, I would listen to Jade talking about her husband Simon. 'I'm in awe of him everyday,' she'd say. I'd get a niggly feeling in my gut. I wanted to be in awe of my partner too.

As my doubts grew, so did my desire to be sexually free. For me, stripping had never been about sex: it was about power. At work I gripped onto mine. I kept my heart closed, having learnt my lesson with Darren. With my mind on the money it was rare that physical attraction slammed through my guard.

Then one night I danced for a young English woman. She had a strong, healthy body with sun-kissed skin and a freckled nose. While I stripped, she clung to the armrest, her chest rising and falling. It was a breathless giggle-fest: I spent most of the dance with my nose in her hair. After four private dances, I wanted to go home with her more than anything. I didn't, but it got me thinking. Here I was, an experienced stripper, supposedly sexually liberated, and I'd never slept with a woman or had a threesome.

I'd been attracted to some of the other dancers before, but had never acted on it. Work was work, and I'd always been in a relationship. An affair would've been too complicated. Over the years I'd witnessed dancers becoming lovers: the atmosphere in the dressing-room would become charged with lustful gazes, soft caresses and lots of mane-tossing. But it almost always ended badly, especially if the girls had boyfriends. Lovers then became sworn enemies, working alternate nights and bitching over who got the busy Saturday. I'd never met anyone I was attracted to enough to risk my relationship or my job.

Then I met Zoe. A dancer from Goldfingers, Zoe had shoulder-length dark curls, muscly limbs and a loud mouth. One night, I came downstairs to find her sitting in the booth next to my chair, smelling sweetly of pot and honey shampoo. Her feet were up on the bench and her long red Lycra dress was tugged aside, revealing athletic legs with a lifetime of little scars. She was arguing with her on-again, off-again boyfriend on the phone.

'Don't fucking yell at me, Joel!' She hung up and turned to me. 'He's never going to tell me he loves me while I'm still stripping.'

'Has he ever?' I asked.

'Valentine's Day last year,' she sighed. 'He bought me a dozen roses. Then I told him I was a stripper and he broke up me with me.'

I couldn't help but smile.

I overheard plenty more yelling matches before Zoe called it quits with Joel and started saving for a round-the-world ticket. She was plucky and determined, and she hated her job as much as I liked mine.

In the girls room I would watch her brush on blusher, bold as a life-drawer. She'd watch me agonise over my eye shadow. I'd admire the definition of her arms and the jut of her hips, my belly tight and my groin pulsating. She'd toss her curls and exhale deeply. Up on the floor I'd pause for her Tomb Raider show, watching her nail new pole tricks with gusto. She'd linger for my shows too, watching as I repeated my repertoire of basic inversions. Conveniently we didn't need to mentally undress each other.

Unsure if I was opening to possibility or self-sabotaging, I decided to involve Tom. He invited Zoe over for dinner and they hit it off instantly. We three became lovers effortlessly.

We got together once a week under the guise of a meal. It was exciting, the sex wondrous. Then I grew frustrated about having to share Zoe. She would've preferred if it was just the two of us too.

We made up for it at the club. I had never done lesbian dances before. Now I couldn't believe I got paid to do them! Zoe and I would prowl the floor, arms entwined. We'd bat our lashes at the guys and offer 'a sexy girl-on-girl show'. (It wasn't actually girl *on* girl: back then lesbian dances were more a game of nude Twister, each girl trying to remove the other's clothing with minimal skin contact.) The guys lapped it up. They'd grin wonkily as Zoe and I undressed each other with fiery smiles. 'You two really are lovers, aren't you?' they'd say. Sometimes we were so into each other the guys felt left out of their own fantasy. It was, as ever, a fine line.

Then one night in the red room, on my knees before Zoe's chair, I looked up from pretending to lick her pussy to find Carole staring daggers at us from the doorway. House rules maintained that if it looked like you were doing it, then you were as good as doing it. Evidently, we were making it more than faking it.

Carole waited until our customer had left before she strode in. 'Come with me, right now.'

Zoe and I raised our brows at each other and trailed Carole in the upstairs toilets. Shit, I thought, we're about to get fired.

'What are you two playing at?' Carole demanded. 'You might as well have been fucking each other in there! Are you?'

I didn't think that was against house rules, but denied it, just in case.

'If I catch you again you're both suspended,' she said. 'Got it?'

We nodded.

'Really, Juliette, I expected more from you.' Carole slammed the door on her way out.

I turned to Zoe. 'I don't want to lose my job.'

'I don't care, I'm leaving in a month anyway. But yeah, probably best to keep it out of here.'

Despite this, we had just one more threesome. Zoe was 'too busy' – I sensed she'd tired of the tryst. (Ironically, the only person who hadn't was Tom.) Becoming 'just friends' wasn't difficult, not like it sometimes was with guys. Still, I missed Zoe when she left for France.

Bored at work and at home, I began to fantasise about taking a lover of my own.

Blair was a new security guard. A Kiwi boy in his early twenties, he was clean-cut and self-disciplined. Plenty of morally upright boys work in strip clubs; to restless dancers, they were to be toyed with, like a cat with a mouse.

A bit of harmless flirting with Blair got me through a routine shift. A gaze held too long, a suggestive smile ... these things spiced up the blandness. It must have been confusing for him trying to determine if I really was interested. Perhaps he was flattered; perhaps he was bored too. When I learnt his girlfriend worked behind the bar I was relieved to have an out. Then one Wednesday after too much champagne, I slipped Blair my number. After putting me in a taxi, he texted, *Sweet dreams, babe. See you soon.* Thrilled, I texted back, *Thank you, gorgeous. Can't wait.* While this wasn't on par with Harlow's textathon, it was a step towards somewhere I sensed I shouldn't – but probably would – end up going.

The following night, hoping for a voice of reason, I confided in Jade.

'No good is going to come from it, babe,' she said. 'Not for him and not for you.' She was right. Remembering how Fletcher and I had ended, I decided to go no further. Tom deserved better. He was my best friend, the perfect stripper boyfriend and my partner in global adventure – an adventure that was now just weeks away.

I came home from jogging after lunch to find Tom slumped on the couch, staring blankly at my phone. He looked at me, his eyes filled with tears. 'Who is Blair?'

My heart raced. 'He's a bouncer at work, but it's not what you think.'

'I don't know what to think.'

'Nothing has happened! Just a bit of silly flirting. That's it, I swear.' I didn't ask why Tom had been going through my phone, though it crossed my mind; I'd been distant since meeting Zoe. Until then, I'd never given him reason to doubt me. He sat there, staring at me confusedly, trying not to cry. His hurt was crushing. I wanted to apologise but didn't know how to without making it sound like an admission of guilt. I had been so stupid.

'I can't think clearly right now,' Tom wiped his eyes. 'I'm going away for a few days.'

'What about the bike trip?' I said, panicky.

Tom shrugged. 'I don't know.'

Our house felt horribly empty without him, the industrial furniture, bohemian prints and Turkish rugs meaningless. More than ever I appreciated how Tom had created a home for us.

At work I was agitated, unmotivated. I ignored Blair completely. Now I was checking my phone for texts from Tom, which never came. Did I have the guts to do the trip on my own? Did I even want to?

Tom arrived home three days later. He looked exhausted. We eyed off across the living room.

'I don't know if I'm making the right decision,' he said finally, 'but I don't want to give up on us, on this. We've worked too hard.'

I felt sick with relief.

Tom was unusually quiet for a few days then he put it behind him. He had never been one to hold grudges.

A week later we moved our belongings into storage. I left The Men's Gallery ten days earlier than I'd planned. I was really so rattled I couldn't bring myself to work another shift. While I didn't plan on returning, for the first time ever, I didn't throw out my shoes.

11.

I T WAS WINTER 2004 AND I HAD A BAD CASE OF THE
post-bike-trip blues.

Tom and I had been back in Melbourne for a month and I
was obsessively writing a book about our cycling adventure. Its
publication was going to transform us into overland legends – and
award me with a new identity, that of author. There was only one
problem. The bike trip hadn't gone to plan.

A year earlier, Tom and I had cycled out of London with a
combined forty-three kilos of gear. We sweated across Europe
during the hottest summer on record, then shivered across
Turkey's snow-coated plateaus, ill with gastro. The daily starvation
continued in Iran with Ramadan. We exited Bam just days before
the devastating earthquake that killed over 25,000. Our bikes were
left on a train in Pakistan and we survived a bus crash getting them

back. It was one wild ride, and incredibly, after 10,000 kilometres, we were physically unscathed. Emotionally, though, we were ruined, our relationship as tattered as the prayer flags strung out across Dharamsala.

In India we were forced off the road every day, and one afternoon Tom snapped – hurling a rock through the windscreen of an oncoming truck. The driver stopped, yanked me off my bike and demanded payment. Admitting responsibility would've been daft amid a fast-swelling rural crowd who spoke little English. Only the intervention of a local saved us both.

That moment broke us. Barely speaking, we limped into Kathmandu before conceding we could go no further. Despite eight months on the road, I felt like a failure. Tom was less goal fixated, more concerned about saving our relationship. I couldn't bring myself to break up with him, to botch that up too. Not knowing what else to do, we returned to Melbourne.

* * *

Back on familiar ground, our friends and families were toasting us as a successful team, a tandem unit. It was easier to pretend we were than to admit we weren't. The cycle trip had given my family and I something positive to talk about – I didn't want to disappoint them again. Before Tom and I knew it we had rented a house together in North Fitzroy. Reluctantly, Tom went back to his old job. I buried myself in writing. But the story I had wasn't one of beautiful vistas and triumph over adversity, it was the diary of an imploding relationship. This was not the tale I wanted to tell.

The denial went deeper. It had been a whole month and I still hadn't rostered on for a shift at the club. Perhaps I didn't want to strip anymore? But acknowledging that would've felt like self-betrayal. I might've failed at being an adventurer and I could fail at being an author, but I was a very successful stripper. Why wouldn't I want to strip? It sucked my creative juices, yes, but it also afforded me a great lifestyle. Two nights a week at the club would give me five days to write. Surely I had enough energy to do both? Stripping made sense. For once, I had some savings, so it wasn't just about the money. I was buying time.

That Friday I faced reality and returned to The Men's Gallery.

* * *

Opening the door to the dressing-room, I was hit by the smell: that sticky-sweet combination of scorched hair, cigarettes, cheap perfume, fake tan and foot odour. There's nothing like taxidermied eau-de-femme. Once it had been comforting, now it was suffocating.

Stanley was behind the dance supervisor's desk, arranging his Herbalife products for sale, as he did at the beginning of each shift.

'Juliette baby! Welcome back.' He added my name to the roster.

'It's good to be back,' I fibbed. I held out thirty dollars, not ready to do a show on my first night.

Stanley waved it away. 'House fees are forty now, baby, but don't worry about tonight. And there's a fifty-dollar fine for no-shows too.' Dancers needed to give twenty-four hours' notice to cancel a shift or provide a doctor's certificate or pay the fine. I wasn't about to debate it: I'd never pulled a no-show and didn't intend to start.

I headed towards the second booth on the left, but stopped short. In it was a remarkably pretty teenager on speakerphone, bitching about someone to anyone who cared to listen. I didn't care. I backed up into the empty first booth, dug out my crusty old make-up and began to resurrect Juliette, my mouth downturned.

The girl's voice grated on. 'Some bitch stole all of my MAC. Do you know how much it's costing me to be here tonight?'

To my relief, Stanley popped his head in. 'Ruby, darling, do you mind?'

'What?' said the girl, but she switched off speakerphone, which didn't actually help because she was doing all the talking. When she hung up, I made sure I didn't catch her eye. After a year of genuine interactions on the bike trip, I had no patience for drama queens. I concentrated on face painting, eyelash gluing and fake tanning. Thankfully, Ruby went up on the floor soon after, but not before pausing alongside the first booth expectantly, as if waiting for me to introduce myself. I didn't. She then harrumphed, tossed her chestnut mane and almost took out pint-sized Bonnie on the stairs.

'Sweet-cheeks!' Bonnie flung herself at me. I dropped into a squat to avoid mashing her face in my cleavage. Then we condensed the last twelve months into twelve seconds. Bonnie said her daughter had started school, and let me prod her new cheek implants. I couldn't spot the eight-grand difference, but didn't say so. Instead, I said, 'I see there's a new princess in the house.' Bonnie simply lit a menthol and winked.

Around 6.30 p.m., Tiffany and Jade arrived, looking washed out from too many late nights. After updates of real-life events – Tiffany had a new man, Jade had bought an investment property – the conversation shifted to work.

Tiffany was not long back from ten weeks dancing in Roppongi, where competition had been fierce and house fees high. It was touching from the waist up, compulsory to work six nights a week and impossible to make money without drinking. The only time Tiffany had off was when she got alcohol poisoning and couldn't get out of bed for three days.

'The whites of my eyes actually turned yellow,' she said, sounding horrified and awestruck.

Jade snorted. 'Stripper penal colony.'

The dancers stayed in an apartment complex managed by the club. If you'd been placed through an agency, as Tiffany was, there was no getting out of your contract unless you forfeited your return airfare and 'tip out', the percentage of the take on bottles of champagne. Contractual obligations included lunch dates with customers. I screwed up my nose at that.

'Tokyo's not for everyone,' Tiffany said. 'I'm glad I went, but if you have any other way of experiencing the culture ...'

I'd been curious about Japan since For Your Eyes Only, when dancers spoke casually of earning thousands a night. But even then I couldn't have handled the groping or the dates.

Talking of dates, the girls said that Harlow had been fired after going public with her famous cricketer affair. TV crews had swarmed outside the club, keen for a glimpse of her. When Harlow finally appeared, it was teary and devastated on *Today Tonight*. She was rumoured to have sold her story for $80,000. Quite the nest egg, I thought enviously. But then Harlow had never been one to let a golden opportunity slip past her.

While I was pleased to see the girls, The Men's Gallery seemed stuck in a time warp – a gaudy carousel ride going nowhere. In the dressing-room, the same faces sat in the same places. Bonnie's belongings were still strewn about and Carole was still chain-smoking. Upstairs, Vietnam Phil was still propped at the bar and Weatherman John was still keen to eyeball my pussy. 'You look just the same,' he said. Unsure if he was talking to it or me, I said nothing. After a year of trying to ride someplace else, getting back on the painted pony was disappointingly easy. I had an innate muscle memory of what to do, even if I didn't really want to be doing it. Eleven hours later, I hobbled home with a garter full of fast cash, a champagne headache and the horrible feeling that I'd never left.

I soon realised I wasn't alone in my discontent. Like me, most of my buddies were tiring of stripping. Unlike me, they had plausible exit strategies.

Bonnie was studying nursing part time. On slow nights she would huddle over fat anatomy texts, bookmarked with eyeliners. 'Did you know,' she once marvelled, 'that the female clitoris is four inches long? Ours is almost as big as theirs!' To which Diamond replied, 'Not the men I date, babe.' I'd never thought Bonnie that focused, but she was acing her exams and loving her practical placement. She seemed to have genuinely found her calling.

So had Cameron, a willowy brunette with a dedicated stable of regulars and several investment properties. After working on and off at the Gallery for years, Cameron had started a commerce degree. It was a fitting choice for a girl whose quirkiest regular once baked her brownies shaped like dollar signs, because he knew she liked money.

Tiffany was under increasing pressure from Emilio to hang up her G. She had fallen for this forty-something, soon-to-be-divorced customs agent, and she'd met him at the club. But unlike the men who make empty promises to turn their strippers into secretaries, Emilio meant it. He needed a secretary now that his wife no longer worked for him. Emilio turned up almost every night Tiffany did, paying her well so she didn't need to dance for anyone else. This confused Tiffany's regulars, who sulked at the bar like children denied their favourite toy.

Boyfriends weren't allowed inside the club but an exception was made for Emilio. I suspected he was used to being the exception: Emilio once told me that strippers should never date their clients. He was the sort of customer the Gallery liked to attract: well mannered, well dressed and well off. Emilio and Tiffany made a striking couple and would sit together, chatting and sipping champagne. They were discreet, but anyone could tell they were in love. It was only a matter of time before Tiffany left.

Meanwhile, Jade wanted one last bite of the Big Apple. We were in the first booth one night when she said, 'It's time, babe. I've been asking the Universe to show me a sign if I should go. Then last weekend this Jamaican girl I worked with over there turned up here.'

I remembered seeing the girl around. 'Do you think you'll be allowed back in?'

Jade shrugged. 'If I'm meant to get in, I'll get in. I'm changing my name by deed poll.'

For a moment I wondered if I could make it in New York. Jade had once said that you literally had to hold onto your customers on the way to the private booths or dancers would cut in and drag them away.

'This is it, babe,' Jade continued. 'One last shot. Si keeps asking, "When are you going to stop? When are we going to start a family?" If it's still good, I'll work solid for a year. Then it'll be Si's turn to keep me and I'll get big and barefoot and pregnant.' Jade strolled over to where one of the dressmakers had set up and thumbed at an apple-green dress. Watching her, I realised she had something I was fast running out of: belief in her ability to make the right call.

Within weeks Jade had changed her surname, sent her outfits ahead and arranged a $400-a-week couch to crash on. Then she was gone.

The following Friday, I was in the dressing-room with Diamond when Tiffany rounded the corner. 'Jade made it through, no problems. She said she was shitting herself.'

'I bet she was,' I said, relieved. 'Are you going too?'

'Emilio's not so keen, but I'd like to. One last summer in New York …'

Diamond turned around. 'Miami, San Fran, I cleaned up there! But New York, we didn't gel. Brunettes did well, not blondes, if you know what I mean.'

'No,' I said, puzzled. Diamond not doing well was like Barbie having flat feet.

'The vibe was more sophisticated,' Diamond said. 'I just wanted to dance and have fun.'

'Is it lap dancing in New York?' I asked.

'Yeah, it's grinding,' said Tiffany, 'but you don't take off your G.'

'I'd want to if I were you.' Diamond nodded at Tiffany. 'You've got a designer vagina.'

Tiffany chuckled. 'A *what*?'

'A model-perfect pussy! I was watching you doing a table dance before and I couldn't help but look. If mine was half as good as yours, I'd be showing it off all over town.'

Diamond was the current Miss Erotica Victoria, the Sexpo sexpot. How she could possibly show hers off more than she already was, I didn't know.

Tiffany had turned bright red, but Diamond didn't notice. 'Some girls prefer to keep their G on,' she said. 'I don't care either way.'

'Me either,' I said. 'I'm not sure about grinding though.' This was basically getting a guy off in his pants – not something I'd done or wanted to do.

'Oh, why not, Juliette?' said Diamond. 'You've got the booty for it.'

'You're incorrigible, Diamond,' I said. She let out a whoop and made for the stairs. Diamond had been stripping five nights a week for at least five years. She was the only girl I knew who hadn't tired of the game.

* * *

I felt jaded, but I was only twenty-nine, which in stripping terms meant I wasn't yet a senior citizen. Harlow had been thirty-one when she'd started. Several girls were almost forty, including Lulu, a twenty-year industry veteran and lapsed beautician. Lulu was writing her third unpublished manuscript, which made me doubt my priorities. Occasionally Weatherman John would ask me, 'How long have you been doing this for again? You can't do it forever.' Then, in the very next breath, 'You look the same as the day I met you.' I'd reply, 'So do you, minus the knee socks.'

Starlets like Ruby reminded me of how assured I'd been at nineteen, how fast I'd wanted to grow up. But stripping doesn't let you grow up. As I got older, I acted younger and less assured. Lulu acted the youngest of us all. She might've looked like Jerry Hall but she talked like a little girl.

One Friday I was hit by a triple-whammy of over-the-hill reminders. First, I arrived to find the dressing-room had been poster-bombed: *Calling Australasia's hottest showgirls to compete for the title of Miss Centrefold Oceania! $50,000 in prizes, including $10,000 cash!*

All the girls were talking about it, especially Ruby. I was sitting with Bonnie and Lulu, pencilling my eyes, when she flounced over.

'Juliette, are you going to enter?'

I glanced up, wondering if Ruby was serious. 'No.'

'Why not?'

I turned back to the mirror. 'Because I won't win it.'

'You don't know that,' she said, all faux innocent.

'Yes. I do know that.'

Ruby paused expectantly.

'Are you going in it?' I asked resignedly.

'I think I might.' An enormous smile lit up her face. Lulu and I watched her skip back to her chair.

'She won't win it,' said Lulu in a low voice.

'I know she won't. That's some serious money though.'

'Imagine what lengths some girls will go to.'

I shuddered. Lulu and I both knew that judging striptease was subjective, the criteria hazy at best. While I was still a showgirl, I wasn't about to flagellate my dying ego – or fuck the judges.

'Lulu.' Ruby was back, prancing around in a cheap blonde wig, looking just like Julia Roberts in *Pretty Woman*. I thought Ruby extra captivating because she hadn't yet learnt restraint. Sometimes I watched her getting ready, watched her watching herself. Her expression would shift from coy demureness to clear disbelief at her own loveliness. I remembered having one of those moments at Rocking Rods ten years earlier. It had been brief, but I was glad I'd had it.

The second blow came when Lulu glided into the booth carrying a gift-wrapped box. She tore off the paper. A Parker pen. Lulu stared at it for a long time. 'It's from Vietnam Phil,' she said finally. 'It's my fortieth birthday today.'

'Happy birthday!' Bonnie and I chorused.

Lulu looked like she might cry. 'I must go and thank him.'

I wondered if I'd still be stripping and trying to write a book at forty. The thought was so depressing I bummed a cigarette off Bonnie and broke my eighteen-month fast. It tasted disgusting, but I persevered.

Then Carole delivered the knockout blow.

'Hey, Juliette,' she sang out, 'do you want to be in the Old Trouts Club?'

'The *what*?' I peered around the corner of the booth at Carole.

'The Old Trouts Club,' said Tiffany, who was leaning against the desk.

'Depends,' I said, missing the pun entirely. 'Who's in it?'

'Me, of course,' said Carole. 'Lulu, definitely. Tiffany, Bonnie. All the old hags.'

'Thanks a lot,' I said.

'Come on, you've been here for bloody ages.'

'You get a lifetime membership to the first booth,' Tiffany said. I supposed you could laugh about it when you were that gorgeous and had an out.

In the first booth, the talk was about marriages and mortgages, babies and botox. One booth back it centred on self-idolisation, footy players you'd fucked and hiding your sexy laundry from your mother. I realised Lulu was old enough to be Ruby's mother.

'I'll think about it,' I said humourlessly, trudging upstairs in search of champagne. It was a glass-half-empty moment. God, that night I felt really old.

* * *

Ruby not only won the Victorian heat of Miss Centrefold Oceania, but also the Australian final. Fifty grand in cash and prizes were hers – and a ticket to the international final in Las Vegas. If Ruby was surprised she didn't show it. She was proof that if you don't believe in yourself, no one will.

In Vegas, Ruby made the top ten. She was photographed with Borat and partied with Hugh Hefner. 'An old bore,' she called him. Back in Melbourne she had her boobs done and got thousand-dollar hair extensions. And she bought a BMW and began parking in one-hour zones outside the club, accumulating tickets in the same perverse way I remembered the Japanese half-smoking their cigarettes at Rocking Rods.

Meanwhile, the old trouts swam on.

* * *

Tom tried to keep our relationship alive, cooking restaurant-quality meals. I left my laptop reluctantly to eat and had little to say. Some days I considered flying back to Nepal and finishing the cycle trip by myself. Then I became unwell. I got heart palpitations and dizziness after drinking coffee. In spring a chest infection forced me to take weeks off work. Antibiotics cured it, but the palpitations continued. A naturopath diagnosed adrenal burnout and suggested I stop working nights. I suspected she was right, but didn't know what else to do.

Inspired by Jade, I asked the Universe to show me a sign. Butterflies – monarchs and painted ladies – began dying under my desk. Was my stripper self or my writing self dead? I couldn't tell. Then my treasured bike was stolen. I cried for days. Five months after I'd started writing, I took a break from the book and never went back.

The sign I was looking for came unexpectedly. Each year, The Men's Gallery produced its own free calendar, an A3 poster featuring its most luscious dreamgirls, topless or nude.

In the past, Carole had asked if I'd like to audition. While flattered, I'd always said no. The photos remained the property of the club and could be used long after I'd stopped stripping. (Its high-profile rotating billboard outside Richmond train station was updated about once a decade.) I hadn't forgotten *The Picture* or *The Press* debacles and nothing had changed to warm me towards auditioning. If anything, there was more reason not to. I was tiring of Juliette. I'd put on weight. And while calendar girls were exempt from house fees for two months, I didn't have to pay a fee because I was still a showgirl.

But when word got around that Lachlan Frank was again doing the shoot I felt compelled to try out. Lachlan was a successful photographer with his own range of sports calendars. I had assisted him with the 2002 Gallery calendar, back when I'd been studying photography. In his mid-thirties with rugged good looks and an easygoing charm, I'd observed Lachlan's fascination for the female form. While I'd suspected his casting couch was well worn, Lachlan had treated me as a creative equal. I'd been grateful – and buoyed by the experience. Now I wondered how it would play out, being on the other side of the camera.

On the designated day, I waited with a handful of other hopefuls on the Gallery's own casting couch until Lachlan called me into the boardroom. It had only been three years since I'd last seen Lachlan, but I almost didn't recognise him. His features were softer, his presence lighter. Lachlan recognised me and, I believe, sensed I was there for a reason that went beyond the calendar. He asked me to strip topless. I did, feeling doctor's-surgery self-conscious.

Lachlan said he liked 'my look', so I wasn't surprised to learn I'd made the cut.

A few days later at Lachlan's warehouse studio it was all as I remembered it – the space strewn with lighting, props and general bachelor-pad disorder. But this time there were also spiritual self-help books by Eckhart Tolle and Neale Donald Walsch. And as I stood at Lachlan's kitchen window, trying to remember how to apply make-up in natural light, he asked me without preamble, 'Do you believe in soul mates?'

I didn't know what I believed in anymore. And I wasn't exactly sure what it was Lachlan was asking. If a soul mate was someone who 'completed' me, then that was a comforting notion. I had, after all, been raised on a diet of monogamy, marriage and till-death-do-us-part.

'Maybe,' I said.

'I believe each of us has a soul mate.' Lachlan's eyes shone; his focus seemed a long way from the calendar. 'They will come into our life when we're ready. And they'll be our greatest teacher.'

Several thoughts flashed through my mind. The first was that I wouldn't mind being Lachlan's soul mate, permanently cast into this slice of creative heaven. The second was of Ben, my first boyfriend and the only time in my life I'd been head-over-heels. Was he my soul mate? The third, and related to the second, was for as long as I could remember I had turned my back on love. Losing it hurt too much. I hadn't realised how tightly I'd closed my heart or the cost of that sacrifice until I saw the love shining in Lachlan's eyes. My own filled with tears.

Lachlan reached out and wiped them away. 'When we search our confusion, it can't hurt us anymore. Let's get on with the shoot. I get the feeling we've got plenty of time to talk about this.'

As Lachlan set up he told me he'd had a near-death experience, which had compelled him along a spiritual path. No longer did he shoot glamour, finding it too contrived. Instead he was fixated on capturing the essence of natural beauty. He put me half in a floral sundress belonging to the girl he said was his soul mate (only she wasn't so sure). As crushing as it was to learn I wasn't 'the one', it was more disturbing wearing her cast-off clothes. I didn't like the *Little House on the Prairie* look either, but I did admire Lachlan's resolve. Yet it was disconcerting for me: if I wasn't being animated or suggestive, I didn't know how to be naked. At last Lachlan got the photo he wanted, of me in profile, gazing into the distance. All that was missing was the straw hat.

Afterwards we curled up on his couch and talked for hours about love, truth, beauty and soul mates. I hadn't thought about these concepts in years, some not at all. It felt natural to reveal more of myself. The sundress came half off again. But while I was eager to connect in mind *and* body, Lachlan had reservations and couldn't be swayed past second base. Considering how Tom might have felt about this for the first time, I put my clothes on reluctantly and went home.

I walked in with a chin raw from stubble rash, which not even stripper-grade make-up could disguise. Tom took one look at my sandpapered face and said quietly, 'Did you sleep with him?'

'No.'

'But something happened.'

'Yes.' I tried but failed to feel guilty.

Tom considered me. 'Perhaps we should start sleeping with other people.'

'Perhaps we should.' I gave him a thin, relieved smile.

He smiled too, trying to be brave. 'The old photographer's trap! I can't believe you fell for it.'

'I can't believe I did either,' I said, although it didn't feel like a trap, it felt like an awakening.

* * *

That December, I hung out at Lachlan's studio at every opportunity. I was hungry for knowledge – and for him. Lachlan had other ideas and decided on a period of celibacy. This was devastating to someone used to turning men on, but probably for the best. Instead of hijacking his life, I needed to recreate my own. I just didn't know how.

Lachlan believed that if I didn't enjoy stripping I should quit, otherwise I was perpetuating a cycle of harm between the sexes. I lied and said I still liked it. He didn't believe me, but did encourage me to consider myself a sacred healer, to connect with the customers instead of fixating on the transaction. I sort of grasped what he was saying, but didn't think I was the stripper for the job.

'We're not a charity, Lachlan,' I said shortly, trying to hide the fact my heart wasn't in it.

Nevertheless, Lachlan got me *thinking* about stripping. Truthfully? When I wasn't defending the industry or my choices, I didn't know what to make of it anymore. Sometimes I adored it;

sometimes I was bored by it. Most of the time I was too tired to think about anything other than basic bodily needs. Eat. Sleep. Fake tan. Stripping was an all consuming vortex where I didn't have to have opinions or beliefs. I just had to smile and take off my clothes.

* * *

Tom and I moved into separate rooms. He'd started bringing lovers home and that proved too confronting for me. I wasn't as open-minded or sexually liberated as I liked to think I was. This probably hurt even more because given that my amorous photographer-interest was no longer amorous or interested, I'd stopped hanging out with him. And although I'd started this turn of events, I needed it to stop. We decided I would move out.

I found a flat nearby and arranged to move in on New Year's Eve.

That Christmas, Tom couldn't afford to fly to New Zealand to be with his parents, while mine had dropped a bombshell, announcing they'd separated.

Mum broke the news in a rare trans-Tasman phone call. She wasn't coping and wanted my support. But I struggled to relate and hadn't the energy to get involved. Mum and I had never talked about the tough stuff. Now I just didn't know how. Nor, I suspected, did Dad. And it was all a little too close to home. My parents hadn't seemed happy together for years and the thought that I might have modelled my own relationships on theirs made me uncomfortable. I refused to take sides or decide who to have Christmas dinner with. I was staying out of it.

Tom and I spent Christmas Day at Melbourne Zoo, drinking ourselves sober. We watched the male gorilla toss shit around and tried not to think about the year before, when we'd celebrated high in the Himalayas, listening to the Dalai Lama speaking on loving-kindness. I felt sad, and a bit lost.

It was the end of 2004. I was single, almost thirty and still stripping.

12.

YOU'VE GOT TO BE DESPERATE FOR CASH OR
company to work New Year's Eve. I arrived to find the men's
toilets had overflowed into the girls' locker room. My costumes
were soaked. I started the shift – and 2005 – in borrowed undies.
That night there was a sweet rapport among the dancers and part
of me was glad to be there. Nevertheless, at midnight I stayed
down in the dressing-room, avoiding opportunistic face-planting
by random customers. I sat there for twenty minutes, skolling
free champagne and trying not to feel sorry for myself. Back
on the floor, the men were all kissed out and the money was
consolingly continuous. I exited when the hard-core partiers
entered at around 5 a.m.

It was my first night in my new flat, unsettling enough without
the roar of traffic. Realising I would have to live with it, I began to

cry. By 8 a.m. I was a blubbering mess. In desperation I phoned Tom, who was out of town, catapulting him into a glorious hangover.

'You just need sleep,' Tom reasoned. 'Let yourself into my place.'

So I stumbled down the block, collapsed on his couch and passed out instantly.

I had a few days' break but it only highlighted how lonely I was. I'd always prioritised stripping, and now I really wanted to work, if only for the familiarity. I signed up for extra shifts. On a January Tuesday, after an hour-long run, I was primed to hustle. Up on the floor, though, I froze. Customers asked me to repeat my name. Conversations stuttered. I seesawed between the main bar and the dressing-room, unable to sit still. I'd had bad starts before, but not like this.

En route to my first podium, a pesky little man, Andrew – aka the Cockroach – blocked my path. Sometimes Andrew was kicked out for touching; a week later he'd be let back in. I had stopped dancing for him after he'd licked my chest. Now he grabbed my wrist.

'Don't touch!' I yanked free.

Andrew cackled, too loudly, followed me to my podium and held up a twenty. I could have refused but most of the few customers were watching. I knelt before Andrew and took the money. It was a fast three minutes: the song hadn't even finished when I sidled out of reach. Andrew sat there, seemingly stunned by my ingratitude. I ignored him, dressed and tried to look like I was having the time of my life.

After the podium, I propositioned two blokes standing at the bar. The moustachioed one snickered. 'I'm gay.' This was a popular diversion tactic – used, I suspected, by homophobes with untapped tendencies. It wasn't funny but I laughed anyway. 'You are not.'

'I am – you can ask my friend.'

'He is,' said the clean-shaven one. I turned away.

A swarthy man in a suit was sitting near table 2. I went and sat beside him.

'I'm Mo,' he said.

'As in *The Simpsons*?'

'No – as in Mohammed.'

'Oh, right.'

Mo patted my hand. 'I'm okay, thanks.'

Fruitlessly, I persevered. By 10 p.m., dancers were yoyo-ing to and from the private area, but my playdar was well off: I was emitting a crackpot charge. After a guy winced on my approach, I stumbled towards the girls room, holding back tears.

'Fluffy!' called a familiar voice. It was Liam, an old regular.

I pecked his cheek, relieved to see him. 'How are you? It's been ages.'

'Good,' he said. 'Better.'

Liam used to come in every other night, miserable with his real estate job. Then he quit to work in a music store and his unhappiness slipped away. I hadn't seen him since he'd brought me a fluffy toy cat months earlier. 'A small thank you,' he'd said, 'for hearing me out at a difficult time, when no one else would.' I'd appreciated the gesture, but also wondered why other girls got expensive gifts and all I got was a stuffed cat.

'Time for a cigarette?' Liam held up a pack. We found a quiet corner and lit up.

'Fluffy, are you okay?' he asked, so genuinely I couldn't brush him off.

I sighed. 'I'm just unsettled. I feel like I'm slowly self-combusting, you know?'

'I know that feeling.'

I told Liam about the failed book, about breaking up with Tom. Liam heard me out and while he didn't offer advice, it was good to talk. He was the first person I'd confided in.

'Do you want to meet for coffee?' I asked.

He hesitated. 'You've always been so professional … Think about it, okay?'

'I have thought about it,' I said, confused.

'Well, you know where I work. Call me sometime.' Liam sounded ambushed; I knew then I'd never call. 'Don't worry, you pussycats always pull through.'

I did pull through, that night anyway. I filled myself with champagne and stopped struggling. Chatting with customers, I held my own space instead of leaning hopefully, hopelessly, into theirs. I got dances. But the men I attracted were sleazy and egotistical and our interactions were as bright and brittle as candy.

Aside from Liam, the only honesty came from a guy who wanted a private dance after my 2.30 a.m. podium. I writhed manically onstage to demonstrate my vivaciousness. Afterwards, the guy said, 'No offence, but is the dance going to be any good?'

My jaw dropped.

'It's just that some girls give awesome private shows, slow and sensual –'

'I'm a *very* sensual private dancer!' Then, remembering how this game got played, I reeled him out. 'But it's up to you ...'

The guy sighed and flicked me a fifty. I danced sensually, like I normally would. He complimented me on everything from my eyes to my butt, as if remorseful for slicing me up with a piece of the truth. It was a horrible note to end the night on, but I was done.

And I was coming undone, both mentally and physically. I couldn't predict my response at work anymore: some shifts I'd freak out, others I'd be fine. Then I'd get sick: colds and flus, ear infections. In eight years I'd rarely cancelled a shift, now I was always cancelling them. Despite the new no-show rule Carole never asked me for a doctor's certificate or to pay a fine. But the day I did the unthinkable and asked to leave after my first podium she did ask what was wrong.

'I don't know,' I replied. 'I just can't be here.'

Wordlessly, Carole crossed me off the roster. That was worse than being yelled at. I cried all the way home and half the night. What the fuck was wrong with me?

The blood tests came back normal, the dizzy spells continued. The naturopath suggested rest. I'd sleep till midday, then feel guilty. At 1 a.m., I was always wide awake, writing my diary or reading self-help books. Had antibiotics weakened my immune system? Could I be suffering from stripper burnout, a kind of shellshock for exotic dancers? Surely not – I worked two shifts a week, at best.

While reluctant to admit that stripping might be the problem, given it had become my entire world, I did consider finding another job. The thought was terrifying. I wasn't capable of doing what was familiar, let alone anything new. Journalism was a long shot, even without the four-year gap on my CV. And I didn't know what else I would rather do. Waitering was pointless: it would take a week to earn what I'd make in one good night at the club.

Briefly, I contemplated subletting my flat and flying to New York, but Jade said all the money was in the champagne lounge now. That sounded scary to a girl having trouble spitting out her stage name.

What about breaking the lease and flying to Canada? I was still eligible for a working holiday visa; perhaps I could work on a ski-field like a normal person. I put a picture of a polar bear on my fridge as a motivator, but suspected I needed to stick this one out. Wherever I went, there I was. There was no getting away from me.

Perhaps if I took a more professional attitude towards stripping I would feel better about myself.

Perhaps if I toned up …

I joined the local gym.

That lasted until a customer said, 'I saw you the other day.'

'Did you now?'

'Don't you want to know where?'

'Not especially.'

He was smiling smugly, like he'd caught me shoplifting. 'The YMCA.'

'Oh yeah. Do you go there often?'

'Most lunchtimes.'

The act of being seen didn't bother me; the man's covert response did. I was probably being paranoid but I enjoyed my stalker-free status. (Twice, Cameron had taken out restraining orders.) I stopped training at lunchtimes, then I stopped going altogether.

The day I decided to quit smoking I had conveniently run out of cigarettes. Every dirty ashtray went into the wheelie bin out the back of the building, so if the urge overtook me, extracting the butts would be a humiliating public exhibition – one that would require a long, conscious walk first.

I made the walk. That patchwork fag tasted unbelievable. Evidently, I wasn't ready to give them up yet either.

Then I self-imposed show training. Alone in the showroom I would feel momentarily inspired, but I grew increasingly self-conscious when I performed. I sped up, as if movement could hide me. I prayed that my old routines were still solid enough for me to stay a showgirl. Those six minutes of anxiety had become my all-night peace of mind, my guaranteed no-house-fee. Even if I wasn't up to hustling, I wouldn't leave owing fifty dollars.

Finally, I tried being openhearted with the customers, as Lachlan had suggested. I tried to listen, to hold genuine conversations, to wait for the men to ask me for a dance. When this approach worked, they thanked me sincerely.

One dance I remember was for the 'Are you shaved?' man from interstate. 'Because I'm looking for a woman, not a girl,' he explained bashfully. 'I have two teenage daughters. It wouldn't be appropriate.'

'I understand,' I said, wondering if I did. 'And I'm not.'

'I'll be annoyed if you *are* fully shaved. Some girls have been telling me they're not when they are.'

I assured him I wasn't. Then I looked at his pressed slacks and receding hair and imagined him being raised on 1970s *Playboy* spreads. My little runway stripe was hardly abundant.

Removing my G for him, I felt unusually self-conscious, a feeling I associated more with gynaecological check-ups and bikini waxing. The man stared between my legs, expressionless. My mind darted off: groin, gynaecology, G … what did the G in G-string mean? (The original is obscure.) I recalled Diamond saying she'd pierced her clit to dress it up: 'I thought it could do with a bit of bling.' I had no such glittery treats but the man was still fixated.

'Thank you for your dance and your honesty,' he said quietly once I'd finished. 'I don't have affairs, but you fulfil a need somehow. I'm very grateful.'

'You're welcome,' I said, meaning it for a change.

But if I honoured myself as much as I tried to honour others, would I still be stripping? I honestly didn't know.

By winter I suspected I might be depressed. Yet my life was privileged, of my own making. Not being able to cope seemed like a selfish indulgence.

There really wasn't anyone I could talk to. The girls at work had their own problems: Bonnie's boyfriend was sick of her stripping, while Diamond's ex had dobbed her into the tax department. Diamond had plenty to say about both. 'Every guy thinks they want to date a stripper; no guy likes the reality.' And, 'He's a convicted felon and they take his word over mine? I've *always* paid my taxes.' Zoe was back from overseas but refused to talk shop now she'd reinvented herself as a barista. Tom was all loved-up with a new partner. My parents were divorcing. My school friends were getting married and having kids – not a future I'd ever wanted.

Raised to soldier on and reluctant to admit that I couldn't, I kept putting on my sequins and my smile. I spent ever-increasing chunks of each shift in the dressing-room, feet up on the bench. Dancers started cold-shouldering me in case struggle was contagious.

One night I simply couldn't go up on the floor. I watched Charlie – a cheeky Colombian dancer – step her Thailand-tanned, yoga-toned body down the dressing-room stairs, wearing stilettos and a bra.

'I just danced for Oscar and no, he was not a grouch,' she announced.

From her desk, Carole looked at Charlie pointedly. Dancers weren't allowed to walk around the club half-dressed. Charlie's hands fluttered to her face. 'My pants just got blown off!'

'Well, blow them back on again,' said Carole.

'How is it up there?' I asked Charlie as she strode past, waist-length braids swinging. Willing her to say it was slow.

'Sexsational!' she said.

Her enthusiasm was exhausting. And her motivation made me realise how little I had.

I recalled the forty-something bottle-blonde who had told my nineteen-year-old self, 'This is a tempting industry, but it can be very hard to get out of.' I wondered if this was what she'd meant.

As the weeks went by my savings plummeted; I didn't care. Impulsively I bought a Hyundai wagon, but rarely drove it. I'd read somewhere that if you didn't respect how you earned your money you wouldn't respect how you spent it. Had I lost respect for stripping? Perhaps if I spent *all* my money I'd have to *do* something else.

One morning, after yet another sleepless night, I hauled myself out of bed at 5 a.m. in search of my old yoga DVD. I couldn't find it, but as I emptied a bag of clothes a roll of banknotes bounced out. Two thousand dollars. I couldn't recall putting it there. That floored me. I took it as a divine sign and didn't roster on for a month.

Meanwhile, I started yoga classes at a different gym. Getting up on time was a struggle and I was paranoid everyone could tell I was a decaying stripper – I had flaky tan and chipped nail polish and could flop into straddle effortlessly – but there were moments of clarity. I realised that despite years of being naked I did not know my own body, I was not fully in my own skin. Nor did I know how to look after myself. I tried to smoke less, to cook more. I started doing up a 1920s kitchen cabinet I knew I would never finish. I bought a gold velvet couch. I read a little; I wrote a lot. The days passed.

* * *

I didn't plan on falling in love. Perhaps no one does. At For Your Eyes Only, a customer had once lamented to Larissa, 'I'll never find love,' and she'd declared, 'Oh no, you don't find love – it finds you.' And so it did.

In August I went skiing with Zoe, her on-again boyfriend Joel, and a few of his mates. We spent three glorious days at Falls Creek in alpine Victoria. The mountains were where I always felt my happiest, yet I hadn't been skiing in years. I was reflecting on this out on the balcony one night when Joel's mate Matt joined me. Matt was a brooding, troubled man with gentle hazel eyes and shaggy brown hair. I'd felt an instant affinity with him; we seemed to 'get' each other. We huddled at the railing in companionable silence, smoking and stargazing.

'What makes you happy?' I asked.

'I'm grateful for every day I'm not in hospital,' Matt said finally. 'I'm happiest when I'm manic.' Beneath his hoodie, his eyes looked haunted. 'Some days, it's all I can do to wash my clothes or go to the supermarket. I'm so afraid of getting it wrong.' He butted out his cigarette and hurried inside.

I watched him leave. I knew Matt had something called bipolar disorder. I also knew he'd spent every dollar he had – and some he didn't – on this holiday. He needed it more than I did: one of his flatmates had just died of a heroin overdose.

While often close to tears that weekend, Matt also laughed a lot. He had a warm belly laugh and a subtle, intelligent sense of humour. He was complex, emotionally real – and reckless. While I cruised the slopes, mindful of shattering my fragile stripping prospects, he hurled himself at jumps, wiping out and cracking a rib. Still, we usually ended up in the lift queue together.

In the backseat of Joel's car on the way home, Matt reached for my hand. Our fingers fitted perfectly. I rested my head on his shoulder. He smelt musty, like he'd been sleeping in his clothes. That was a small thing, compared to how good he made me feel.

A few nights later, I texted Matt while drinking red wine in the bath. He invited me over, with a warning: he was drunk. That was okay. I was too.

Matt lived one suburb over, in a ramshackle two-storey share house. I cycled there to find his room candle lit, a fresh bottle of wine on the mantelpiece. Touched by his thoughtfulness, I sat on the bed beside him and glanced around. Everything was old and worn, lived in. A heaped clothes rack, a desk with two computers, a bookcase filled with paperbacks – Nietzsche and Baudelaire and Borges, names I didn't yet know. There was a record player and a crate of records, which Matt gestured to. 'You can pick something if you like.' I flicked through, not recognising much. Several were without sleeves; some were cracked. I was relieved to find Joni Mitchell's *Blue* intact and put her on.

Matt lay down, one arm behind his head. 'I moved the record player. Now I can change records without getting out of bed.'

Laughing, I lay beside him. Music was lost on me – it had become a mere prop I danced to.

Matt's fingers found my skin. His touch was warm and unhurried, like a tropical wave. I surrendered to it.

'I love you,' he murmured into my hair.

'I love you too,' I said.

Afterwards, he tucked my crown beneath his chin, my nose to his chest and fell asleep almost instantly. I'd never slept this way before. For a long time I lay in the candlelight, in the tangle of sweaty sheets, listening to him wheeze. I felt like I'd found my soul mate.

A few weeks later, I was back at work and the dizzy spells had stopped. I was still practising yoga, and was even thinking of becoming a yoga teacher – there was an open day coming up at a local academy. And I'd applied for a Canadian visa, because change finally felt possible. I knew Matt had some financial problems but secretly hoped we could go together.

We had slipped effortlessly into each other's lives. Matt worked part time in administration and often skated to my place afterwards. We would sit in the nearby park, drinking beer, chatting away and casting curious, wondrous glances at each other. Other times, I would cycle to his house and we'd go for long walks into the night. He showed me his graffiti tags, sprayed high on railway overpasses. 'Without destruction, there's no creation,' he said. Unsure, I said nothing.

I said nothing too when he smoked pot in front of me, shamefully at first. I watched as he drew back, set the foetid water bubbling. Watched the crease between his brows smooth over. Watched, while the judgemental part of me stayed dormant.

We never talked about his bipolar either. I had asked, 'What is it, exactly?' He sighed heavily and his bottom lip trembled. Not wanting to hurt him, I never asked again. And we never talked about my work. He said once, 'If I could do it, I would.' I took that to mean he didn't mind. We didn't even talk about being together. There was just an innate understanding that we wanted to be, that our lives were better for it.

It was as if Matt had opened a portal into a better way of being. He'd introduced me to hip-hop, philosophy and composting, to his housemates and his squatter friends. Like him, they didn't have much money yet they seemed rich compared to me, and lived fuller lives. Some were activists with socialist opinions and political agendas. They had an honesty I lacked – I felt like a fraud around them. I had unintentionally defined myself by Juliette for so long

I didn't know who I was or what I believed in. Still, Matt's friends were accepting. They shared what they had, as did Matt. Inspired, I made an effort to share too.

At my place soon after we started seeing each other, he spent time inspecting the cycle trip photos Blu Tacked to my wall – Tibetan monks, Indian rickshaw drivers, Pakistani shopkeepers. 'The places you've been.'

When he plucked the polar bear picture off the fridge, I said, 'Canada. I'm thinking of going.'

Matt smiled wistfully. 'You should. Think of all that powder.'

'You can get a visa till your thirty-first birthday. How old are you?'

'Thirty-one,' he said.

'There goes that, then.'

'What about cash in hand?'

'I don't know. You even need a visa to strip.'

'Is that what you're thinking of doing?'

I shrugged. 'Maybe.'

If I went, it would have to be on my own. I felt torn – grateful to be able to move at last, unsure if I wanted to. Being with Matt was such simple joy. It was more than enough, more than I remembered having.

* * *

One Thursday I arrived at work to find someone sitting in my chair. She was late thirties, sinewy with a bleached crop. I took the seat beside her and said a grudging hello. Unfazed, she held out her tiny hand.

'Crystal.'

Another has-been stripper, I thought, as she buckled on big black sandals that matched her little black dress, picked up a leopard-print rug and glided up the stairs.

An hour later, I was still dawdling downstairs, contemplating myself in a new red lace two-piece, purchased as a pick-me-up. Unlike my other 'uniforms', I actually felt sexy in this. Suddenly, I didn't want to share that feeling with a bunch of desperados, I wanted to share it exclusively with Matt. Was I *done*?

Just then, Crystal rounded the corner. 'Can I walk out?'

This was my area of expertise. 'Why not tell Carole you'd like to go? That way you can come back.'

'I don't want to come back.' Crystal sat down. 'This is *it*. I've been dancing for seventeen years and tonight is my last night.' She clasped my hands in delight. 'Thank you for sharing this moment with me!'

This was huge. Dancers often made these declarations then came crawling back, but I sensed Crystal had been through that already. We sat holding hands and smiling for several long moments.

'What are you going to do?'

'I'm a trained yoga teacher, but I wanted to dance a little longer. I started here, so I wanted to finish here.'

What a coincidence! And the timing ...

'I was just considering leaving,' I admitted.

'Well, you have to honour your own truth.'

My skin prickled. 'You're a messenger.'

Crystal laughed. 'Yes, I've had messages for girls all week! Monday and Tuesday, I sat there,' she indicated the second booth, 'but tonight, my spirit guides told me to sit here.'

I wanted to know more about these mysterious guides, but I was late for a podium. Wishing Crystal good luck, I dashed upstairs. Onstage, I danced with a newness I thought I'd lost. There *was* life beyond stripping! Afterwards, I rushed back to the dressing-room, but Crystal was gone. On my chair were her leopard-print rug and a note: *Hey beautiful. Thank you. Remember, listen to your truth. Love and light, Crystal Blaze xxx*

A week after that, I was just hanging in when a gangly apprentice with narrow eyes and a cracker smile came up to me. 'I'd like a dance, because that's as close to knowing you as I'm ever going to get.'

His words made me inexplicably sad.

As I stripped, the boy said, 'I reckon you're attracted to me.'

I tried not to laugh. 'Why do you reckon that?'

'I just do. I can tell.'

'I'm not attracted to you.'

'Yeah you are, just a little.'

'Listen, I'm not going to insult you by lying. This is my job.'

The boy watched me dress. 'We had a moment, that's all,' he said plaintively. 'Let me have that moment.'

Perhaps I should have. Instead, I wanted to tell the truth. 'Let me tell you a story,' I began, and told him about stripping for Fletcher's friend in London. 'It didn't matter that he was charismatic; it didn't matter that he was good-looking. I simply didn't *see* him. Do you understand?'

The boy stepped out of the shadows, his eyes filled with hate. 'That's a horror story. A horror story! I hope I *never* see you again.'

Mortified, I watched him leave. Who had I become? If I could no longer respect the customer or honour the transaction then I shouldn't be stripping at all.

I went straight down to the dressing-room, up to Carole's desk. 'Can I go, please?'

Carole sighed. 'Yes, but I expect you to call management tomorrow. I've had enough of this.'

'This is *it*.'

I went and emptied my bowels of all the shit I didn't know I'd been holding onto. Then I gutted my locker and charged out into the night, loaded up like a bag lady. Disappointingly, G. I. was the only person to witness my grand exit.

'Toots! Where are you going?' he called.

'I don't know!' I laughed madly. The air smelt unbelievably sweet – like spring. Like new life.

The fantasy still smelled sweet in the morning as I fabricated my CV. I was going to land the dream job selling crystals, tarot cards and self-help books – I'd read plenty, after all. I went door knocking with my head held high. Two metaphysical shops spoke promisingly of openings but the calls never came. I tried to stay optimistic. I did a lot of stiff downward dogs and wrote loose poetry.

And I applied for jobs online. Finally a market research company offered me work. It started well enough. After learning the how-to, I was allowed 'out on the floor' (a comfortingly familiar term) to make some calls about egg-buying trends. While I didn't manage to 'get any' (not so familiar strip club parlance), responses were civil.

The following night – a Monday – I was yelled at continually. 'How dare you invade the sanctity of my home!' one man ranted. 'You people are absolute scum!' Agreeing silently, I apologised.

My teenage supervisor came and stood over me. 'Now I know you're new, but you need to lift your call rate.'

'You're joking, right?' I was going as fast as I could.

She scratched her nose. 'Why don't you take your ten-minute break now?' Ten minutes was barely enough time to go pee then find my desk again. After that, the refusals stacked into the hundreds.

Club customers had told me I was good at sales. I'd joked it was because I believed in my product. Whatever I did with my energy stripping, it was not as predatory or meaningless as this. If my eggs were all in one basket, then so be it. I stuck out the four-hour shift, then quit.

* * *

Like a runaway child skulking home, I tried to sneak past Carole's desk.

'Well, look who's here!' Carole grinned. Then she said seriously, 'What happened?'

Embarrassed, I shrugged. 'I just needed a break, that's all.'

'Well, it's good to have you back.'

I was grateful that was all she said, all that needed to be said.

I rounded the corner of the first booth to find Bonnie fussing with her curls and Lulu sipping a cup of tea. Cameron was there too, as poised and meticulous as ever.

'Juliette!' Bonnie hugged me. 'We missed you, didn't we, Lulu?'

'We did,' said Lulu.

'I missed you too,' I said.

'I couldn't believe it when Carole said you'd left,' Bonnie told me.

'I knew you'd be back,' Lulu said, with just a hint of satisfaction. I tried not to feel irked — I'd only been gone for six weeks. 'Well, having time off has made me appreciate this place.'

Cameron looked up. 'There aren't many jobs like it, are there? Where you can choose your hours, make good money and still have your days free.' Unlike me, I don't think she ever took stripping for granted.

'And get paid to drink and hang out with your friends!' Bonnie giggled.

I laughed, actually happy to be back. 'How's it been?' The standard stripper question, asked nonchalantly but with razor-like attention on the answer.

'Much the same,' said Lulu, to my relief. She headed for the stairs.

Beside me, Bonnie painted her eyelids peach. I stroked my face with foundation until every pore was coated, every blemish covered. Wiping the slate clean. A familiar surge of adrenaline caught my breath. *Back.*

Up on the floor, Weatherman John was loitering near table 2, looking like a glow-worm in glasses and a short-sleeved white shirt. He tried to hide his delight. 'I didn't think I'd see *you* again! The other girls told me you'd left.'

'I hadn't left!' I snorted. 'I was simply having time off.'

'Don't worry, my dear, I'm fully aware that any given Friday could be my last.'

We headed towards John's favourite chair (the most brightly lit). He sat down, paid and looked at me expectantly. I smiled and stepped towards him. The same old moves, the same old music. The same old John, grinning appreciatively. This wasn't so bad.

As the night unfolded, I was warmed by stripping's small idiosyncrasies. Diamond selecting a sandwich from the 2 a.m. tray, sniffing it and declaring, 'There's no love in these.' Stanley replying, 'Some people say that about the private dances.' Diamond toasting Stanley's quip with her sandwich then tossing it in the bin. George murmuring '*Om Namah Shiva*' during my 5 a.m. massage as 'Private Dancer' by Tina Turner came on. Someone groaning, 'I hate this song.' Walking to my car behind three guys leaving the Gallery, eavesdropping on their conversation: one asking, 'Who's up for Goldfingers?', another saying, 'There's only so many tacos you can eat in a Mexican restaurant.' And stopping at 7-Eleven for milk. The attendant taking in my painted face, asking, 'Where do you go tonight?' Me giving him my least suggestive smile. 'Home.'

Home.

* * *

In late October I took the weekend off work. Tom's housewarming was on Saturday. Matt and I were going together and I was picking him up at 11 a.m. That morning, though, Matt arrived on my doorstep at 5 a.m., cuddly, completely shitfaced and somehow convinced I'd forgotten to collect him. I led him to bed, mildly flattered he'd let me see him so drunk. When my alarm went off at 10 a.m. he lurched up, more hyped than hungover. Weary from working three nights in a row, I admired his stamina. It didn't occur to me that Matt might be unwell.

I made us coffee. Matt put on The White Stripes' 'Seven Nation Army' and sang along loudly. He was especially enthused about going to Wichita. Only we were going to the Yarra Valley, outside Melbourne.

It was a relaxed gathering and by mid-afternoon most people, including Matt, were merrily sozzled. But by the evening, Matt had become argumentative, with a strange glazed look in his eyes. I insisted we leave: the yoga teaching information session was at midday and I wanted to be fresh for it.

We stopped for felafels and took them back to his place. I ate cross-legged on the floor of his room. Matt didn't eat. Instead, he paced up and down, and scratched at his stubble. 'I have to tell you something. I can't lie to you.'

'What is it?' I asked.

'I *have* to tell you,' he said agitatedly. 'Even if it means we're over.'

I put my food aside. '*Matt*. Tell me.'

'I slept with someone else. I didn't mean to. It just kind of happened.' His ex had dropped by two weeks earlier when I'd gone to get a prescription for the contraceptive pill, of all things. 'I was still in bed, and …'

I crawled under his desk. With my vision blurred with tears, my head hit the wall. I stared unseeingly at the carpet. How had something so good gone wrong so fast?

Matt tugged at my foot. 'Leigh?'

I didn't move or utter a sound.

He tugged again. I still didn't move.

'It's unbecoming, you being like this,' he said, turning away.

The shift in his tone broke my stupor. What right did I have to be so upset? We hadn't agreed not to sleep with other people, I'd just thought neither of us would. Slowly I crawled out and wiped my face.

'Do you still love me?' Matt's voice wavered.

'I love you so much,' I said, almost wishing I didn't.

He cried then, his ribcage heaving like a trawler in a storm. I held him and wondered what had been broken.

Intending to rest, I lay down on Matt's bed and tried to comprehend. I'd read that promiscuity was a sign of mania, but did sleeping with your ex count? And Matt's behaviour at Tom's – guilt and intoxication might explain that, right? Briefly I wondered where the line between wellness and illness lay. Then I passed out.

When I woke up it was 11.30 a.m. There was no time to go home, shower and change my clothes. Unbelievably, I arrived at the yoga school bang on midday, still fingering parsley out of my teeth. The receptionist tsked and told me I was an hour late: daylight savings had started. But the director – who was in her sixties and wore a black leotard – clapped delightedly when I peered around the studio door. 'We've been waiting for someone to do that all day!' She bounced out of lotus and plumped up a floor cushion for me. 'We've been talking about life purpose and how to find yours.'

Leotards aside, I was intrigued. Where was my life purpose lurking?

I glanced around. It was an odd bunch: a sharp-talking man with scraggly hair, several plus-sixties with beatific smiles, a few corporate types. Most people were wearing all black, including a darling redhead called Van who brought me cups of pungent tea and was super-excited I was considering 'answering the call'.

Was that what this was? After a year of murmuring 'mayday' into the ether, had the Universe finally answered? I might've been more discerning had I not felt so wrecked. I burst out of there, feeling reborn, application in hand.

There was a letter waiting for me at home: I had been granted a Canadian visa. Yoga teacher training didn't start until June, which meant I could go to Canada for six months. I loved Matt, but after what had just happened … Impulsively, I bought a plane ticket, leaving in five weeks.

Matt was sitting at my kitchen table when I told him. I was cooking vegetarian curry.

He stared at the floor. 'Are you going to come back?'

I dropped to my knees before him. '*Of course* I'm coming back.'

He pulled me onto his lap and smiled courageously. 'I'm jealous of you and wish I wasn't. I wish I wasn't in debt, that I had options, that I could come with you.'

'I wish you could too,' I said, and meant it.

13.

THERE'S NOTHING LIKE A CANADIAN WINTER TO make a girl yearn for her sweetheart. For five weeks I trudged around the snow-coated countryside mortified by just how much I missed Matt. I wasn't even sure *why* I was in Canada. Had I run away? Or was I seizing my last chance to have a fully clothed working holiday? It was, it turned out, too late for that. The going rate for ski-field lifties in Alberta was seven dollars an hour: this pole-doll wasn't freezing her tush off for that. Not working was a waste, stripping wasn't supposed to be a first resort and going home felt like failure.

I signed up for a ten-day silent meditation retreat, hopeful it would help me decide what to do. It was held near Merritt, a logging backwater deep in the Rockies, and I caught a lift there with a meditation convert named Ariadne. As we churned over icy mountain passes, between snowdrifts as high as houses, we smoked last cigarettes – then last-last cigarettes – and shared our stories. Ariadne was a weaver who sold her wares at markets all over the Canadian Interior. I told her I was a stripper.

'Fuck off, you're not,' she said.

'Why not?' I asked.

'All the strippers I know are *big*. Big hair, big tits, big drug habits. You're ... sedate.'

Ariadne wasn't the only person to make me question stripping in North America. Everyone I'd met on the road had advised against it: I was too nice; the clubs were too hands-on. Hopefully meditating would shine some light on the subject.

For ten days I sat and tried to focus on my breath. There was no talking. No reading, no writing, no internet. No caffeine, no alcohol, no cigarettes. Limited food and little sleep. It was the toughest thing I'd done, *ever* – and all I was doing was sitting with myself. At least once a day I wanted to storm out, but we'd been snowed in. I wasn't going anywhere in a hurry.

Each evening after a hard day of doing nothing we would listen to an hour-long recorded teaching. Bizarrely, these usually related to the profound yet obvious realisations I had made that day. The morning I knew with certainty that I needed to quit stripping, the nightly wisdom was about *ahimsa* or nonviolence. Even if I could honour myself and every person I stripped for (unlikely), the act of selling my sexuality (also a no-no) could encourage violence against women. This might seem obvious from outside the girlie fold looking in, it was anything but from the inside looking out. I could live with harming myself; harming others was harder to handle.

The second realisation was that I wanted to go home to be with Matt. This was as simple as bringing forward my flights through Montreal and New York.

By the time I left Vancouver, though, I was already doubting my decision to quit stripping. I ended up outside Club Super Sexe in Montreal one night, the temperature well below zero, gazing longingly up at the neon explosion, like an alcoholic outside a bottle-o. I yearned to get in there among my people, drop my pants and gyrate in some John Deere-cap-toting guy's lap. But I didn't. My recent realisations needed to be nurtured, not abandoned.

Two days later in New York, it happened again. I lingered on Broadway outside the club Jade and Tiffany had stripped at – where they'd both finished stripping at – while the city screamed around me. Horns honked, screens flashed, spruikers touted. Ah, Broadway! What if I had Fosse talent lurking inside my seizing joints? Was I selling out by not selling? I stood slack-jawed before the Gods of Neon for a long time, while habit tried to one-up my heart.

The answer didn't really matter. I was flying home the next day. My costumes would stay crumpled at the bottom of my backpack. I would never know if that over-polished apple was tasty or rotten to its core, because my time munching on such temptations was over.

But on the plane, as I sped towards my respectable future, the mind chatter kicked in ten-fold. Perhaps I hadn't seen the light; perhaps I'd been snow-blinded. It wasn't realistic to boycott stripping. I would have to use all my savings to pay for yoga teacher training. Wouldn't it be better to strip for three months until my course began? I could stockpile some cash while getting used to the idea of a fully clothed existence. It would be a three-month, in-the-buff buffer zone. I had decided: three more months then I was out.

* * *

The moment I saw Matt, time literally stood still. As did I, holding up a planeload of people when I abandoned my trolley to gaze into his eyes. Matt was just as captivated. All day he kept whispering, 'It's really you! You're really here.' When we climbed onto his roof to watch the sunset, he stroked my hair. 'You give me hope for something more.'

'You too,' I said truthfully.

Not for a second did I regret cutting short my trip, although there were a few shortcuts I would regret. I had been dreaming of a share house with a vegie garden and a communal kitchen. Instead, I agreed to move into a townhouse Matt's parents had bought in inner-city Abbotsford, because it was close to yoga school and because Matt wanted to live with me. Then I agreed not to tell his parents I stripped, even though I hated lying. I'd only met them twice, but they'd welcomed me warmly and I liked them a lot. They reminded me of my own parents: hardworking, socially conscious baby boomers. The contact I had with my own family was increasingly sporadic. We stuck to 'safe' topics and they did most of the talking. I'd noticed it was the same with Matt's family but, unlike me, he had more realistic expectations. 'I understand what you do,' Matt had said, 'but they won't. If you're quitting in three months is it really worth upsetting them?' So I said I worked at Tunnel nightclub – not a place parents would ever pop into. I told myself these compromises didn't matter. They mattered more than I realised.

The day we moved in, Matt's parents arrived with new couches and a dining suite in tasteful navy. There wasn't room for my retro kitchen furniture or my gold velvet couch. Matt and I weren't moving in together: I was moving in with him.

I felt ungrateful, but also trapped. It was an ideal pad for most thirty-something couples and Matt's parents were generously charging us minimal rent. But I was back trying to live up to parental expectations. I gave away some of my furniture, Matt threw out some of his. He hid his bong on the balcony and made mutterings of cutting back. We set about creating a home but I couldn't shake the feeling I'd made a mistake.

* * *

Back at The Men's Gallery, my stilettos punched the carpet every Thursday, Friday and Saturday. Juliette had rekindled like a trick birthday candle. After the previous year I was relieved to have a focus and to be accepted back by management – especially as Lulu had been let go without warning while I'd been overseas. There was limited job security in nudie-land, the downside of super-flexible working conditions. I had renewed appreciation for the Gallery and for regulars such as Weatherman John, who told me he'd asked his wife to laminate my calendar pic (she'd refused), and Kevin from Origin Energy, who held up his VB and declared,

'This stands for you: Very Beautiful,' because – cheesiness aside – Kevin only wanted to make me feel good.

Unlike The Wizard. Once, I would've avoided The Wizard, but now that every dollar counted, I relished nailing him. He had a wiry beard, beady eyes and exceptionally large hands, which he would slo-mo towards my vagina mid-dance like a parent aeroplaning food towards a child. 'Mmm, what do we have here, a treasure trove, a right Pandora's box,' he'd murmur.

I'd dodge the incoming aircraft and say brightly, 'Well, there's always hope.'

One time, The Wizard produced a sheaf of photos of erect penises. 'Cor, get a load of these.' His eyes sparkled.

I averted mine. 'Why don't we show those to management?' The Wizard put the selfies away, sulked and never danced with me again.

His favourite dancer was Chantilly, a former hairdresser with stringy locks, a comely smile and a no-nonsense attitude. Chantilly had twice been arrested for having sex in a public place. She was also the only Gallery girl who'd stripped for a blind man and his seeing-eye dog, a guy with a pet blue-tongue lizard and a disabled patron who shat himself mid-dance.

Watching Chantilly and The Wizard finish up on table 2 one night, George the masseur appeared beside me. The old man's knobbly fingers were on Chantilly's hips while she backed up and wiggled her vagina centimetres from his face. The Wizard's droopy cheeks rounded into plums of rapture.

George chuckled and shook his head. 'Why do men spend their whole lives trying to get back into where they came out of?'

I just laughed. After thirteen years in the business it was still a great mystery.

* * *

I would get home from the club to find little notes on the kitchen bench or a flower Matt had picked while out skating. His tenderness made the tough nights easier, but Matt wasn't used to seeing me so driven.

And I wasn't used to seeing him so depressed. Matt was facing court charges, trying to pay off debts and regain the driver's licence he'd lost driving drunk – all while staying sober. I hadn't realised the extent of his troubles. Nor did I understand the effects of alcohol withdrawal or the intricacies of bipolar disorder. Matt saw a psychiatrist and was in regular contact with his parents, who were all far more experienced with his condition than I. But while they wanted him to go back on medication, I respected Matt's decision not to. He didn't want to take drugs that hadn't worked for him in the past, that had horrible unavoidable 'side' effects. He was the smartest person I knew: if he seemed to be self-medicating with marijuana instead, who was I to say he shouldn't? I wanted to trust his judgement. I didn't realise it might have been reluctance on his part to accept his illness.

The one thing I did realise was that on a part-time wage, Matt's financial burden was more than depressing, it was crippling. I helped where I could, short of paying his debts. Matt's parents believed bailouts didn't address the cause, and I agreed. When Matt struggled to get out of bed, I'd entice him with breakfast. When he cried and said he couldn't go on, I'd kiss his tears and insist he could. I bought organic groceries in an effort to become healthier and if we went out for dinner I insisted on paying.

We did things that didn't cost a lot, like going for walks or to the library or watching movies on TV. Most of the time it was just the two of us, which was fine by me but more difficult for Matt, who was mostly on his own when I was at work. Joel and Zoe had moved to the country and Matt was trying to stay away from his old drinking buddies. Smoking pot seemed his only relief.

As autumn moved towards winter, Matt's debts slowly shrank while my savings grew. The grout in the shower turned brown from fake tan and the lines around my eyes deepened. Sometimes I woke to find Matt clutching me tightly in his sleep. We had sex less than before. I wasn't sure if this was because of me stripping, because Matt was depressed or because we were always together. I couldn't believe it had happened so fast, but three months after I'd returned from Canada, the honeymoon was over.

* * *

In the dressing-room the talk centred around home ownership. Bonnie had bought a house with her boyfriend before leaving to become a nurse. Cameron was renovating a beachfront terrace while other dancers were building. They compared paint swatches as often as new shades of MAC, and swapped tradies' cards gleaned up on the floor. It was all very in-house.

One night, I got chatting to a lawyer-turned-potato-farmer. He told me his girlfriend used to strip. She'd got in, saved a hundred thousand, got out and bought a block of land. 'You girls can set yourselves up for life if you're sensible.' Suddenly, I wanted a place of my own. I wanted something to show for all these years nude. I wanted to be *sensible*, damn it.

But I was about to quit stripping and become a student. I talked to Cameron, our resident property mogul.

'You still can buy a house,' she said. 'Dance hard for two years and save. You need a decent deposit anyway.'

Cameron was right. If I was studying yoga for the next fifteen months, why not combine the two? Teacher training was three evenings a week, plus every second weekend. It would mean an eighteen-hour Saturday, four hours' sleep then another three of yoga, but it was doable. Other dancers successfully juggled work, study and a relationship. I wanted to have it all too.

* * *

The first day of teacher training I dressed in uniform black and stood at the bathroom mirror, simultaneously gulping coffee and brushing my teeth. I hadn't seen the right side of 7 a.m. since the bike trip. My guts were a bucket of nerves: I craved a cigarette, but I'd quit again. I'd also stopped practising yoga. Had I made a mistake, committing thirteen grand on a whim? So much was riding on this.

That morning I was dismayed to find a lot of middle-aged women with expensive hairdos wearing Lululemon. Where were the artists, the ferals, the socialists? Then it dawned on me that they couldn't afford the fees to be here. Who was I to judge? I had conveniently forgotten I'd bought my way in, too.

As the day progressed I felt my frostiness thawing. While the lessons were painfully slow – there was even colouring-in to stimulate right brain function – I recognised truth in the teachings. By 5 p.m., I'd been swept up in the collective positivity.

I arrived at the club radiating good vibes. I was amped to work, to sprinkle all with love and positivity like an auric golden shower. But while I conversed easily and was treated with respect, I couldn't get a dance. Not one! Were the men drawn to our vacuousness? Did they want to rescue us, fill us up and hold us under, all at the same time? I didn't know. But I wasn't about to have all I *did* know wiped out in a single day. I shelved my real smile, got my sexy on and ignored my soul crying out. My filling garter was capped by a 3 a.m. finish.

At 9 a.m. I felt like a porcelain doll that had toppled off the shelf. The other trainees were still buzzing from the previous day; I sat in the back row and sulked. I didn't want to do partner work – I'd been doing partner work all night! The slow pace and boundless optimism did my already-done-in head in.

It seemed once again I had jumped without thinking; once again I was paying someone else to tell me what to think. I couldn't give up the crazy-beautiful club for people sipping ionised water and talking about their feelings! But I would need to find a balance – to be more present and less goal fixated – otherwise I would short-circuit. Sadly, I realised years of stripping had made me less open-minded and more disparaging of new people and situations. Being judged had made me judgemental, the very opposite of what I wanted to be.

* * *

Matt tensed up whenever I mentioned the club now. He didn't find my anecdotes amusing – not even the one about Weatherman John, whose wife had told him, 'You're just another John to her.' Sometimes when I left for work, Matt looked close to tears. And I hadn't yet told him I was going to keep stripping.

When I did he wasn't happy. 'I don't think you're aware of how much of yourself you're actually selling,' he said.

'Everyone sells themselves,' I said defensively.

'But not everyone sells their sexuality. You have a choice.'

'And one I'm comfortable making.' I remembered Diamond's words: 'You think we're being exploited? Try working for minimum wage.'

Matt didn't reply.

'I'd like to buy a house one day,' I said.

'You have a house. This is our house.'

'No, this is *your* house, in family trust for you. It will never be part mine.'

'It won't?'

'No,' I said.

'I thought you couldn't teach yoga and strip?'

'Maybe I can.' I shrugged. 'Besides, I'm not teaching yet.'

'You could get another job.'

'I already have a job.'

'It's not just a job! It's a big part of who you are, and I love you for it. But I'm tired of you always being tired.'

'Don't you think I'm tired of you always being depressed?'

Matt's eyes welled up. 'Don't you think I'm not tired of it? I have to *live* with it.'

I saw what I was doing, stopped and apologised. 'Are we okay?'

Matt squeezed my hand, hard. 'We're *more* than okay.'

I gave him a wan smile and wondered why he was only bothered by my stripping now. I couldn't understand what had shifted for him any more than I could grasp what had changed for me.

A few weeks later, Matt said too casually, 'I'd like to come in and see you at work sometime.' His tone made me cautious. He was trying hard not to make a big deal of it.

Matt knew boyfriends weren't allowed in the club; he also knew exceptions were made. I sensed he wouldn't cope, but knew that dissuading him would make it sound like I had something to hide. 'If it's a quick visit,' I said, 'I suppose it's okay.'

The following Saturday, around 1 a.m., while doing a podium set on the main stage, I saw Matt in the crowd. I flashed him a huge smile. He downed a tumbler of whiskey and turned away. So he was drinking again. Well, a drink or two was probably inevitable tonight.

When I came offstage, I saw Matt had dressed up. He wore a black shirt and suit jacket over black jeans, and the Italian shoes he'd found in a skip. He looked different, harder around the edges. So did I, in my blue sequins and heavy make-up. With my stilettos on we were eye to eye.

'Hi,' I said, catlike with conspiracy.

'*Hi.*' Matt reached out and squeezed my butt.

I grabbed his hand. 'Hey, you can't touch me in here.'

He yanked me to him. I steadied myself against his shoulder, like a ragged waltz. He reeked of whiskey.

A couple of my bread-and-butter customers were watching us with interest. I wriggled out of Matt's grasp. 'Come on, let's go for a dance.'

To my relief, he followed me into the private dancing area. I settled on one of the poky cubicles with frosted glass walls – not where I wanted our first dance to be, but his behaviour made me want to hide. What had got into him? The only other time he'd been like this was Tom's housewarming.

Matt sat down and thumbed the green vinyl with disdain. 'Making a lot of money?'

'It's been all right,' I said honestly, easing onto the arm of his chair.

'Be careful you don't touch me.'

I stood up. 'Would you like me to dance for you or not?'

'Yes. I would like you to dance for me.'

I did, and it was like imitating an imitation. I was hyper-conscious of every move, of all points of contact and the spaces in between, knowing he would be imagining others in his place. Simultaneously, I yearned to dance my best because *it was him* and to dance my worst. I was removing my G when Matt froze, wild-eyed with fear.

'Who *are* you?' His voice rose above the music. 'I don't know you.'

My mouth dropped open. 'Yes, you do. Matt, *it's me.*'

He grabbed my wrist and held me out from him. 'Who the fuck are you?'

'Matt! *Let go.*'

His eyes flickered. He let go.

'Bend over for me,' he said coldly, craning his head.

Hesitantly, I did. In another context it could have been erotic. I hoped he'd suddenly grow playful. He didn't, and I couldn't remember the last time I'd felt so used.

I hung my head and put my clothes back on. Then I smoothed my skirt and considered him.

'What do we do now?' Matt asked.

'Well, we could have a drink.' He didn't need one, but I certainly did. 'Then I'm going back to work.'

We stood at the bar and watched Diamond's genie show. I was glad she was performing, proud of her professionalism, but Matt was unimpressed. Afraid he would make a scene, I wished he would just leave. Instead, he lurked about in the shadows while I worked the floor. As soon as I was rostered off podiums, I took him home. Matt was jovial in the taxi, as if relieved it was all over.

When I woke up mid-morning, my chest ached like I'd smoked too many cigarettes. I shook Matt awake, needing to know why he'd behaved that way.

He cradled his sore head and gazed at me lovingly. 'Did you look amazing? I bet you looked amazing ...'

I stared at him in bewilderment. 'You don't remember?'

'I sort of remember arriving ...'

'Do you remember me dancing for you?'

'You danced for me?'

I nodded sadly. I wanted us to reach an understanding about my stripping. But how could we discuss it now?

* * *

Despite the growing tension between Matt and me, there were many moments of sweetness and generosity. That Christmas, Matt couldn't decide which book to buy me, so he bought them all: nine exposés on stripping, from Dita Von Teese's *Burlesque* to Juliana Beasley's *Lapdancer*. The books affirmed to me that striptease was a complex subject, with a multitude of perspectives and experiences.

At the club, as I moved from one customer to the next, I pondered stripping and where my own ever-shifting truth lay. I knew it depended on my motivations, which were now focused on studying and saving for my future. I didn't want to listen to Matt's misgivings. I wanted to believe that stripping wasn't all bad.

Strip clubs profited from and promoted sexist behaviour – I knew the negatives only too well. They were also spaces where men could relax and be vulnerable, where women could be powerful and take charge. I told myself that strip clubs were one of the few places where women could be unashamedly sexually expressive, and where men could actually *look*. Our culture worshipped physical beauty and used sex to sell; if stripping was a reflection of those fucked-up values, was it fair to blame the strippers? And beyond desire, I had also brought comfort. I'd danced for quadriplegics, for a man released from prison who was dying of AIDS, for a peacekeeper in post-war Iraq who'd told me, 'Yesterday I was in Dubai. Today I'm here, trying to relearn how to relate.'

Over the years I had formulated my own code of ethics, my own responsible service of striptease: make believe, but don't outright lie; maintain control over what happens in a dance; and don't steal, either time or money. I tried not to take advantage of others, but if there were drunks with a hundred dollars burning a hole in their pants I couldn't rescue them from themselves.

Outside of ethics and my relationship to anyone else, there was my relationship with myself. At thirty-one there was finally a grace to the way I carried myself. I luxuriated in my body, in the dance. Yoga teacher training actually made me a better stripper. A toned physique, mental clarity and emotional detachment were alluring qualities; it was no wonder so many strippers had 'yoga kicks asana' stickers on their lockers. Yoga brought the ability to both accept and transcend my reality. The previous year I'd felt old and stiff in my stilettos; now I felt ageless and assured.

I recalled Larissa saying in London, 'You know that feeling, when you just flow and the night flows with you?' I didn't then, but I did now. I would surrender and each night became a continuous stream of encounters, of soft smiles, of propositioning and thanking, of arching and turning and twisting, of unfastening and fastening. I would cease to move, become movement itself. How could that be wrong?

While I continued to doubt the morality of stripping, when it was just me in my panties in the purest of heart-spaces, I knew what I offered was an intimate gift.

Like the time I table danced for a fortyish Chinese woman in a windcheater, jeans and a bum-bag; stripping was banned in China and The Men's Gallery was on the tour bus itinerary. Her pretty face was earnest, which said more than any common language. I was careful not to be overly explicit, but she was bending her head to peer between my legs before my G was even off. Not shy, this one. We exchanged genuine smiles and she returned to her group, beaming.

Or the herculean guy I table danced for, his skull and piercings gleaming. I counted four: a lip stud, two brow bars and a bull ring. He looked up at me with ridiculously soft eyes. I liked him instantly.

'Do you have any other piercings?' I teased.

'Just what you see.' He stuck his studded tongue out at me then grinned. As I danced, emotions shifted across his face like clouds across the sky. He was bemused, playful, enraptured. I draped my hair across his head, went to sit back and realised I was snagged.

'Oh fuck,' I giggled.

'Don't worry,' he said. 'Happens all the time.'

When I was truly present, I felt stripping didn't diminish my relationship with myself or with Matt. But staying truly present: that was where things got tough.

* * *

By 2007 Matt had repaid his debt, got his driver's licence back and started work as a cable technician, a job that involved a lot of driving. This was risky: the Victorian Police had introduced drug testing, and a judge had warned Matt that another DUI charge would most likely result in jail time. Matt still smoked pot daily and drank himself blind occasionally – usually when I was at work – even though it was excessive use of marijuana combined with alcohol that tipped him over the edge.

There was another hiccup after I told Matt's parents I stripped. For me the lie had become impossible to live with and, like my parents years before, they refused to discuss it. Matt was also upset, still hoping I would quit, while I still hoped he might come around to my way of thinking. That was why I agreed to him coming into the club a second time if he promised not to touch and not to drink.

Matt didn't try to touch, but he was drunk. In the taxi on the way home, he said he'd been tongue-kissed in the lounge bar by a girl on her hen's night. Had he said that to make me jealous? I wasn't. Then he said Diamond had tried to persuade him to have a private dance, saying, 'I want you, baby, I want you now.' He added proudly, 'I know you'd never say that.'

I thought I'd won a victory of sorts – until the next day. It was Chinese New Year, the Victoria Street Festival. I spent the afternoon napping. Matt spent it drinking at the festival, and came home around midnight. He wanted to make love, but I was too tired.

'Can't you just try?' he said. So I tried. But I wasn't feeling it and refused to fake it, not with him.

Matt jumped up and began pacing the room. 'How can you do that? You make me feel so fucking low!'

I tried to catch his hands, but he shook me off.

Then it all came out, all the words he could never say when sober or straight. Matt didn't stop until I screamed so loudly it popped my ears. He saw me doubled over, fists in my sodden mouth, and grabbed me. I kicked out at him; he held me straitjacket tight until I went limp.

I crawled across the floor and under the doona. Matt got in and held me. Then he began to cry, softly at first, then great wracking sobs. 'I want you, I want *all* of you, and you don't fucking want me. What do I do with this sexual energy? Do I go out and sleep with other people?'

Maybe he should; I didn't know anymore. He got more of me than anyone ever had, yet it still wasn't enough.

'Every time you go to work, I'm in agony.'

'What do you want from me?' I asked.

'*Commitment,*' he said.

Once I'd thought that was something I wanted. I was no longer sure.

14.

MANIA: AN ABNORMALLY HEIGHTENED MOOD characterised by increased energy, irritability and rapid speech, sometimes accompanied by recklessness, promiscuity and delusions. I thought severe mania would be easy to spot, but I was too close to see clearly. And I wanted so much for Matt to be well that I took any sign of activity as proof that he was improving. Until it became obvious he wasn't.

That winter I came home from the club most weekends to find Matt still out. The lights would be on, the heater too, the balcony door open. I would follow the trail of empty glasses and beer bottles, trying to gauge his state when he left the house. Then I'd call his phone, but Matt rarely answered – perhaps because I'd stopped taking his calls at work, which were often requests to visit. He would usually trip in the door around dawn, crawl into bed and turn from me. Where he went, I wasn't sure. Bars and pubs, he said. Occasionally other strip clubs to understand me better, something I thought was a waste of money.

I thought about speaking to his parents, but I didn't want to worry them or betray Matt, who was generally okay for work by Monday. And I didn't want to cop the blame. So I said nothing. Not after the night Matt staggered home with a black eye; not even after the night when he didn't come home at all.

I told myself Matt's psychiatrist would pick up on it. He already had, as had Matt's parents. His psychiatrist asked me to encourage Matt to start medication or else he would lose control. I tried, but of course he wouldn't – after months of feeling like shit, he was on top of the world.

I've never seen a tornado but I imagine severe mania is like that. An upward spiral that collects everything in its path, flinging it skywards. Afterwards you're left sifting through the wreckage for clues of your former life.

Matt's job went first. Then everything sped up until he couldn't sit still or sleep. When he was finally hospitalised – voluntarily, on the condition that there was a piano – he was beyond reasoning with, and his parents and I were exhausted.

I visited him most afternoons to find the medication was slowly bringing him back down. Matt would convince the harangued nurses into letting him go out for another walk. He would hurry towards the city and I'd try to keep up.

The afternoon Matt strode into Allans Music, I knew my old regular Liam would be working. He was. And I could tell from the look on his face that Matt had been there before. We watched Matt sit down at a baby grand.

'Hey, Fluffy.' Liam had filled out; his goatee was tinged grey.

'Is it all right, him playing?' I asked.

'Yeah, it's fine. He plays well, which is more than I can say for most.'

'Do you still play?'

'Nah, working here has put me off. Are you still at Men's?'

I nodded. Liam touched my shoulder. 'Tell him he's welcome here any time.'

Tearing up at his kindness, I watched Liam walk away.

Despite everything, I was grateful to be able to work, knowing Matt was safe. That Tuesday, the small habitual preparations held me: the dusting of a cheek, the affixing of a garter, the baby-wiping of a shoe. I performed each task with care and gratitude.

Up on the floor I worked with empty efficiency. Then, around 11 p.m., I played the poor-stripper card for the first time ever.

A cherub-faced man gestured for me to join him. He looked a boyish forty, wore jeans and a polo shirt, and had a can of Red Bull in front of him. 'I've been watching you. You are a hard worker, but not impolite.' He held out a fifty. 'Take this – you deserve it.' I took the money and thanked the man, whose name was Sandeep. He was from India, but I pointed out his accent was slightly American.

'You are perceptive!' He chuckled. 'I have a hotel in Florida.' Then he laughed again, this time at a dancer glowering at us from table 3. 'Look, she's jealous! I'd better go and cheer her up.' Sandeep bounced out of his chair, slipped her a fifty, bounced back. 'She's a pretty girl, but she's young.' He clasped his stubby hands over his belly. 'What else do you do? I can tell you do something.' I said I was studying to teach yoga. He laughed loudly. 'Yoga! In India that is commonplace, everyone does yoga.' Then he bought me a champagne, himself another Red Bull and said, 'I'm thinking of opening a hotel here. My family owns hotels. I am lucky, I have money.' He said this without a hint of pride. Then he said, 'I'd like to go out with you sometime, Juliette. What do you think?'

I thought the question had come much earlier than expected. 'I don't think my boyfriend would like that.'

'He can come, no worries,' said Sandeep. 'I don't know many people in Melbourne. I like to make friends.'

'To be honest, my boyfriend is unwell. He's been hospitalised.' I met Sandeep's eyes. 'I can't afford to take time off.'

The lie was out my mouth before I knew it.

Sandeep looked concerned. 'What's wrong with him?'

'He has bipolar disorder.'

'Oh, that is not good. What would it take for him to be well?'

'That's an excellent question. I don't know.'

'You must love him very much.'

'Well, yes.'

'If you love him, then he must be a good person.'

'He is,' I said, feeling anything but.

Sandeep handed me another hundred and the talk turned to India. Before leaving, he asked when I was working next. I said Friday, depending on Matt. Sandeep asked how much I made on a Friday.

I lied and said eight hundred.

He patted my hand. 'Friday, I will pay you eight hundred dollars and you do not need to worry about working to support your boyfriend. Just talk with me and have some fun.'

Suddenly, I wanted to work Friday if I could.

Matt came home on Thursday. That evening when the Crisis Action Team made the first of their home visits, I asked if I should continue dancing. They didn't see why not – Matt's medication knocked him out for ten hours each night. Scowling, Matt turned away.

By Friday, my anticipation had turned to remorse. I left for the club feeling guilty for hurting Matt and lying to Sandeep. I found Sandeep at the main bar with a bottle of Veuve. I didn't feel like drinking, but it was expected and perhaps bubbles would lighten my mood. Sandeep was in an exceptionally good one – he'd found a potential site for his hotel. As time passed – time I was more aware of, having been prepaid – many dancers stopped to chat, knowing Sandeep would tip them or buy them drinks. I didn't mind. Although I was trying, I couldn't rouse much frivolity.

By 2 a.m., I was the unhappiest eight-hundred-dollar stripper in the house. Sandeep and I had retired to a quiet corner and were pretend-relaxing. I'd stopped drinking; every glass made me more miserable. Smart man that he was, Sandeep noticed. He pressed something into my hand. A Visa card.

'I want you to have this. Take as much as you need for your boyfriend to get well.'

'Sandeep, I can't accept this.' I tried to give the card back.

'Juliette, please. Put it in your wallet and forget about it. One day you may need it.' Sandeep looked at me earnestly. 'I have a lot of money. What's the point of having money if I can't help people?'

I sat there staring at the card. It had finally happened. I'd heard of customers buying dancers convertibles, financing businesses, paying off debt, but I'd never known how it was done. All I'd had to do was lie convincingly.

Sandeep then gave me his business card with his pin number written on it. 'If you need more than the daily limit, call me and I will make the deposit.'

'Thank you.' I stared at him, stunned. 'Why would you do this? You hardly know me.'

'Yes, but I know people and I can tell you help others. Now it is my turn to help you.' Sandeep patted my knee. 'Go home – you are tired. When I am next in town I will come and see you and we will go out, you and me and your boyfriend.'

Well, I knew that would never happen. I tucked the card into my wallet and, surprisingly, forgot about it. Months later, I would find it and cut it up, unused. I would never see Sandeep again.

* * *

I graduated as a yoga instructor, two weeks after Matt's hospitalisation. I felt relieved the back-to-back weekends were over, to have more time to myself. Although I was qualified, the thought of actually teaching yoga scared me shitless. I didn't feel ready.

Six months later, Jeremy a yoga instructor friend, asked if I would like to teach a weekly Monday evening class. He had found a room for hire in a nearby church and was looking for someone to go halves. I still didn't feel ready. Jeremy persuaded me to say yes.

The room was a carpeted alcove adjacent to the nave, with high ceilings, leadlight windows and sturdy bookcases full of Christian literature. I wondered if my class should come with a disclaimer, to assure students that the only practice I was trying to convert them to was yoga. I set to work creating a flyer and mailbox-bombing the area. That generated a single inquiry. Then Matt's brother and his girlfriend said they'd come. Matt was keen too. I had four students.

The first class, I wore my black uniform by default and instantly regretted it. I felt like I was masquerading as a disciple of some fringe Christian yoga cult. After I'd vacuumed up pieces of biscuit and what looked like dried cucumber, I lit some candles. Then I sat up front trying not to hyperventilate while Matt reviewed the church brochures with sardonic good humour. Before I knew it, my student family had arrived and were looking at me expectantly. I instructed everyone to lie down so they couldn't see my terror. Then I began parroting my teachers' words, saying some of those truly stupid things such as 'touch the ceiling' and 'let your sit-bones melt'.

The only thing melting was my lotus-shaped candelabra, on the altar behind me. A gust of wind had swept under the door and set it on fire. Class paused while I emptied my water bottle over the flames then carried the smouldering remains outside.

To my amazement, everyone enjoyed the class, at least more than I'd enjoyed teaching it. It was great to have Matt proud of me too. And I was touched by his family's support. They formed the core of my class while it lasted.

Each week, at least one new student came along, but despite positive feedback they all stopped coming. I didn't blame them.

Possibly, a small class was too intimate; perhaps the venue was wrong. Certainly, I was giving off a weird vibe.

After six weeks, my nervousness had only increased. I dreaded Mondays. I worried I'd get busted as a stripper. Deceiving students was un-yogic, difficult to brush under the crumb-coated carpet, but it wasn't enough to warrant my almost paralysing stage fright. What was going on?

Then one night during class, I spied a heavy bronze crucifix on top of a bookcase. Memories flooded back and at last I understood what was happening. When I was sixteen I'd lost my virginity in a church. It hadn't been planned nor was it exactly consensual.

I'd been part of an interschool performance troupe. Our show was African themed and we stomped around whooping and hollering. Lots of the girls were smitten with Jeff, a tall Islander who looked sensational in a loincloth. By then I was used to being noticed by the opposite sex and was fast figuring out that could be as powerful as it was annoying. I flirted with Jeff, hot and cold, the way precocious teenage girls did. He invited me over to his boarding house one night. I snuck out of my own boarding house and loitered near Jeff's school gates till he emerged from the darkness. In a tracksuit instead of a loincloth he wasn't so appealing. We stared at each other awkwardly. He offered to give me a guided tour. Jeff was on lock-up, which meant securing all the school buildings. I trailed him around, getting more bored by the minute.

The final building was the Victorian chapel. Instead of locking the heavy doors, Jeff pushed them open. I followed him up the aisle towards the altar. Now I was interested. This was one place

I definitely shouldn't be. Wordlessly, we began kissing. It felt awesomely illicit to be making out in a church. I almost giggled at my audacity. My hero Madonna might have done something like this. Soon Jeff and I were rolling around under the altar, half-naked. Then before I knew it, he was forcing his way inside me.

Instinctively I froze, from the shock as much as the pain. Why didn't he ask? I thought. Should I tell him to stop?

I wasn't sure I wanted him to stop. Nothing this significant had happened in years. And losing your virginity was a hot topic at school. Now I would have a good story to tell, if that – this – was what I wanted.

I considered my situation: no one knew where I was; no one would hear me; Jeff was stronger than me. The thought that he might not stop if I protested was worse than pretending to be willing. So I just lay there and looked up at Christ on his cross. Afterwards, I took a scalding shower and binned my knickers.

I endured a lecture from the irate doctor who prescribed the morning-after pill, and told Jeff I didn't want to see him again. To my astonishment, he cried. I took responsibility. Then I moved on and eventually it ceased to be a big deal.

In this other church, confronting my past while people looked to me for guidance, I understood I hadn't had closure, and I wasn't okay with what had happened. Which in its own way was okay too.

Not for the first time I considered what impact the experience had on my initial decision to strip. I'd read enough to know that a high percentage of strippers and prostitutes had a history of sexual assault. I also knew plenty of strippers who didn't, as well as women who had been assaulted and hadn't chosen sex work.

While the encounter was probably a factor, I felt it was more a case of stripping allowing me to embrace the parts of myself that I had been discouraged from being at eighteen – extroverted, sexual and individual.

Slowly I stopped blaming myself, under the guise of ownership, for what had happened.

When Jeremy decided to let the space go, I was glad. He went to Peru and drank ayahuasca, a medicinal plant that induces purging, which sounded horrible. Before he left he offered me a class at a suburban YMCA on Tuesday nights. I took it. They were thirty strong, mostly in their fifties and sixties with enough life experience to know that everyone has to start somewhere. Slowly my confidence as a teacher grew. I dropped back to Thursday and Saturday nights at the club. It was a precarious balance, tightrope walking between the light and the shadow, but I'd finally started moving forward.

* * *

There was one setback: I had snared myself a devoted regular. I'd never had one, never wanted one, before Thursday Man. At first he had come into the club every second week and danced with me and several other girls. He was polite, respectful and shy. While I knew he was from Malaysia, drank Carlsberg and had fifty-dollar dances, I couldn't remember his name.

In January, after a four-week break, all that changed. I was on table 3, clinging to the pole and struggling to settle back into my stilettos when Thursday Man sauntered in. Tall and slim, he moved easefully in his tan summer suit. Glancing around, he saw me and smiled. My face lit up. I was saved! After my set, I charged over to his table and pecked his waxy cheek, catching a whiff of day-old cologne, something nautical. Then I sat opposite, cupped my chin and tried to look embodied. We chatted for a while and I asked him if he wanted a dance.

'Oh, yes please.'

With that, I was out of my chair, into a private room. Thursday Man opened his wallet like a spinnaker to the wind. He pulled out a fifty; I caught myself licking my lips and was momentarily horrified. How indiscreet! Slowly, I began to strip. His undemanding appreciation soothed me. I could do this; it was going to be okay.

The club was quiet, so I made an exception and sat with him again. He told me he was a financial analyst for the Royal Australian Navy; I told him I'd worked for the public service in London. We had another dance. Then he requested a third.

'You're spoiling me,' I said, pleasantly surprised.

'I'm making up for lost time,' he said.

At 11 p.m., just as the customer-to-dancer ratio improved, he sailed out the door.

From then on, Thursday Man came in every week and only danced with me – three fifty-dollar privates, sometimes four. He arrived before the club got busy, so I was content to sit and chat first. It helped with the transition from Matt-and-yoga time to sexy time. And Thursday Man was easy to talk to, uncomplicated.

He laughed when I admitted to forgetting his name.

'It's Joseph,' he said. 'I know yours isn't Juliette, but that's okay.'

'It's Rebecca.' My second name.

He told me his age (forty-five). I told him my real age (thirty-three), not my stripper age (twenty-seven). He said he caught the train to work, except on Thursdays when he drove partway then trammed in and out to collect his car. 'Such effort!' I said.

'It's worth it to see you,' he replied.

He also told me that his elderly mother lived with him. 'I hope I'm not putting you off,' he added. I said, 'I think that's very good of you.'

I'd never played a regular before, not deliberately. But when Joseph asked me out for dinner, I said I'd think about it. Honestly? I liked the idea of going out with him, somewhere discerning and understated, a Teppanyaki restaurant perhaps. Other girls fantasised about marriage proposals or gang rape. Not me. I wanted a paid date and wagyu, that's how dysfunctional my life had become.

When Valentine's Day fell on a Thursday, I put my regular ahead of my relationship. I didn't believe in Valentine's Day and my love for Matt had never been about commercial gestures, yet that Thursday night in February I left some heart-shaped chocolates on the kitchen bench with a note: *Happy Valentine's Day, because this nonbeliever believes in you.* And I did, even if guilt motivated me to express it.

At the club, Carole's desk was coffin-coated with flowers. More than one person had bought lilies. Liking the irony, I glanced at the cards. None was for me. Would Joseph bring me flowers?

In the first booth, a red satin cushion had been tossed in the bin. *Be Mine!* it declared. Then one of the day girls, Harley, held up a pair of slippers. 'Anyone want these?' Harley never took presents home out of respect for her husband. 'Vibrating slippers, anyone?'

'Hah! Yeah, maybe,' I said, recognising that despite statements to the contrary, I did want a gift. I put on the slippers. The pulsing felt weird. Nice weird. Good quality fur too. The guy must've thought this one out.

Up on the floor there were fewer groups, more single men. These lonely hearts were glad to have a Valentine, even one they had to pay for. Unsurprisingly, 14 February was a solid moneymaking night.

Joseph brightened when he saw me. 'I didn't know if you'd be here.'

'I didn't know if you would be either,' I said. 'I thought you might be out on a hot date.'

'Me? No.' But I could tell he enjoyed the suggestion.

Joseph hadn't bought me anything.

Matt had. I came home to a big bunch of peonies and a note. *I wasn't going to buy you flowers because there's nothing special about today. But I realised I was just being spiteful and there's so much that's special about you, so Happy Valentine's, my Valentine! Thank you for being in my life and bringing me so much joy. I miss you tonight but I'm so happy I'm the one you're coming home to.*

My deception worsened. After I skipped a Thursday and had no way of letting Joseph know, I suggested exchanging phone numbers 'as a courtesy'. This was a contractual no-no although other dancers did it; some even had separate mobiles. I trusted Joseph wouldn't text or call unnecessarily. But the next time I danced for him he said, 'I love you,' so joyfully I couldn't pretend not to have heard.

He said it again; I gave him a distant smile. Then his eyes sought mine. 'I love you, Rebecca! Why do you think I come here?'

I winced. 'Joseph … I don't know what to say.'

I felt awful. I was so bothered by my complicity in this I went home after Joseph left.

'Console yourself with the knowledge he's spent a couple of grand on you,' Matt said. It wasn't consoling. I half-expected not to see Joseph again, but if I did, the deception had to stop.

The following Thursday, Joseph was back. He pulled a disappointed face and said, 'I don't know what to do with you.'

I sighed. It was pointless reminding him that that was precisely the point: he didn't get to *do* anything. 'Perhaps you should stop coming here,' I said. 'You're a wonderful man, but this is my job.'

'Thank you for your advice, Juliette,' he said evenly. 'I appreciate it.'

I searched Joseph's face. 'This is supposed to be enjoyable.'

He permitted a small smile. 'It's still enjoyable.'

The next week Joseph was oddly distant, walking away after our first dance instead of booking me for another. I let it go. All regulars have a use-by date and he was souring as fast as spoiled milk.

Joseph was still in the venue an hour later, so I went up to him. He raised his eyebrows.

'Would you like another dance?' I asked, more meekly than intended.

'One more.'

'I wasn't sure …'

'Tonight, I thought I'd leave the asking up to you,' he said coolly, 'to see if you wanted to dance for me.'

'Oh, okay,' I said brightly. Why wouldn't I? *You pay me.*

A part of me wished Joseph would just go away. Another part wanted him to keep coming in. The more yoga I taught, the less I wanted to hard-hustle. Joseph was a known quantity, navigable despite his occasional outbursts. I liked that he kept me busy when the club was quiet, that increasingly he paid me to discuss politics and bad TV. If there was ever a patron saint of strippers, Joseph was it.

Three months turned into six, then nine. By September, Joseph looked away when I removed my G, while I ignored his declarations of love. The charade weighed heavily, though. I was thinking of cutting back to just Saturdays when Joseph announced he was going to Las Vegas on holiday.

'I'll miss you, Rebecca,' he said. 'Three whole weeks without you.'

'You'll be in Vegas! It's the showgirl capital of the world.'

'But you won't be there. I love you, I really do.'

My mouth twisted. 'Joseph ...'

He put a finger to his lips. 'You don't need to say anything.'

'No, I do. I feel bad sometimes. You know I'm seeing someone, don't you?' Knowing he didn't.

His eyes hardened, but that was all. 'Thank you for your honesty, Juliette, it's overdue.'

I felt rage then. Look at where you are! A *strip club*, into which you freely walked!

Seeing my scowl, Joseph spent more on me that night than he ever had.

The professionalism I'd prided myself on had faded. I wondered how low I'd go, and what would be left.

One night a middle-aged Pakistani man strode up to me and began humping my leg like a dog. That had never happened before – I'd never emitted the sort of vibe that encouraged it. I watched him, curiously detached.

'I am so close to orgasm,' he puffed. 'Can I come while you strip?'

You peculiar man, I thought, wanting to come in your pressed pants. 'Be my guest,' I said. Then I stripped a metre away while he thrust at the air.

'You did not keep your part of the deal!' He frowned.

'I said you could come,' I said coldly. 'I didn't say I'd help you.'

'You are a liar.'

'Yeah? Well, you're a filthy pig. Fuck off before I call security.'

He did.

Another night I pretended I was Russian and spoke little English. Partway through the dance I dropped the act. The guy was furious. I didn't care.

I didn't care when Joseph returned either.

'You know what I've missed most? Our conversations,' he said, smiling. I planted one stiletto on his chair and ground my cunt centimetres from his face. His mouth pursed. 'That's enough, thank you, Juliette,' Joseph said tightly. He stood up and walked out. I thought it was about time. But the following week, he was back.

* * *

By November 2008, I was teaching two weekly yoga classes, plus covers. And I was taking classes with a popular yoga teacher, Anthony, who had taught me back in 2000. He'd been a choreographer and understood the lure of the stage. Anthony's classes were a delicious blend of movement, mantra, visualisation and breath work, spliced with laugher. Anthony himself was an overflowing bubble-machine of joy. He sported a Hare Krishna ponytail, numerous tattoos and brightly coloured threads. Anthony was proof that life beyond the stage was potentially richer than I'd imagined.

One day Anthony encouraged us to perform a fire ritual – to burn something that symbolised what we would like to let go of, then light a candle to something we'd like more of in our lives. I built a funeral pyre out of old costumes, then lit a candle to more permanent classes. Within hours, I'd been offered two, both on a Thursday night. I let go of Thursdays at the club, believing – almost hoping – it would be the end of Joseph.

It wasn't. Joseph swapped to Saturdays, my one remaining night. Saturdays were still the busiest night, so our chats grew shorter. A once-weekly dive into club-land was paid playtime, a welcome relief from the responsibility of teaching. I could've kept it up, if I hadn't been spotted.

I was onstage when I noticed one of my students observing me from the bar. I ignored him, hoping that context would skew any connection. After our next yoga class, he asked, 'You don't by chance moonlight as a table dancer, do you?' I laughed. 'Why, do I look like someone you know?' Embarrassed, he changed the subject. But I knew it wouldn't be long before I was outed. Melbourne's yoga community was close-knit and world class. If I wanted my peers to take me seriously, I needed to practise the *yamas* and *niyamas*, yoga's ethical codes. That included *brahmacharya*, 'rightful use of sexual energy'. And that meant quitting my public flashing for money.

Friends of Matt's had opened a café and were looking for a part-time kitchen hand. It was dish-pig pay with 7 a.m. starts, but they were prepared to roster around my classes. Before I knew it, I had another class, then another. I had planned to strip occasionally, but there wasn't time and I was making enough to scrape by. Although I could see the neon lights of King Street from the café, the club seemed a world away. Instead, I spent Saturday nights with Matt. We would go out for dinner or a movie, or stay in. I still wore Lycra, only it was mostly black. And at the café, in sinks of hot, soapy water, I washed myself clean.

15.

TEACHING YOGA GAVE ME PURPOSE. IT BROUGHT
moments of deep contentment and joy knowing I was helping
others. It was also stressful: I'd spent most of my training half-
asleep, absorbing information by osmosis. Determined to deliver,
I committed the ultimate spiritual sin, shunning my shadow
and striding blinkered towards the light. Yoga became another
performance, another podium set. I stretched on my smile, faked
some positivity and tried to inspire. It was exhausting.

So was my relationship with Matt. Quitting stripping hadn't
improved his mental health. While he was now taking a new
prescription medication, he was still struggling and still self-
medicating. By late 2009, we needed a break, a holiday, perhaps
both. We booked flights to Thailand for January, thinking the land
of smiles would be relaxed, easy travel. But by the time Matt and

I arrived on remote Koh Phayam, he was too depressed to enjoy himself. He smoked a little pot, hoping it would lift him. It did: into three weeks of mania. I lost Matt for days. It was no holiday: I spent my waking hours searching the island, trying to find Matt, petrified he had been arrested. Fortunately he reappeared, delusional but unharmed. Once he stopped partying, his medication kicked in and he stabilised. We went on to have a week in Chiang Mai as planned, and I fell in love with the northern city's Buddhist temples, diverse populace and vibrant yoga community. I vowed to return.

We went back to Melbourne broke, and broken. I was bitter and Matt was full of remorse, yet still unable to overcome his addictions. I wondered what that might take, and if I should leave him. I still believed he could get well. And against all rationale, I hoped he might be able to live and work overseas with me. That was my new plan: to save up, go to Asia and teach English.

I was thirty-five: I reasoned that this was my last chance to dance my way into my next manifestation. After months of the minimum wage I just wanted to go back to what I knew and to be rewarded for it.

I dug out my suitcase of costumes from the back of the wardrobe. Inside were the hallmarks of my former self: the blue sequinned three-piece, the cat and army show costumes, the manky PVC thigh-highs. Seeing these items again I realised I was always going to go back.

Stripping was my safety net, my back-up plan when all else failed. Yoga hadn't sustained me. Love hadn't cured all. But stripping, stripping had never let me down. Eighteen months after the sacrificial bonfire, Juliette rose from the ashes.

* * *

I walked into the dressing-room in time to hear two dancers discussing anal bleaching. A second pair's topic was designer babies. 'I get so frustrated with people who deplore embryonic stem cell research on ill-thought-out religious grounds.' The other laughed. 'You're going straight to hell, firstly for bagging the religious right and secondly for being a stripper.'

I smiled. It was good to be back, whether Matt liked it or not.

I didn't recognise many faces. The old line I'd flipped at customers appeared to be true: every time you walked into the club, the girls got younger. Except for me – and Harlow. I couldn't believe she was back after the cricket scandal. She must've done some serious butt-kissing. She was also training the new girls. Penance, perhaps?

'Sometimes you need to go and do something else for a while, don't you?' she said, after we'd air-kissed. 'I had five years out of the industry, babe. Five years! I needed a break, but I'm so happy to be here.' And she looked it. She had returned to retail in the interim, saying her ex-boyfriend had forbidden her to dance. I couldn't imagine anyone telling Harlow what to do, but then I'd thought that about myself once.

Remembering Harlow's dream house in Brighton, I asked her what she was saving for. 'You know me,' she chuckled, 'always a goal. I want to pay off my new convertible, then I'm saving for my retirement. Five more years and I'll never have to work again.'

'Wow,' I said, wondering if I should push on and pay off the investment property I'd finally bought. I shuddered at the thought.

At Harlow's age, it almost made sense. She must've been forty-five. The only telltale signs were the creases around her mouth. In the darkened club, with the help of plastic surgery, botox and great genes, Harlow looked her stripper year (thirty-two). She was more age defying than a Revlon commercial.

(Meanwhile, I'd given myself a serious waxing and had been shocked to discover my labia had wrinkles. Surgery wasn't tempting, but sadly it appeared age affected all vital organs.)

Harlow told me that the old crew had disbanded. Cameron had a full-time job in finance but still did the occasional shift, while Diamond had moved interstate seeking a fresh start. I knew it was unlikely I would see Diamond again: most full-timers cut ties with the industry when they quit, like a bad habit.

Carole had also left, wanting to spend more time with her kids. The new house mum was an ex-stripper called Dani. She reminded me of Sunny McKay: quiet, librarian sexy with thin hair and thick glasses. Dani was down-to-earth and I liked her instantly, but I missed Carole's upbeat quirkiness – the way she decorated the roster with star stickers, the way she believed in second chances.

My other surrogate parent, Stanley the MC, had stopped spruiking Herbalife and started vending MonaVie. All the girls were going gaga over the açai berries' concentrated energy boost. Finally, Stanley was onto a winner.

George the masseur hadn't been so lucky. He'd been fired after skipping too many Saturdays for bush doofs, and hadn't been replaced. I missed his healing hands at the end of a long shift.

A surprise addition was the new chef, Jules. He was a beautiful bear of a man who minced around in short shorts and dished up fairy bread at sandwich time. The girls lapped up his love, even if some of the customers looked confused by his presence.

Unsurprisingly, they hadn't changed. Vietnam Phil was still propped at the end of the bar, though I didn't bother acknowledging him anymore. Weatherman John still appeared most Fridays and some Saturdays. 'I couldn't really see you teaching yoga,' he said. 'Not even nude yoga?' I asked rhetorically. Ralph still came in too. He'd cancelled his life insurance, which meant he could afford two more private dances a month. 'Do you have life insurance, Juliette?' he asked. Thinking, *No, Ralph, I have stripping*, I shook my head. Ralph smiled, reassured he had made the right decision.

I had been back a month when Joseph sauntered in.

'Juliette! I never thought I'd see you again.' He managed a small smile. 'The other girls have been looking after me, but it's not the same.'

Joseph could have called me; I was grateful he never had. And I was relieved he was happy to see me – it made the afterlife much easier. This time, though, I didn't have the energy for grey areas or guilt. I told Joseph my travel plans upfront, which technically gave him a year to rescue me. He was still number crunching, still single, still looking after his mother. And soon he was coming in every Saturday to see me. This time, as every dollar went towards my future reality, I had no problem selling Joseph a fantasy.

There was a cold detachment to the way I worked now. Juliette was all smiles, but soulless. I felt empty, like the goodness had been sapped out of me. Increasingly I struggled to care. The little remaining hope I had for a fully clothed, functioning future with

Matt faded with every passing week. I knew that if I continued to strip I would stay numb, my sadness at bay. It was a horrible way to live, but an effective way to work. I was untouchable, unaffected. There was just a sliver of my heart left, frozen deep inside, waiting for the tropics to thaw it out. I suspected when that happened there would be plenty of tears.

* * *

The Men's Gallery was changing and the first major change was to group functions. Function girls were to attend a compulsory information session. One Friday, about fifteen of us trudged into the VIP room and sat around the massive table while Dani outlined the upgrade. In addition to standard fifty-dollar functions, the club would be offering eighty-dollar 'raunchies' or $240 'lesbians'. Raunchies meant using ice, candlewax or shaving cream on yourself and the buck. My main issue with getting mucky was to do with aesthetics: raunchies would ruin my Sally Hansen fake tan. At thirty dollars a can, it almost cancelled out the financial gain. And lesbian pseudo sex? I wouldn't be able to sell Matt on the idea. Could I sell myself?

'You'll be getting a hundred and twenty dollars each for a lesbian, so they need to look real,' said Dani. 'To give you an idea of what's expected, Eve and Brooke are going to demo.'

A group cheer went up. There aren't many workplaces where your colleagues strip off at staff meetings and feign sex on the boardroom table. Eve and Brooke were two unashamedly sexual young strippers rising up the ranks. They were girls who could handle themselves – and each other. While we watched, the pair undressed one another with unbelievable enthusiasm. They writhed around, suggesting positions and sequencing, as if enacting a *Dummies Guide to Soft-core Smut.*

Brooke lay back. 'Just lick your own fingers, like this,' said Eve, then pressed her hand between Brooke's thighs. Brooke affected a porn-face of pleasure. With strategically placed hair and hands, it was a convincing simulation. It was also difficult to tell where said simulation ended and actual stimulation started, for there was plenty of tongue kissing and nipple grazing. The guys were in for a treat.

'If you'd like to do lesbians, think of a dancer you'd like to do them with,' said Dani. 'They have to look real, so you need to be comfortable with each other. You can't just do them with anyone.'

I glanced around at the other dancers, most of whom I didn't know. There wasn't anyone I felt comfortable sort-of chowing down on.

Still, I was curious about the legalities. 'Dani, Carole always said if it looked like we were doing it, then we were as good as doing it,' I said, all patent-leather prim. 'That meant instant dismissal, because the club could lose its licence.'

'Don't worry, you can do it now,' Dani said airily. 'It's all changing.'

And so it was. The popularity of the internet – especially live chat – was forcing strip clubs to reinvent themselves. But I decided to stay a stock-standard, vanilla-function kinda girl, attempting to preserve my tan, what was left of my relationship with Matt, and my tenuous definition of dancer dignity.

Soon the stage shows got raunchy too. Every second showgirl was scorching her labia with candlewax or soaping herself up. Previously water shows had been banned; now the stage was awash, a virtual theme park of fantastic proportions as dancers slippery-slid from pole to pole like bare-bottomed toddlers. The guys in the front row lurched back from the slops and we older girls tsked, 'You never used to be allowed to do *that*.'

In comparison, I was still flogging the same two 'clean' shows – army and cat. These were at least five years old now. My army girl had become a veteran, my cat Garfield. I hoped that if I kept my head down and my butt up, no one would notice I wasn't doing my portion of the stage washing.

Then one night Dani took me aside and said, 'If you want to keep doing shows, you'll need to come up with a new one.'

'Sure. I've been meaning to anyway,' I lied.

Truthfully? I didn't want to do shows anymore. It was paralysing being visually consumed by so many men at once when I already felt hollowed out by all that Matt and I had been through. During shows I struggled to keep the discomfort from my face, but I wanted to pay a house fee even less. With fees now seventy dollars, there was no shortage of prima sellerinas. I knew Dani was serious about this and that I had to make an effort.

The only way for me to go was highbrow, with a more elaborate costume and props. Years ago in Venice I'd bought a masquerade mask from an old *mascareri* who'd insisted he was the master craftsman behind the film *Eyes Wide Shut*. The half-mask was gold leaf, edged with resplendent green-black feathers. It would cover both the cracks in Juliette's persona and my bottom line.

I tied my hair back and teamed the mask with a satin corset, a hooped tutu, my PVC thigh-highs and opera gloves tipped with Thai dancing talons. The black-and-gold outfit was the most breathtaking I'd ever worn, and not just because of the boning. While Lady Gaga pokerfaced and Goldfrapp ooh la la'd, I scratched and preened like a hybrid human-bird.

There was great comfort in wearing the mask. Now I understood why so many strippers covered their eyes with 'secretary' glasses. Why we wore fake tan like a second skin, shedding it in the shower at the end of every shift. We might've been naked, but we weren't revealing all of ourselves.

I didn't want to take the mask off. From a sales perspective, though, the customers needed to know who that weird bird was. I waited until the last thirty seconds of my six-minute act and tried to keep my expression soft.

In contrast, I ripped the corset off straightaway. For the first time in my un-career, I let myself become a faceless vessel for sexual fantasy, perhaps because I had so little left to give. Flirting with self-destruction was freeing, but bitter anger rose up inside me as I stared at my audience with glassy, cock-eyed coldness. Most stared back expressionlessly, some looked a bit freaked out. I had to stop myself from taking it too far – lashing out or storming offstage. Even if I was struggling with being seen, every person watching was still worthy of recognition. If yoga hadn't taught me that, then stripping certainly had.

After a few weeks of applying my old choreography to the new show, I decided it was time to up-skill, to make a last-minute ladder climb and go back to school. Pole school.

Pole dancing hit the mainstream in the mid-2000s. In 2004, an ex-stripper had opened Melbourne's first studio chain, Pole Divas. Pole Princess and Dolls on Poles were hot on its tush. By 2010, pole dancing had become the latest fitness craze. Girls who had dissed stripping were strapping on Pleasers and exposing their butt-cheeks in broad daylight. Some had even made the transition to table dancing. And as these so-called amateurs began showing us professionals up, we began taking pole classes too. Many strippers were inspired by the swift global success of Perth girl Felix Cane.

Diamond had returned from the west in 2006, prophesying the meteoric rise of a young dancer called Felix who could do extraordinary things with the pole. 'She's gonna be the next big thing, mark my words,' Diamond had said. So when The Men's Gallery brought Felix to Melbourne, I was keen to watch her perform. Looking like a young Liza Minnelli à la *Cabaret* in a trench coat and bowler hat, Felix moved with sinuous agility, scaling the pole with gravity-defying grace. She was self-contained; she possessed an un-stripper-like humility. The other girls stood open-mouthed, not knowing whether to befriend her or ask for her autograph. Felix went on to win Miss Pole Dance Australia in 2006, then Miss Pole Dance World in 2009. Like many fans, I scoured YouTube for clips of her awesomeness.

While I knew I wasn't about to become a Cirque de Soleil aerial artiste in my advanced years, I hoped pole school could teach me a new trick or two. My co-workers recommended Pole Divas. Its website was as pink and fresh as a thirteen-year-old girl's bedroom. 'Unleash your inhibitions and inspire your inner feline to come out and play,' it encouraged. My inner feline had been out for years: it needed to be caged or retired. Nevertheless, I read on. Pole Divas offered beginners, intermediate and advanced classes. *All* students had to start in beginners. I already got paid to pole dance and I didn't see the point in paying to start over. Surely I'd be eligible for recognition of prior learning? I phoned up to find out.

'We'll need to grade you,' said the receptionist, with bucket-loads of enthusiasm that left me cowering in my own living room. 'Can you come in Wednesday at 5 p.m.?'

I could.

That Wednesday I stuffed my rotting thigh-high boots and a pair of pink running shorts into a bag and headed for Pole Divas, Prahran. Pushing open the front door I was met by the tinny sound of the Pussycat Dolls deep-throating 'Don't Cha'. So far, so similar. The reception area was lined with racks of Pleasers, including high-heeled runners no self-respecting stripper would be caught dead in, as well as singlets and skimpy shorts emblazoned with the Pole Divas logo. I didn't think I could get my size-twelve self into any of those shorts. Not so similar, after all. At the far end of the room was the reception desk with the super-perky receptionist. She nodded towards the studio itself. 'You can warm up in there if you like. Jenny will be here soon.' Warm up? I thought. And that was where any similarity ended.

The studio had freshly painted cream walls and a row of large windows. Stepping into it was like stepping into a panty-liner commercial. A revolving mirror ball sent shards of pink light across the sunlit space. Twelve steel poles – pristine by strip club standards – spanned from floating floorboard to five-metre-high ceiling. At the front was the instructor's raised dais, backed by a wall of slimming mirrors, in which three toned teenagers were watching themselves writhe and dangle. One winked at herself. I stifled a giggle.

Then I saw that she wasn't wearing shoes. In fact none of the girls were. They were gripping the poles with their thighs, knees and shins. I couldn't do that; I relied on non-slip PVC. But my boots were going to look as out of place as a heavy metal t-shirt in a roomful of cashmere sweaters.

Valiantly, foolishly, I headed onto the floor barefoot. My nervousness only made my palms more slippery. I was alternating between palm-wiping and downward-spiralling when a lithe blonde arrived toting a Mary-Kate Olsen–sized takeaway coffee. Presumably this was Jenny. She pulled off her spike-heeled boots and tight jeans, revealing lean brown legs and tiny pink shorts (at least I had the shorts half right). Then she glided around the room, fiddling with the stereo, texting, and throwing practised smiles and words of encouragement to everyone except me. I went up to her.

'Give me five minutes,' she said.

I went back to greasing the pole and watching her sip her coffee. Jenny had mastered the art of looking exceptionally busy while not doing much. When at last she came over, I was inelegantly full-body humping the pole in an effort to wipe it with the edge of my shorts.

'Can you do a funky monkey?' she asked.

'Huh?' I said.

Jenny spun upside down, caught the pole with her armpit and reached back for her feet. She hung there, as if velcro'd on, before righting herself without so much as a milky burp.

'I don't think so,' I said, but I gave it a go, burning my armpit and almost dislocating my shoulder.

My grading continued in this vein. Jenny would name a terrifying-sounding move I'd never heard of – such as 'crucifix climb', 'death lay' or 'Chinese flag contortion'– then demonstrate. I would hurl myself at the pole, slide off, pick myself up and stare at her with confusion. The only thing hurt was my pride. After ten minutes Jenny scrunched her thin nose and said, 'Why don't you just start in beginners?'

For an hour every Tuesday morning for eight weeks, I swapped shadowy strip club for shiny pole studio. My instructor was another intimidatingly young, petite, tanned, blonde taskmaster with a double-jointed pelvis; my classmates were in their early twenties, ranging from a giggly housewife to a super-serious contemporary dancer. It was a full house. And I was the token stripper – the only one wearing used stilettos. My Pleasers were fake-tan brown and smelly, unlike the other girls' sparkly new shoes. I remembered the days when Pleasers were made in the United States; now they came from China at one-third the price. One girl had actually bought the high-heeled sneakers. In fact, pole school was a bit like spinning class: it was healthy good fun and provided an unexpectedly intense workout.

For some girls it was a serious boost to their self-esteem. It was a harsh reality check on mine.

I was an amateur at something I was supposed to be good at, which packed extra ouch factor. It also bothered me that the instructors were so revered. I wasn't about to kiss any sinewy, super-toned butt.

Speaking of butts, there was a lot of half-arsed booty slapping going on. Which got me wondering just who we were being bootylicious for. There seemed to be an imaginary audience in the house – the ghost of every girl's fantasy or spurned heart. Pole dancing might've been marketed as the babes reclaiming their smoking hotness, but it was still reinforcing a male-defined view of female sexuality. Not that I had a problem with that: I'd made my living from it, after all. But having come across from the dark side, there was something pointless, something holier-than-thou about pole dancing. It wasn't an Olympic sport and not everyone could be a Pussycat Doll. Then again, perhaps I was just jaded and old.

Despite my cynicism, I enjoyed myself. I learnt a few new moves and some cool sequencing. After eight weeks in beginners I received an invitation to the next level. Pragmatically I decided against it. At Pole Divas we spun in an anti-clockwise direction, while at work I'd always spun clockwise. Now I found that during my shows I'd lunge for the pole and freeze, not knowing which way to go. My pelvic alignment might have been grateful, but my ego was not.

It was time to face facts: this diva was on her way down. I was at least a decade too old to be starting afresh. To me, pole dancing was as different from stripping as day was from night. There was a central axis around which both spun, and that was where the similarities ended.

* * *

At the club, I had a new crew to putty up with. These girls had no time to dwell on the ethics of stripping or booty slap on their days off. They were too busy leading real, fulfilling lives.

There was Lila, a sturdy Canadian lass who was doing a Masters in clinical psychology. Lila had been at Richmond station, wondering how she was going to pay her foreign student fees, when she'd seen a sign, the Men's Gallery sign. Any money Lila had leftover she spent on wakeboarding. She was the only stripper I met who once came to work with concussion and gave private dances with cerebral spinal fluid dripping out of her nose.

Lila was best mates with Yaz, a body builder and ex-pharmaceutical rep. Yaz prescribed our booth free Duromine during the Grand Prix to keep us racing. I slept about three hours in two days and swore I'd never scoff diet pills again. Yaz ate them like lollies. She also dished out training advice during dances to musclemen turned on by her abs. Yaz took her training regime far more seriously than she did stripping. She had a parrot finger puppet called Mr CanCan, which she would produce whenever a guy wanted her to find a good-looking bird for his mate. 'Who wants a good fingering?' she'd cackle. After too many party boys freaked out, Mr CanCan was retired to the wings.

Cecile also sat in the first booth. A French jewellery designer, Cecile could be found invoicing or emailing on her laptop during quieter moments. She was friends with Zara, an Iranian filmmaker and performance artist. In her mid-forties, Zara more than anyone embodied the dancer qualities that Lachlan the photographer had been keen to bring out in me. Rachel was a personal assistant by day and a magnet for oddballs by night. Her regulars included Hair

Fetish Man, who stroked her waist-length hair, and Foot Fetish Man, who sniffed her feet and tried to suck her toes. There was also Stu, a guy on sickness benefits who bought Rachel chocolate from The Reject Shop and thought the club was his second living room. Stu never paid Rachel to sit and chat, she was simply concerned about his welfare. Rachel made time for everyone.

Intelligent and warm hearted, these dancers were drawn to humanity in all its wackiness. We would spend our breaks driving Kinder Surprise cars around the booth, giving Yaz dating advice and motivating each other to score 'just one more' private dance at 6 a.m.

Dawn was our witching hour, when exhaustion gave rise to sheer silliness. At 5.45 a.m. one Sunday, I danced for a cute boy with spiky blond hair. He said he was Swedish (he wasn't). I said we were neighbours – I came from Lapland. Then he said he was a dog person. 'But I have no backyard, so I have a token dog. A cat.'

'Do you call your cat Dog?' I asked.

'You're really very silly,' he said, smiling and giving me another fifty because, 'We guys need a little attention sometimes. It's not about the nudity, I can get that online. You can put your clothes back on if you want to. I just want to talk.'

Another guy who wanted to talk was that night's taxi driver. He told me he was from Lebanon. I didn't tell him I'd been.

'Do you party?' he asked. 'Some girls, I drop them at the clubs after they finish work.'

It was 7 a.m. 'After a twelve-hour shift? No.'

'But you are young! You should go out, dance, have some fun!'

'Do you like going for a nice long drive on your day off?' I asked pointedly. He stared at me as if I was mad.

Half an hour later, I stood at the kitchen window, freshly showered, chugging down a honey sandwich and wondering if perhaps the taxi driver wasn't right. Maybe I should be having more fun. Then a lithe Asian girl in hot pants jogged by, ponytail swinging. A middle-aged man with a dog and the paper walked straight into a parked car. After an all-nighter, that was enough amusement for me.

* * *

The silliness at work was in stark contrast to my home life. Matt and I were coexisting. We didn't say a lot, for fear of saying the unthinkable. I'd taken up stamp collecting. Matt had taken up quitting pot. I wanted to believe him. In spring, his depression again shifted to mania and this time when he stabilised – fortunately without hospitalisation – he asked for help. Matt's parents agreed to do so with conditions attached. It was soul-destroying watching him struggle, yet I knew I had reached my limit.

I had to get away from all of it – Matt, the Gallery, Melbourne.

As the year 2010 drew to a close I boxed up my belongings again, sold my car and bought a one-way ticket to Thailand. Before I left, Matt gave me a small Buddha statue inside a pink heart-shaped box. On it, he'd written, *To Leigh, with all my heart, Matt.* It was the most beautiful gift anyone had ever given me. And so I left him without actually breaking up with him.

I wandered Thailand like another lost Westerner. The idea of teaching English was now the last thing I had in mind. I practised yoga – and wrote. In beach huts in the south, I tried to shape years of stripping diaries into a manuscript. It was almost anti-climactic to discover that writing was what I most wanted to do.

In Chiang Mai the international yoga community welcomed me with the fierceness, love and generosity they bestowed on all travelling kin. Overnight, I had an instant family. Inspired, I kept writing. Five months later, when my visa ran out and my money was fast following, I headed home to Melbourne to study an associate degree in writing and editing.

16.

AFTER TWO DECADES I HAD COME FULL CIRCLE.
By the middle of 2012, I was once again studying, stripping and single. Fortunately, I loved the writing course and I didn't feel like I was a loser. Sure, I had wasted a lot of time down the rabbit hole, but I had also learnt some important life lessons. I knew that people deserved to be treated equally regardless of their social or financial status, or appearance. I knew that stripping could be both empowering and disempowering to women. And I knew that ultimately there were no shortcuts to any place worth going. If anything, my stripping shortcut to a writing career had proved the long way home.

As for my physical home, I was living in a Brunswick share house with friends of stripper friends, a fashion designer from Austria and a community worker from Belgium. Our house had all the good things I'd been craving but had been unable to create: a big backyard, a vegie patch and a communal kitchen. It was a place where I could be myself – all of myself, the light and the shadow. Where my creative self was nurtured, and my destructive self – the part of me that was drawn to the darkness – was acknowledged as real and valid, something to be learnt from, not denied.

I had finally broken up with Matt. He was trying hard to get well and it hurt seeing him, and seeing him suffer. After seven years I didn't want to cause him any more pain. It was better to keep my distance and start over.

I made the decision to stay single for a while. I didn't have the energy to strip and take a lover, let alone invest in a relationship. Yes, I'd returned to The Men's Gallery. I'd inadvertently committed to the one thing that required no commitment. Making the call had been nerve-wracking, not knowing if they would take me back at thirty-seven. To my relief they had, though this stint would be my last.

I'd changed my stage name from Juliette to Jasmine. It wasn't an ode to Asia, but to Melbourne. The heady scent of jasmine on a hot summer night: it represented the promise of new adventure, and encapsulated years of my own unfolding. Accordingly, Jasmine was savvier and more sexual than Juliette. She wasn't as naïve or romantic.

That there was little love left in my dances bothered only me. I did what I could and I did it by rote, flashing my smile on and off like a rainbow strobe. It helped that I'd taken to curling my hair and apparently resembled someone called Taylor Swift, which was making a few nineteen-year-olds' fantasies come true and, once

I'd googled the songstress, helped bolster my own aging alter ego. Thankfully my regulars were still loyal. One text to Joseph and he was back to kickstarting my Saturdays. And Weatherman John and I had become Facebook friends – he under a pseudonym, me under my real name. I figured if John was going to stalk me, he would've done it by now.

I'd stopped doing shows and functions even though house fees had gone up to eighty dollars on weekends. I simply couldn't be centrestage anymore. Or spend that much time sculpting cellulite at the gym. My energy went into writing. In the months I'd been away, the pseudo-lesbian action had come out of the boardroom and onto the big stage. The showgirl duos and trios seemed to be genuinely having a good time, rolling around like newborn kittens – eyes closed, tongues out. They weren't faking it anymore, and lick-outs were too-stiff competition for an ossified showgirl. (Nor did I want to risk an STD. That would've given new meaning to being an independent contractor.) After years of doing the Mr Whippy clockwise, my pelvis was permanently twisted, one scapula higher than the other. Continuing to do shows would've been foolish on body, mind and spirit. The house fee was easier to accept than the degeneration.

The club was degenerating too. The locker room flooded regularly; the girls' showers were black with mould. Upstairs, the private dance armchairs were splitting, snagging the odd pubic hair. More than once I tripped on a threadbare patch of carpet en route to a private dance, catching myself with a trite, 'Oops, I'm falling for you.' The playlist was more trance than pop now, the volume too loud for conversation, which helped attract drugged-up musclemen who kept the bar afloat with antifreeze-green vodka monsters. The patron dress code had gone, as had the free happy hour buffet, and the no-questions-asked evictions of badly behaved customers. Increasingly, it was every girl for herself. All this indicated that Peter would run the club into the ground, then build apartments. Melbourne was booming, King Street prime real estate. Yet it saddened me to see how the club had been let go – saddened me, too, that I was no longer proud to be associated with it.

But stripping still remained the best part-time job option I had, so I stayed.

For two years I trotted Jasmine out on weekends, spread my smiles then returned to my books, drained of energy but fiscally solvent. But by the end of 2013, seesawing between 6 a.m. finishes at the club and 9 a.m. starts at uni was taking its toll. I had constant backache, despite my own sporadic yoga practice. And I was older and wider, while there were more dancers and fewer customers than ever before. One Friday during unhappy hour, I counted eighteen girls and seven men. It became almost impossible to get a dance without agreeing to being touched. That was one thing I'd sworn I would never do, and I was doing it.

Clammy-handed foreign students grappled my hips, ice users with rank breath nuzzled my neck. I toughened up and became more sexually aggressive. My cougar tendencies were whiskey-fuelled. One double-shot a night became several, at work and at home. Too many Saturdays I arrived hungover after student drinks. I'd wallflower in the smokers' room until Joseph arrived, scabbing fags to stoke my inner fire. Friday sessions made Saturday stripping less of a head-fuck, more a continuation of my social life. Which, increasingly, it was.

It was also a poor substitute for a sex life. Over time I tried to enjoy the touching, to take part rather than take control. My boundaries might have been worn down, but I discovered I still had my limits.

The men expected more for four hundred dollars an hour, a new booking the club had recently introduced. Savvy young strippers were all over this option like junior investment bankers. I'd find them in the fantasy booths lying prone atop their customers, planking towards the dawn. One night, a retired Perth schoolteacher booked me for two hours. I got smashed on whiskey and submitted to a hideous grope-fest. Days later I was still carrying the auric detritus. I didn't promote bookings after that. The pay-off wasn't worth it.

Another night, a customer began massaging my shoulders during a private. A tradie turned body worker, he'd sensed my tension and knew just how to shift it. I melted under his command, going all gooey and glassy-eyed. He laughed. 'You're looking at me like I'm your ex-boyfriend and you want me back!'

I laughed too, but it was more sad than funny. After three years, I still missed Matt. Now drug and alcohol free, Matt had moved to the coast, had a new job and surfed most days. He was happy and healthy. I still loved Matt more than anyone. But I was still stripping. I had to let him go.

Sometimes Weatherman John would ask after my love life.

'I don't have one,' I would say. 'This is it.'

'Darling, you could have anyone you want. I think you're being far too picky.' I didn't think so – on either count.

Joseph was my faux date for four hours every Saturday. Fifty dollars a fortnight in 2006 had become hundreds each week by 2013. Given what he paid – and what he saw happening around us – he demanded little. He seemed content to have me perch on his chair, chatting about what movies I'd watched or what I'd eaten for dinner. (And I preferred to perch there, rather than risk being mauled by strangers.) Our interaction was banal, curiously asexual. Was Joseph a virgin? I couldn't ask for fear of embarrassing him – or being misinterpreted. At his request, I'd stopped removing my G. It was as if this elevated our 'relationship'.

'Do we have a relationship or is this just business to you?' he asked one night. 'What will happen to us when you leave here?'

What will happen is that we'll never see each other again, I thought. *Do you really think I'm going to move in with you and your mother, watch* The Biggest Loser *and eat nasi goreng? You pay me.*

'Of course we have a relationship,' I said sweetly. 'A business relationship. Although I'm fond of you.'

'You are?'

'I am.' I wondered if I was anymore. I was grateful, unmotivated, and bored.

Joseph's method of manipulation – when he used it, which wasn't often – was passive aggressive and easily sidestepped. 'It's getting harder to find a park,' he would start. 'If it gets worse, I might not be able to come in every Saturday.'

'Have you thought of taking the train?' I would reply.

He continued to tell me he loved me, always when my back was turned. Depending on my mood I'd either ignore it or murmur, 'I know you do.'

When Joseph bought me an iPhone for Christmas, I was moved by his generosity – until he began texting midweek. *How are you? Nothing much to tell, except I'm busy at work.* Unsure how to handle this, I consulted Lila, our booth's psychologist-in-training. Lila thought a degree of play for pay was necessary though, so I kept my replies brief. *I'm good, thank you. Hope you are too.* Then the texts came daily, first thing in the morning. *Please be careful riding your bike out there, it will be windy today.* I grumbled to Lila, 'I've ridden halfway around the world and he worries about me *commuting*? It's too much.'

I told Joseph not to text unless absolutely necessary.

'You tell me what I can and can't do,' he said.

'You know the rules,' I said, annoyed at his reluctance to take responsibility. 'They haven't changed.'

'They haven't?'

We both knew they had.

Despite my financial reliance on him, I became more uncommunicative. I wanted to *dance*, not discuss his mother's ill-fitting dentures or his outings to the mall. The silences grew. Then one night, tired and hungover, I did the unthinkable: I fell asleep and toppled off his chair.

'Jasmine!' Joseph exclaimed. 'Are you all right? What happened?'

I picked myself up, supressing a yawn. 'I'm fine. I slipped, that's all.'

The only thing that had slipped was my standards. I had to raise them. I refused to become like Brooke and her regular, who had given up on dancing *and* conversation. He would hold Brooke in his lap and they'd sit immobile as statues until his time was up, when she'd climb off and wait for more cash. Then back on she'd climb.

What did she think about? And where do you go from there?

Yaz suggested I try dexamphetamine. 'Dexies'll perk you up! They make all the stupid shit the men say hilarious.' She winked and popped me a small white pill. It was the best four dollars I'd ever spent. The slow burn came on mid-podium; I danced like it was 2004. My back pain completely disappeared. And I had so much to say to Joseph! The intricacies of denture construction were riveting. Best of all, I had no problems sleeping afterwards (though I did grind my teeth). One pill a night turned into two, then three. I was finally doing the other thing I swore I'd never do: getting fucked up to do my job.

* * *

Ayahuasca. Some people believe that the South American plant medicine forms a relationship with you before you drink it. By 2014, I kept noticing references to ayahuasca in spiritual texts and online. Friends who had participated in ceremonies reported life-changing shifts in consciousness. One had been cured of chronic fatigue. Curious, I trawled forums and watched documentaries, trying to unearth all I could. Many of the writers and filmmakers were intelligent and articulate free-thinkers. Some were academics; some were my parents' age. Several were medical practitioners who reported astonishing results using ayahuasca to help patients with opiate addiction and post-traumatic stress disorders.

This was no hippie trip. Nor was it fun. The rank-tasting vine, taken ceremonially, induced purging and was brewed with psychedelics. Now, the idea of barfing in front of strangers while journeying into unknown realms struck me as seriously mad. Still, it was going to take something strong to cure me of stripping. Gentle practices such as yoga hadn't brought lasting transformation. I wondered if ayahuasca could. The thought bubbled away for months. So when I chanced upon a writer who assisted with ayahuasca ceremonies, I shelved my control freak and signed up.

One Friday evening in country Victoria, I took part in a ceremony with twenty-five others. The room was candlelit, the air thick with burning sage. We sat in a circle, a bucket positioned ominously before each of us. I reminded myself that the bucket was my friend, a potential vessel of glorious rainbows. When the shaman called me forward I knocked back the bitter brew, returned to my mattress, closed my eyes and waited.

At first there was nothing. Then slowly *la madre* uncurled in my gut, like an exploratory snake. My head grew heavy, pulsated with the relentless beat of the shamanic songs being played on CD. The evocations seemed inside me, I inside them – as if my inner and outer worlds were merging.

Somewhere, someone cried. Somewhere, someone threw up. I congratulated myself for being stronger. (Hello, ego.)

At some point I drank again. The vine kicked in then, winding her way from my belly to my heart. In my mind's eye I saw the armour around it shattering, rigid and metallic grey. *La madre* snaked into my smoker's lungs. Then the nausea began, a soft breathlessness. The purge rose, not from my gut but from my lungs themselves. Instinctively, I held on. 'Just release,' a voice nearby instructed, so I surrendered. As I puked, the night sky spun before me, white stars in the blackness.

A didgeridoo started. A great red and black pit opened up in the floor. I stepped back, though I was still sitting cross-legged. My jaw began to dissolve. One eyeball roamed off into the ether. I hugged my knees to my chest and held on. Someone murmured, 'I'm so confused.' Someone replied, 'No, you're not.' Someone laughed. I exhaled and let go, into cosmic fractals, sacred geometry and ley lines. Everything was One. I morphed into an Indian temple dancer, adored and adoring. Threw back my head, back and back. Then I *was* back. Outside, the wind danced with the trees. Bucket in hand, I padded out to watch. A lone gull rose. I smiled, saturated with bliss. Inside, I found my mattress and slept.

In the morning, every sense was vibrant. At home I heard the train from two suburbs over, saw the leaves on the trees photosynthesising. I plunged my hands into the earth and gardened for hours. For a full week I felt an assured sense of connectedness with everything. I couldn't fathom what had happened, but knew it had been profound. My backache was gone. I wasn't self-conscious in public. The thought of stripping held no emotional charge. It lay like an old postcard in my mind, flat and faded. I could go there; I could not. My eyes had been opened to possibility.

There would be more ceremonies, more purging and more insights. That night was the beginning of a new way of being.

* * *

The Men's Gallery – always home to the walking dead – had started to resemble a morgue. In March 2014, the Grand Prix – the most bankable weekend of the year – left more than one dancer in the red. By April, girls were regularly not making their house fee. Harlow had semi-retired. It was so slow that even some of the Russians had quit. And word was our club was busier than most.

To ease the Great Depression, Dani plastered the dressing-room with inspirational pictures and quotes. My favourite was stuck on the back of a toilet door: 'When you think of quitting, think about why you started.' I sat there, wondering why I *had* started. Two decades on, it was almost impossible to remember.

Door numbers continued to plummet. Dancers self-promoted tirelessly on social media, Instagramming gams and offering hump-day play. Management began manically rewriting the rules.

The first was permitting tattoos, now regarded as über-cool. For years the dancers had to cover their tatts with stage make-up. There had even been a prominent sign in the dressing-room: *All visible tattoos must be covered*, which was redundant unless your ink was on the soles of your feet. This was great news – I'd recently got a half-sleeve tattoo and was tired of swabbing Dermablend across my Persian lady.

It was unclear just how the regulars would respond to the girls revealing their body art. I knew that Joseph would see it as proof I'd been keeping things from him. And I knew that Weatherman John loathed tattoos. John knew of my lady's existence thanks to Facebook, and I fully expected him to end our fifteen-year association when he saw her in the flesh. Instead he simply flinched and said, 'Ew, stand on my other side.'

Joseph was initially wounded I hadn't confided in him, then conceded, 'She suits you. Yes, she does.' His sanguine response was only a little unexpected.

Exposing my tatt also made me instantly popular with youngsters still working up the courage to get inked. Allowing body art had been a smart move by management.

Another change was introducing theme nights, including Costume Fridays. I hadn't worked a Friday all year, but during mid-semester break I decided to try my luck. June was fairytale month and I went with Princess Jasmine from *Aladdin*. I YouTubed clips of Her Highness flouncing around in turquoise pyjamas and claiming she wasn't living up to her full potential. Cringingly apt. Then I ordered the outfit on eBay from China (2XL, just in case) and hoped no one would care that I was blonde.

Weatherman John didn't care. 'Grant me three wishes,' he said, eyeing my see-through pyjamas.

'I don't think Princess Jasmine does that,' I said. 'All I do is smile and wave. Nothing very meaningful or difficult.' Actually, removing the pyjama bottoms *was* difficult. It required all of my flexibility to fold myself forward and pull trousers over toes while mooning sveltely. Weatherman John looked suitably impressed. Then after the dance he asked who I was supposed to be.

'Haven't you been listening?' I said.

'Darling, I've been too busy staring at your pussy.'

'But I can speak many languages!'

Not knowing the quote, he wandered off, confused. That was the problem with Costume Fridays: with dancers in double disguise, it was too complicated.

It was also the end of the financial year – a year in which the Federal Government had delivered unexpected budget cuts. The Friday I made one hundred and fifty bucks in ten hours was my last. Not long after that, the club canned Costume Fridays.

The third major change was making the Top Forty topless. Like most dancers, I objected to this boob-fest on technical grounds – the *point* of stripping was that we stripped. Ripping our bras off like bandaids before taking to the stage undermined our art form. Now all that stood between us and a private dance was a bejewelled triangle of lycra.

The shitty titty parade was mandatory, so I embraced it. It was the old adage of owning your exploitation. We older girls would fembot around the stage with sage smiles, while enthusiastic teens honked each other's tits like a flock of cornered geese. One busty young dancer regularly dropped to her knees and slapped her breasts across random customers' faces. The parade would politely halt until she'd rejoined the ranks. One night they trialled a new MC. I couldn't tell if he was taking the piss or numerically challenged. 'It's every girl onstage at once!' he roared. 'Thirty-two dancers! Sixty-six breasts! It's a *tsunami* of boobs!' Delirious and a bit drunk, I wondered if fake breasts were a buoyancy device in bad weather, like a built-in life raft.

* * *

Not that long ago, every second customer had told me I was beautiful. I'd accepted those compliments without thought, like breathing. I took their absence the same way, noticing it only when a rare flattering comment reminded me. My face had hardened, my body softened. Old irregulars like Ralph made excuses; the Chinese tour guides waved me away. Dani had stopped giving me podiums on the main stage. I didn't know why and was afraid to ask. Instead, I hid behind my first-ever long black dress. My body was maturing, thickening in ways I disliked but hadn't the energy to try to slow. After years of not thinking, I was relishing using my brain again. I wanted to spend my precious energy on writing. I actually wanted to act my age.

One night two teenage hipsters sat down at my podium then glanced up. 'Look at the arse on that troll,' said the skinny redhead. I ignored him, but was still stunned that was how he saw me. Maybe it should have bothered me more than it did. With my baseline covered by Joseph I had become good at ignoring and being ignored. Most Saturdays after Joseph left, I would circuit the club, half looking for someone I wanted to dance for, knowing there was no one. Then I would head for the smokers' room, shoulder into a corner, light up and blank the customers.

I listened in to conversations and was shocked by what I heard. Way too many men called their wives 'fucking cows', their mothers 'old hags' and the dancers 'slippery, money-hungry cunts'. I could excuse a throwaway comment from a kid who didn't know better, but not from grown men en masse, not when that was all I heard. Despite tinnitus and the bad techno, my ears were suddenly open.

Had the talk always been so hateful? Or had the guys stopped trying to impress me now that I wasn't 'their bag'? Could it have been the change in clientele? Whatever the reason, I was sick of it.

Sick of them, sick of myself. Sick of still stripping and still smoking. While the wind swirled in through the mesh grating, I'd stare out at the bin-lined laneway and wonder what fork in the twisted path had led to this. At what point should I have gotten out? And where to from here? I had writing, but I had no idea if I could earn a living from it.

Sometimes when I crawled into bed at dawn I considered getting fucked for money. I could still work for myself, still earn a weekly wage in one night. Perhaps I had more to offer as a prostitute than as a stripper – being youthful wasn't as essential. I liked the idea of sex as art. Then again, I'd thought that about stripping once. Once, it had been. But if stripping was so hard for me to quit, then prostitution was the point of no return. Deep down I knew I couldn't handle being touched by strangers, inside or out.

Weatherman John confided that there were dancers offering after-hours services, and one in particular who encouraged him to put his fingers inside her.

'Did you?' I asked.

'No. I wasn't comfortable doing that because she's married.'

'You're married too.'

He chuckled. 'Somehow that didn't bother me as much.'

It bothered me. So did another comment he made: 'You and Cameron are the only girls I don't touch now. I respect both of you too much.' Had I sugar-coated John? Or was he, like me, simply adjusting to a changing climate? I still needed to respect him to respect myself, or else I felt it invalidated the past fifteen years. That would've been a sucky, sour-cherry note to end on.

In spring I received a text from Dani: *Hey lovely, sorry but you'll need to clear your locker as they're only for girls who work a minimum of two nights.*

It wasn't personal, yet I felt like I'd been asked to pack my bags and leave. There would be nothing that marked my place, nothing to come home to. I would be back to snail-shelling it. Two weeks passed before I could tear the scrap of paper with 'Jasmine' scrawled in pink highlighter off the door. I'd squirrelled away four boxes of latex gloves, six cans of Sally Hansen tan, two packets of baby-wipes, one can of hairspray, a bottle of mouthwash, two curling wands, one straightening iron, a set of hair rollers, a back-up pair of stilettos, a back-up back-up pair of stilettos (really?), a hip-flask of vodka (score!), a bottle of body wash and a mouldy exfoliating glove. Plus all of my costumes and make-up. Everything was coated in a sticky film of fake tan. I had mixed feelings, equally push–pull, like cleaning out a closet after someone has died. A part of me *was* dying, a big part of me. No wonder some dancers never emptied out their lockers when they left. It was simply easier to close the coffin and walk away.

Just before Christmas 2014 rival strip club Bar 20 permitted touching from the waist up. Many of its distraught dancers moved to The Men's Gallery. Overnight, there were one hundred serious hotties on the roster every Saturday. Some weren't making their house fee, and I wouldn't have made mine if it weren't for Joseph. I despised this dependence, but was determined to tolerate it till January, when I'd decided to leave. The dances were getting more and more grubby. Management was just turning a blind eye.

Joseph wasn't. Once, he mimicked Brooke's regular by trying to cuddle me; I slithered out of his embrace. Another night, he grabbed the back of my neck and tried to kiss my forehead, scraping my eyeball with his glasses as I twisted away. 'Ouch, that really hurt!' I retreated to my chair, head in hands.

'I shall have to wear my contacts,' he said.

'No – you'll have to not do that!' I scowled. I refused to accept his apology. To compensate, Joseph spent more, as I'd suspected he would. I forgave him before he walked out the door, but knew I was the one who needed to leave.

Dancers were being let go without explanation. Both Lila and Rachel had taken time off and couldn't get back on the roster – it was 'full'. Every Monday when I texted mine I couldn't relax until it was confirmed. With so many dancers, I needed to jump before I was pushed.

The clincher was an increase in house fees from eighty to one hundred dollars per shift. That was it. I could not be that reliant on Joseph. The week after my fortieth birthday would be my last.

The few dancers I told weren't convinced. Neither was Weatherman John, although he booked me for an hour as a final farewell. 'It's been a pleasure knowing you,' he said. 'I think a lot of you as a person, even if I disagree with so many of your thoughts and ideas.' I chuckled at that. It had been a pleasure for me too.

I didn't dare tell Joseph I was hanging up my G – couldn't bring myself to shatter his illusion. I said I was going to visit my family. 'I'll miss you!' he whined. 'Twenty-seven whole days till I see you again.'

And then some, I thought.

At 4 a.m. on my last shift I was in the dressing-room, sitting in the first booth by myself, my feet up on the bench, a whiskey in one hand and a coconut water in the other. My back ached, I was clean out of dexies and it was dead upstairs. I sat there, silently saluting my nude sisters for sharing the road, for being my other family, for making me feel like I belonged. These women had been truly extraordinary. I'd watched girls raise children; immigrants with limited English become fluent, property-owning citizens; students put themselves through every school imaginable, from medicine to circus to horse massage. I'd seen philanthropists found charities; budding artists and musicians become self-employed professionals; actors, burlesque performers and comedians support themselves in the off-season. I'd worked with teenagers through to almost-fifty-year-old women. We came from all ranks, from all over the world. Money might've been our motivation for becoming strippers, but it wasn't the sole reason why we kept doing it. It had been a privilege knowing so many outrageous, spiritually generous women.

And I thought of all the men. Their motivations for 'going to the strippers' were multifarious. Some wanted to be heard and valued, or to dominate and manipulate. Some were on a cultural road trip or a journey of sexual discovery. Others wanted time out, simply to be entertained. Others still were there under duress, for a buck's night or an office break-up. But whether they were looking for love, a little physical contact, a hint of intimacy or just to perve at a pretty girl's pussy, one thing was clear: few of them wanted their perception of sex and gender roles to be challenged.

'Check this out.' Krystal, an exquisite 25-year-old, glided into the booth, jolting me from my thoughts. She held up a cotton nightie and rolled her eyes. It was a gift from her latest regular, a businessman who'd given up fucking hookers and was trying to fuck strippers. The nightie read, 'Where there's a will, there's a way.' I laughed. *Krystals still have messages for me*, I thought.

Krystal binned the nightie. I binned my shoes. Then I scrubbed off my second skin for the last time, packed up and headed for the stairs.

Stanley was behind the dance supervisor's desk, uploading the roster onto his iPad.

'Night, Stan,' I said.

'Night, baby. See you next week.'

I didn't correct him, I just kept walking.

If I was lucky, my life was half over. I'd spent enough of it playing dress-ups and make-believe. I wanted real connection. An authentic relationship – real love, genuine intimacy. A meaningful existence. Greater work/life balance. A kitchen cupboard that wasn't full of overpriced supplements. White sheets that weren't stained brown with fake tan, a face free of toxic chemicals. Pubic hair. A broader definition of female beauty. Words that meant something. Difficult conversations. A better rapport with my family.

It wasn't going to be easy. But at last leaving felt easier than staying. At last I knew there wasn't any reason good enough to go back.

ACKNOWLEDGEMENTS

THE SUPPORT AND GENEROSITY OF A GREAT many people made this book possible. I'm grateful to you all.

Thank you especially to my family, to Lynne for sharing your love of storytelling and nurturing my own, and to Gary for encouraging me to explore the world. Thanks to Gary and Rae for the loan of your beach pad, which helped enormously with completing later drafts. To Neil, Mel and the girls, thank you for being a welcome sanity check between bouts of seclusion.

My heartfelt thanks to the staff and students of RMIT's professional writing and editing programme, in particular Penny Johnson and Sian Prior.

Sian, this book wouldn't have happened without your unwavering encouragement and sound guidance – thank you! To my Thursday ladies, Alison Jones and Lucy Callaghan, a special thank you for your love and support from concept to completion.

A massive thank you to Nic Low for your enthusiasm, wisdom and generosity, and for the wondrous adventures between edits. This book and my sense of self are much better for it.

To my editor Melanie Ostell, thank you for turning my melodramatic ramblings into a story fit for print. I'm indebted to you for your ruthless good judgement and for going beyond the call of duty. To Sophie Hamley, Tom Bailey-Smith, Karen Ward and all the team at Hachette, thank you for taking me on board and for getting behind this book with such gusto, dedication and trust. I will be forever grateful.

Numerous people provided feedback on early drafts. Thanks especially to Naomi Bailey, Andrea Gillum, Cam Hassard, Melanie Joosten, Rajith Savanadasa, Myfanwy McDonald and Erin Stutchbury, for keeping the dream alive.

To my Brunswick homies Katrien Van Huyck, Pamela McGraw, Cameron Kelly, Tim O'Connor and Wendy Jenkins, thank you for tolerating me turning my room into a perpetual workspace and for never asking 'are you done yet?'

Thanks to the Chiang Mai yoga crew for making me feel so welcome. Thank you, Koraly Dimitriadis and Sista Zai Zanda for inspiring me to speak my truth. To Ian Nelder, thank you for being a constant presence in my life. My deep thanks to Tim McDonald for your love and bravery.

And of course thank you to my nude sisters for continually wowing me with your daring, determination, open-mindedness, humour and heart. You fierce goddesses, you've enriched my life immeasurably. Shine on!

Leigh Hopkinson is a New Zealand–born, Melbourne-based writer and editor. Her articles, stories and photographs have been published in newspapers and anthologies on both sides of the Tasman. *Two Decades Naked* is her first book.

hachette
AUSTRALIA

If you would like to find out more about
Hachette Australia, our authors, upcoming events
and new releases you can visit our website, Facebook or
follow us on Twitter:

hachette.com.au
facebook.com/HachetteAustralia
twitter.com/HachetteAus